Studies in modern capitalism – Etudes sur le capitalisme moderne

The politics of the world-economy

Studies in modern capitalism · Etudes sur le capitalisme moderne

Editorial board · Comité de rédaction

Maurice Aymard, Maison des Sciences de l'Homme, Paris
Jacques Revel, Ecole des Hautes Etudes en Sciences Sociales, Paris
Immanuel Wallerstein, Fernand Braudel Center for the Study of Economies,
Historical Systems, and Civilizations, Binghamton, New York

This series is devoted to an attempt to comprehend capitalism as a world-system. It
will include monographs, collections of essays and colloquia around specific themes,
written by historians and social scientists united by a common concern for the study
of large-scale long-term social structure and social change.

The series is a joint enterprise of the Maison des Sciences de l'Homme in Paris and
the Fernand Braudel Center for the Study of Economies, Historical Systems, and
Civilizations at the State University of New York at Binghamton.

Other books in the series

Maurice Aymard (ed.): *Dutch capitalism and world capitalism/Capitalisme hollandais et
capitalisme mondial*
Iván T. Berend, György Ránki: *The European periphery and industrialization, 1780–1914*
Pierre Bourdieu: *Algeria 1960*
Andre Gunder Frank: *Mexican agriculture 1521–1630: transformation of the mode of
production*
Folker Fröbel, Jürgen Heinrichs, Otto Kreye: *The new international division of labour:
structural unemployment in industrialized countries and industrialization in developing countries*
Caglar Keyder: *The definition of a peripheral economy: Turkey 1923–1929*
Peter Kriedte, Hans Medick, Jürgen Schlumbohm: *Industrialization before
industrialization: rural industry in the genesis of capitalism*
Bruce McGowan: *Economic life in Ottoman Europe: taxation, trade and the struggle for the
land, 1660–1800*
Ernest Mandel: *Long waves of capitalist development: the Marxist interpretation*
Michel Morineau: *Ces incroyables gazettes et fabuleux métaux: les retours des trésors
américains, d'après les gazettes hollandaises (16e–18e siècles)*
Henri H. Stahl: *Traditional Romanian village communities: the transition from the communal to
the capitalist mode of production in the Danube region*
Immanuel Wallerstein: *The capitalist world-economy: essays*

This book is published as part of the joint publishing agreement established in 1977
between the Fondation de la Maison des Sciences de l'Homme and the Press
Syndicate of the University of Cambridge. Titles published under this arrangement
may appear in any European language or, in the case of volumes of collected essays,
in several languages.

New books will appear either as individual titles or in one of the series which the
Maison des Sciences de l'Homme and the Cambridge University Press have jointly
agreed to publish. All books published jointly by the Maison des Sciences de
l'Homme and the Cambridge University Press will be distributed by the Press
throughout the world.

The politics of the world-economy

The states, the movements, and the civilizations

Essays by

IMMANUEL WALLERSTEIN

Director, Fernand Braudel Center for the Study of
Economies, Historical Systems, and Civilizations
at the State University of New York at Binghamton

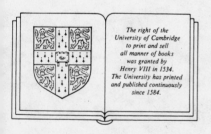

The right of the
University of Cambridge
to print and sell
all manner of books
was granted by
Henry VIII in 1534.
The University has printed
and published continuously
since 1584.

Cambridge University Press

Cambridge
New York   New Rochelle   Melbourne   Sydney

Editions de la Maison des Sciences de l'Homme

Paris

Published by the Press Syndicate of the University of Cambridge
The Pitt Building, Trumpington Street, Cambridge CB2 1RP
32 East 57th Street, New York, NY 10022, USA
10 Stamford Road, Oakleigh, Melbourne 3166, Australia
and
Editions de la Maison des Sciences de l'Homme
54 Boulevard Raspail, 75270 Paris Cedex 06

First published 1984
Reprinted 1985, 1987, 1988

Printed in Great Britain at the University Press, Cambridge

Library of Congress catalogue card number: 83–20853

British Library Cataloguing in Publication Data

Wallerstein, Immanuel
The politics ofthe world-economy. –
(Studies in modern capitalism=Etudes sur le
capitalisme moderne)
1. Capitalism – Political aspects
2. Economic history – 1945–
I. Title   II. Series
330.9   HB501

ISSN 0144–2333

ISBN 0 521 25918 5 hard covers
ISBN 0 521 27760 4 paperback

ISBN 2 7351 0073 1 hard covers (France only)
ISBN 2 7351 0074 X paperback (France only)

CE

Contents

Acknowledgments   *page* vii

1 World networks and the politics of the world-economy   1
2 Patterns and prospectives of the capitalist world-economy   13

I. The states and the interstate system
3 The states in the institutional vortex of the
   capitalist world-economy   27
4 The three instances of hegemony in the history of
   the capitalist world-economy   37
5 The withering away of the states   47
6 Friends as foes   58
7 The USA in the world today   69
8 The world-economy and the state-structures in
   peripheral and dependent countries (the
   so-called Third World)   80
9 Socialist states: mercantilist strategies and
   revolutionary objectives   86

II. Antisystemic movements
10 The future of the world-economy   97
11 Eurocommunism: its roots in European working-class
    history   112
12 Nationalism and the world transition to socialism:
    is there a crisis?   123
13 Revolutionary movements in the era of US hegemony
    and after   132

v

III. The civilizational project

14 The quality of life in different social systems:
    the model and the reality   147
15 Civilizations and modes of production: conflicts
    and convergences   159
16 The dialectics of civilizations in the modern
    world-system   169
17 The development of the concept of development   173

    Index   187

Acknowledgments

We are grateful to the original publishers for their kind cooperation in granting permission for publication here.

1 Amos W. Hawley (ed.), *Societal growth: processes and implications* (New York: Free Press, 1979), pp. 269–78 (copyright 1979 by the Free Press, a Division of Macmillan Publishing Company)
2 Originally prepared for Seminar on Economy and Society in the Transformation of the World (second international seminar of the United Nations University Project on Socio-Cultural Development Alternatives in a Changing World), held in Madrid, 15–19 September 1980 (copyright United Nations University)
3 *International Social Science Journal*, 32:4 (1980), pp. 743–51 (copyright 1980 by UNESCO)
4 *International Journal of Comparative Sociology*, 24:1–2 (1983)
5 *International Journal of the Sociology of Law*, 8:4 (1980), pp. 369–78 (copyright 1980 by Academic Press Inc. (London) Ltd.)
6 *Foreign Policy*, no. 40 (Fall 1980), pp. 119–31 (copyright 1980 by the Carnegie Endowment for International Peace)
7 *Contemporary Marxism*, no. 4 (Winter 1981–82), pp. 11–17
8 *Anthro-Tech: A Journal of Speculative Anthropology*, 1:3–4 (1982), pp. 11–12, 38
9 Edward Friedman (ed.) *Ascent and decline in the world-system* (Beverly Hills and London: Sage, 1982), pp. 289–300 (copyright 1982 by Sage Publications Inc.)
10 Terence K. Hopkins and I. Wallerstein (eds.), *Processes of the world-system* (Beverly Hills and London: Sage, 1980), pp. 167–80 (copyright 1980 by Sage Publications Inc.)

11 *Contemporary Marxism*, no. 2 (Winter 1980), pp. 1–7

12 *Third World Quarterly*, 5:1 (1983), pp. 95–102

13 Originally prepared for Seminar on Culture and Thought in the Transformation of the World (third international seminar of the United Nations University Project on Socio-Cultural Development Alternatives in a Changing World), held in Algiers, 13–17 December 1981 (copyright United Nations University)

14 C. K. Blong (ed.), *Systems thinking and the quality of life* (Washington, D.C.: Proceedings of the Society for General Systems Research, 1975), pp. 28–34

15 *Theory and Society*, (1978), pp. 1–10

16 Originally prepared for Ninth World Congress of Sociology, Working Group "Civilizations: One or Many?", Uppsala, 14–19 August 1978

17 *Sociological Theory*, 2 (1984)

1 ❧ World networks and the politics of the world-economy

The antinomy between state and society is often asserted to be a defining characteristic of the modern world. Some argue that the contradictions deriving from this antinomy following the French Revolution underlie the contrasting ideologies that arose in the nineteenth century, and that sociology itself as an intellectual discipline represents an attempt to analyze and resolve this antinomy. The concepts "state" and "society" refer usually to two structures that presumably coexist within a single set of boundaries (ultimately juridical boundaries). These structures are thought to be organizations of collective energy – one formal, one not, but both real – that operate on and are operated by the same set of individuals. If one starts with such an assumption, which has been widespread, indeed dominant, in Western, indeed world, thought since the French Revolution, then one can pose questions about the degree of fit between the values of the state and of the society, and seek to explain why the fit is far from perfect. In terms of policy, one can prescribe what one prefers to make the fit more perfect. This set of categories then becomes the basis of "comparative political sociology."[1]

The lack of value fit was perceived by many to be a lack of boundary fit. It followed that if the boundaries of the state were changed – diminished, enlarged, or redrawn – thus creating different juridical units, the fit would become greater. This is where the concept of nation and its allied terminology have come in. "Nation" refers in the last analysis to a "society" that has a state to itself, or has the moral right to have a state to itself (the so-called right to self-determination). Since

[1] This is made very explicit in one well-known reader: Reinhard Bendix *et al.* (eds.), *State and society: a reader in comparative political sociology* (Boston: Little Brown, 1968).

1

there has been considerable difference of views over the past two hundred years as to which were the essences which had these moral rights to existence, there has been as we know enormous and often violent conflict about these issues.

But the very fact that there has been endless, passionate debate about which "entities" constitute which concrete "societies" throws fundamental doubt, it seems to me, on the utility of the concept "societies" as a starting point for analysis. States are at least visible, functioning organisms. There exist also visible, functioning collectives of collective identification – call them nations or ethnic groups or what you will – whose boundaries may be constantly changing, but whose existence at any given point in time can in fact be empirically measured. But where can we find "societies" other than in the minds of the analysts, or of the orators? Social science would, in my view, make a great leap forward if it dispensed entirely with the term.[2]

For one thing, we would all then have to justify our unit of analysis instead of assuming it (and indeed frequently assuming it in the vaguest of all manners, such that the boundaries are totally unspecified). My own unit of analysis is based on the measurable social reality of interdependent productive activities, what may be called an "effective social division of labor" or, in code language, an "economy." In modern history, the dominant effective boundaries of the capitalist world-economy have expanded steadily from its origins in the sixteenth century, such that today it encompasses the earth.[3]

The actual measurement of the boundaries of the world-economy is both theoretically tricky and technically virtually unexplored, but logically poses no great problems. It is sufficient at this point to indicate the factors that would have to be measured. A world-economy is constituted by a cross-cutting network of interlinked productive processes which we may call "commodity chains," such that for any production process in the chain there are a number of "backward and forward linkages," on which the particular process (and the persons involved in it) are dependent. These various production processes usually require physical transportation of commodities between them, and frequently the transfers of "rights" to commodities in a chain are made by autonomous organizations, in which case we talk of the

---

[2] In the last twenty-five years, Western Marxists have substituted the term "social formation" for "society." This is just flimflam. It changes nothing. Everything one can say about the ontological vacuity of "society" applies equally to the concept "social formation."

[3] An elaboration of my position is to be found in I. Wallerstein, "Semi-peripheral countries and the contemporary world crisis," *Theory and Society*, 3:4 (1976), pp. 461–83.

existence of "commerce." Commerce is frequent, but far from universal, as the mode of linkage, and is in no way essential to the functioning of a commodity chain, except at the very end when the final consumable product is sold to the final consumer. Both the great merchant companies of the seventeenth and eighteenth centuries and the contemporary multinational corporation have been structures that eliminated much (though seldom all) of the commerce in the interstices of given commodity chains.

Production for this cross-cutting set of integrated commodity chains is based on the capitalist principle of maximizing capital accumulation. It is based on this principle not because all persons share a value consensus that this is a desirable principle on which to make production decisions. Many, perhaps most, do not. Production is based on this principle because, in the absence of a single overarching political structure that could control production decisions at all points in this world-economy, the existence of world market alternatives for what is supplied by any particular production unit constrains producers to obey the law of accumulation (reduce costs to the minimum feasible, expand sales price to the maximum feasible), or pay grievous economic penalties (ultimately bankruptcy, which removes the nonconforming producer from the economy, at least in the role he had been playing).

The primary tool in the reduction of costs is force applied to the direct producer, reducing his income to a minimum and allowing someone else to appropriate the remaining "value" he has produced. The mechanisms of such appropriation are multiple, but they take three main forms. One is forced labor, in which the direct producer receives from the legal "proprietor" part or all of his income in kind. A second is wage labor, in which the direct producer receives from the legal "proprietor" part or all of his income in money. A third is petty proprietorship, in which the direct producer is indirectly forced, often through debt mechanisms, to sell his product at below the market value. In each of these forms, which in turn have a large number of variants, the legal system of contractual property rights is an essential element, and the role of the state machinery in ensuring the coercion of unequal contract is central to the functioning of the system.

The primary tool in the expansion of sales price is the creation of a monopoly, or at least a quasi monopoly, which reduces the alternatives of adjacent actors in the commodity chain. No absolute monopolies can exist in the absence once again of an overarching political structure for the whole world-economy. But quasi monopolies are not merely possible; they are constant and recurring, and this has been so at all points in the history of the capitalist world-economy. Quasi monopolies are only possible by the utilization of state power to constrain potential "competitors" of the holder of the putative monopoly.

Let us review the picture thus far. Production is organized in commodity chains, which should be visualized as a process to which there are multiple product entry points. For example, to oversimplify, there is a commodity chain that goes from cotton production to thread production to textile production to clothing production. At each of these production points there is an input of other productive materials (each of which has to be traced backward) and of labor (which had to be both produced and maintained, and hence there are further elements of the chain, as traced backward). Almost all commodity chains will cross state boundaries at some point, and many (even most) will cross them at many points. At each point that there is a laborer, there is state pressure on the laborer's income. At each point that there is an "exchange" of product, there is state pressure on the "price."

The first kind of state pressure, that on the laborer, governs the relationship between bourgeois and proletarian. The second kind of state pressure, that on exchange, governs the relationship among bourgeois. In a capitalist world-economy, the states are expressions of power. States enforce appropriation of value by the bourgeois from the proletarian, to the extent they are not restrained by organized resistance of direct producers. States favor appropriation of value by some bourgeois from other bourgeois, but not necessarily always the same ones. Thus there are two kinds of politics in the modern world-system: the class struggle between bourgeois and proletarian, and the political struggles among different bourgeois. Insofar as these different groups of bourgeois may control different state-structures within a single world-economy, such intrabourgeois political struggle takes the form of interstate struggle.

The states are not given. They are created institutions, and are constantly changing – in form, in strength, in boundaries – through the interplay of the interstate system. Just as the world-economy has expanded over time, its political expression – the interstate system – has expanded. As the commodity chains have become longer and more complex, and have involved more and more machinery, there has been a constant pressure by the strong against the weak. This pressure has concentrated more and more of the processes in the chains that are easiest to "monopolize" in a few areas – "core" processes in "core" areas – and more and more of the processes that require less skilled and more extensive manpower that is easiest to keep at a low-income level in other areas – "peripheral" processes in "peripheral" areas. Parallel to this economic polarization has been a political polarization between stronger states in core areas and weaker states in peripheral areas, the "political" process of "imperialism" being what makes possible the "economic" process of "unequal exchange."

The strength of states has to be understood within this context. A strong state does not mean an authoritarian state. Indeed, the correlation may almost be inverse. A state is stronger than another state to the extent that it can maximize the conditions for profit-making by its enterprises (including state corporations) within the world-economy. For most states, this means creating and enforcing quasi-monopoly situations, or restraining others from doing the same to its disadvantage. The strength of the very strongest state, however, under the exceptional situation of true hegemony, is measured by its ability to minimize *all* quasi monopolies, that is, to enforce the doctrine of free trade. If hegemony is defined as a situation in which a single core power has demonstrable advantages of efficiency *simultaneously* in production, commerce, and finance, it follows that a maximally free market would be likely to ensure maximal profit to the enterprises located in such a hegemonic power.

It is no accident therefore that, at the moment of Dutch accession to hegemony in the seventeenth century, Hugo Grotius published that "classic" of international law, *Mare liberum*, in which he argued that "Every nation is free to travel to every other nation, and to trade with it," because "the act of exchange is a completion of independence which Nature requires."[4] This ideology was revived under British auspices in the mid-nineteenth century and American auspices in the mid-twentieth. In each case, the ideology was practiced only to the extent that – and as long as – the core power who promulgated it was truly hegemonic. But moments of true hegemony

---

[4] Hugo Grotius, *The freedom of the seas* (New York: Oxford University Press, 1916; 1st ed. 1608). The subtitle is "The right which belongs to the Dutch to take part in the East Indian Trade." The Portuguese and the Spanish, the ostensible objects of the treatise, were declining in any case. The Dutch view was even more hurtful to their rivals, the English (and the French). In 1617 John Selden, an Englishman, wrote a response, *Mare clausum*.

Free trade is a pragmatic matter, as Sir George Downing, England's great diplomatist, observed with acerbity in 1663 about the Dutch, who by that time had supplanted the Portuguese in the East: "It is *mare liberum* in the British seas but *mare clausum* on the coast of Africa and in the East-Indies." Cited in Pieter Geyl, *The Netherlands in the seventeenth century*, part 2: *1648–1715* (London: Ernest Benn, 1964), p. 85.

are rare, and intercore rivalry is the normal state of the world-system. Hence the doctrine of free trade seldom prevailed over the innumerable quasi monopolies instituted by or with the assistance of state-structures.

It has been the case over the history of the capitalist world-economy that the system's growth or "development" has not been constant, but has occurred in wavelike spurts of expansion and contraction.[5] This is observable empirically, and theoretically it is not hard to discern the basic explanation. As production is expanded in the individual search for accumulation, there regularly come points where the amounts produced throughout the world-economy exceed the effective demand resulting from the existing distribution of world income (as fixed by the resolutions of prior acute sociopolitical conflicts). The consequent periods of stagnation both reduce overall production and lead to class struggles which force a redistribution of world income to lower strata within the world-economy. This redistribution expands the market, at least in the core zones, and this can be most effectively compensated for, in terms of the interest of the upper strata, by the incorporation of new zones within the world-economy, adding a new component of ultralow-income-receiving direct producers.

It is important here to see that the link between "politics" and "economics" operates in two opposite directions. The cyclical difficulties in capital accumulation lead to acute class conflict within core countries which over time in fact strengthens the political claims of workers in these countries and accounts for the clear pattern of relatively rising standards of living. But since, at the same time, new lower strata are incorporated into the system, it is unlikely that the world-economy-wide distribution of income is significantly changed; indeed, the opposite is probably true. Nonetheless, expansion serves as a spur to production, and hence renews expansion.

In the course of the periods of stagnation, the system undergoes a shakedown, in which producers of weaker efficiency are eliminated. This is what accounts for the musical chairs game at the top. The "old" dominant enterprises (and the states in which they are located) find their costs steadily rising, because of the costs of amortizing "older" capital investment, combined with rising labor costs resulting from the

[5] There are waves of varying lengths. For a review of the state of our knowledge, and an assessment of the relationships between different kinds of waves, see Research Group on Cycles and Trends, Fernand Braudel Center, "Cyclical rhythms and secular trends of the capitalist world-economy: some premises, hypotheses, and questions," *Review*, 2:4 (Spring 1979), pp. 483–500.

growing strength of workers' organization. "Newer" enterprises (and the states in which they are located) thus constantly overtake "older" enterprises in the quasi-monopolistic world market, and this "overtaking" is most likely to occur in periods of stagnation.

The game of musical chairs is not restricted to states at the top. It is also played by other states. There always are – indeed there must be – states somewhere in between on various criteria. We may call them semiperipheral states. The enterprises located within them are divided between those engaged in "corelike" processes and others engaged in "peripheral" processes. In moments of expansion of the world-economy, these states find themselves attached as satellites to one or another core power and serve to some extent as economic transmission belts and political agents of an imperial power.

The periodic difficulties of world capital accumulation present *a few* semiperipheral states with their opportunity. For one thing, the world squeeze on profit intensifies competition among core powers and weakens their hold on given semiperipheral states, who are freer to play among the rivals and erect new quasi-monopolistic constraints. However, the other side of this coin is that the semiperipheral states are cut off from some of the normal sources of income, of capital and technology transfer, etc. Those that are too weak eventually succumb and return to the imperial fold chastened. A few, one or two at the most, are strong enough to impose themselves as new core powers, usually displacing over time some falling core power.[6]

The key thing to notice about the game of musical chairs, as played at the top or in the middle, is that even though who plays what role may change, the distribution of the roles (how many in each role: i.e., core, semiperiphery, periphery) has remained remarkably constant, proportionally, over the history of the world-economy.

In an interstate system, states are clearly in some sense actors. But states are themselves organizations, and we must discern who in fact does the acting. The state machineries of course reflect the pressures of the multiple enterprises whose ability to survive in a capitalist world-economy depends in very large part on the degree to which they can get these organizations, the states, to represent their interests. By and large, the enterprises have been remarkably successful in their efforts, or at least some of the enterprises – those that have flourished. But

---

[6] My arguments for these propositions on semiperipheral states are to be found in Immanuel Wallerstein, "A world-system perspective on the social sciences," *British Journal of Sociology*, 27:2 (1976), pp. 343–52.

direct producers can also attempt to assert political strength, either by resisting the state machinery or seeking to seize it and use it for their own ends.

Thus, we cannot meaningfully discuss the politics of the interstate system without analyzing the ways in which populations are grouped for political purposes. It is here that the Weberian trinity of class, status-group, and party can serve as a preliminary mode of classification.

I shall put forward some very schematic propositions about classes, status-groups, and parties, forgoing elaboration or even justification, in order to relate group conflict to the existence of an interstate system as the political framework of the capitalist world-economy.

Classes are usefully defined as groups that have a common relationship to the economy. But if the effective "economy" (in the sense of a long-term, relatively integrated set of production processes, that is, a social division of labor) is in fact a world-economy, and if we accept the argument that the existence of "national economies" has been more rhetoric than reality, then it follows that classes – classes *an sich* – are classes of the world-economy and not of states. Since, however, class consciousness – classes *für sich* – is a *political* phenomenon, and since the most efficacious political structures are the sovereign states (or the sovereign units whose creation is sought by strong, organized movements/parties), it follows that class consciousness operates largely on a state level, which per se intrudes a constant element of false consciousness into most expressions of class consciousness.

This is the structural basis of the confusion between, the contradiction between, class consciousness and national/ethnic/race consciousness, a confusion/contradiction that is both pervasive in the modern world and pervasively discussed and debated. It may well be that under certain conditions, and at certain moments, national/ethnic/race consciousness is an expression – even the most realistic expression – of class consciousness, and at other moments of historical evolution, it is precisely the opposite. And such moments may be successive in time, running one into the other without any easy demarcation lines.

Indeed, because of the axial division of production processes in the capitalist world-economy, the core–periphery relations that reproduce themselves constantly and everywhere, the antinomy of class – *an sich* in a world-economy, but *für sich* in the states – forces *most* expressions of consciousness to take a national/ethnic/race form. Nationalism is the "modern Janus," as Tom Nairn, calls it: "all nationalism is both healthy and morbid. Both progress and regress are inscribed in its genetic code from the start." But what do we conclude from this? Do we conclude, with Régis Debray, that "to discard nationalism along with its oppressive aspects means courting disaster"? Or should we conclude, with Eric Hobsbawm, that "The temptation to discover that [nationalism] can or must be [a detour on the way to revolution] is great, but so also is the danger that the detour will become the journey"?[7]

Should, however, the question be put primarily in voluntaristic terms? It is more to the point, it seems to me, to look at the factors which have made capitalism so durable as a system. Capitalism, overall, has been more exploitative (that is, extractive of surplus labor) and destructive of life and land, for the vast majority of persons located within the boundaries of the world-economy, than any previous mode of production in world history. (I know this will evoke howls of dismay among many as it seems to go against the grain of the "obvious" expansion of human well-being in the last two centuries. But this expansion of well-being has seemed to be obvious because it has been true of a highly visible minority, largely located in the core countries, and the perception of this rise in well-being has left out of account the populations that have been decimated and pauperized, largely in peripheral zones.)

When one wonders about the durability of a system so obviously detrimental to the vast majority, is not one of the explanations to be found in the unclarity (the social "veil") that is involved in a system whose economic parameters are worldwide but whose political organization is largely channeled into competitions for control of state-structures, and into inter*state* conflicts?

Nor is this the only unclarity. Since there is a game of geographical musical chairs, there is hope for "mobility" despite "polarization" – mobility for states as well as for individuals. What is usually omitted from the analysis is that, in a stratified system, upward mobility for one unit is downward mobility for another. The wonder is not that there is so little class consciousness, but that there is so much.[8]

This brings us to the question of parties. The interstate system has steadily crystallized a process that started with the development of

---

[7] See Tom Nairn, "Marxism and the modern Janus," *New Left Review*, no. 95 (Nov.–Dec. 1975), p. 17; Régis Debray, "Marxism and the national question," *New Left Review*, no. 105 (Sept.–Oct. 1977), p. 41; Eric Hobsbawm, "Some reflections on 'the break-up of Britain,'" *New Left Review*, no. 105 (Sept.–Oct. 1977), p. 17.

[8] I have discussed in much more detail the relations of class and status-group in several essays reprinted in I. Wallerstein, *The capitalist world-economy* (Cambridge: Cambridge University Press, 1979), chs. 10, 14, 18.

strong monarchies in Europe, beginning in the late fifteenth century, and has spread ever outward, the so-called rise of nationalism in the nineteenth and twentieth centuries – always in peripheral and semi-peripheral zones, be it noted (including new peripheral zones located inside the old core states). Parallel to this process has been a spreading realization by class forces that political efforts were more meaningfully directed to gaining control of state machineries than smaller, less structured, entities within these states.

While the multiple political organizational expressions of the world bourgeoisie – controlling as they did *de facto* most state-structures – could navigate with relative ease the waters of murky geographical identity, it was precisely the world's workers' movements that felt obliged to create national, that is statewide, structures, whose clear boundaries would define and limit organizational efforts. If one wants to conquer state power, one has to create organizations geared to this objective. Thus, while the world bourgeoisie has, when all is said and done, always organized in relationship to the world-economy (which accounts for all of the "strange alliances," from those of the Thirty Years' War to those of the Second World War), the proletarian forces – despite the internationalist rhetoric – have been far more nationalist than they claimed or than their ideology permitted. The marriage of socialism and nationalism in the national liberation movements of the twentieth century is not an anomaly. These movements could never have been truly "socialist" were they not "nationalist," not truly "nationalist" had they not been "socialist."

And yet these *parties* not only claim to be, but are indeed, a reflection of a world *class* struggle. This is a contradiction, to be sure, but how can proponents of a Marxist world view, like the parties in power in many peripheral and semiperipheral areas of the world, doubt that the contradictions of a capitalist world-economy would find expression in their own actions (just as much as in the actions of other social actors)?

We arrive therefore at the point. The world-system has experienced "growth" in a host of ways over five centuries of existence. Like all social structures, its contradictions both sustain it and undermine it. This is a temporally discrete process, the slow but eventual trans-formation of quantity into quality. A system is born, not suddenly but at some point decisively. It then lives and grows, surmounting its ongoing difficulties – the moments of "stagnation" – by mechanisms which restore its forward movement – the moments of "expansion." But some of these mechanisms of reinvigoration approach their asymptote. For example, new peripheries are created, until we come near the end of new spaces to incorporate in the system. Or semi-proletarian, low-cost labor is fully proletarianized, expanding effective demand but raising the real cost of labor, which sustains the system until it comes near the end of new compensatory processes of peripheralization.

In the directly political arena, there is a slow process of increased awareness. Workers' movements become politicized, seek state power, and then learn the limitations of state power, especially state power in peripheral and semiperipheral zones. There is only so much the state machineries of such peripheral and semiperipheral states can do effectively to alter the unequal exchange mechanisms of a capitalist world-economy. Workers' movements are thus being forced beyond their nationalism to worldwide organization. This last process is in a very early stage, as these movements are caught in a dilemma. They can reinforce their state power, with the advantage of holding on to a foothold in the interstate system, but they face the risk of making the detour the journey, in Hobsbawm's phrase. Or they can move to organize transnationally, at the great risk of losing any firm base, and at the risk of internecine struggle, but it may be that power is only truly available at the world level.

The world bourgeoisie is not without its multiple divisions, to be sure. But their weakness lies less in these divisions than in the growing inability to maintain the world social veil. This decline of the façade was attributed by Marx to the effects of the steady growth of the forces of production, and by Schumpeter to the self-destructive "anti-feudalism" of the bourgeoisie which destroyed the political "protective strata" in order to further the interests of accumulation.

It doesn't really matter whether Marx or Schumpeter was right. Quite probably, they both were. The point is that either analysis is a mode of accounting for the world transition from capitalism to socialism through which we are now living and which will take easily another century to complete.

As social scientists, we can interpret human history and we can project where social forces are heading. But we are not gods, and nothing, however probable, is inevitable. The reality of the world is too complex, and offers too many alternative solutions at minor and major turning points, to efface what has been romantically called throughout history "free will."

Free will, however, is not anarchic option. It is simply the reflection of complexity. Social science is one political mode of treating this complexity. It can clarify it or obscure it. Social science was born out of the interstate system, and social scientists have been historically, despite their rhetoric, closely tied to nationalism and to state-structures. This is inevitable for "professions," and we all know the steady trend to professionalization of all the branches of knowledge.

But social reality is centered in the working of the world-economy, and we will not be able to analyze intelligently any social phenomenon, however "micro" it may seem, without placing it as an element constrained by the real system in which it finds itself.

As, however, world parties emerge, slowly substituting themselves for national/ethnic/race structures as the real expression of class divisions, the logic of professionalization will break down, and social science as we know it may undergo a sea change as great as its earlier separation from philosophy. Indeed, as is obvious, we are in fact living in the midst of this sea change, whose evolution parallels and reflects the worldwide transition from capitalism to socialism.

2 ❧ Patterns and prospectives of the capitalist world-economy

1. The nature of the world-economy

The concept "world-economy" (*économie-monde* in French) should be distinguished from that of "world economy" (*économie mondiale*) or international economy. The latter concept presumes there are a series of separate "economies" which are "national" in scope, and that under certain circumstances these "national economies" trade with each other, the sum of these (limited) contacts being called the international economy. Those who use this latter concept argue that the limited contacts have been expanding in the twentieth century. It is thus asserted that the world has become "one world" in a sense it wasn't prior to the twentieth century.

By contrast, the concept "world-economy" assumes that there exists an "economy" wherever (and if but only if) there is an ongoing extensive and relatively complete social division of labor with an integrated set of production processes which relate to each other through a "market" which has been "instituted" or "created" in some complex way. Using such a concept, the world-economy is not new in the twentieth century nor is it a coming together of "national economies," none of the latter constituting complete divisions of labor. Rather, a world-economy, capitalist in form, has been in existence in at least part of the globe since the sixteenth century. Today, the entire globe is operating within the framework of this singular social division of labor we are calling the capitalist world-economy.

The capitalist world-economy has, and has had since its coming into existence, boundaries far larger than those of any political unit. Indeed, it seems to be one of the basic defining features of a capitalist

13

world-economy that there exists no political entity with ultimate authority in all its zones.

Rather, the political superstructure of the capitalist world-economy is an interstate system within which and through which political structures called "sovereign states" are legitimized and constrained. Far from meaning the total autonomy of decision-making, the term "sovereignty" in reality implies a formal autonomy combined with real limitations on this autonomy, which are implemented both via the explicit and implicit rules of the interstate system and via the power of other states in the interstate system. No state in the interstate system, even the single most powerful one at any given time, is totally autonomous – but obviously some enjoy far greater autonomy than others.

The world-economy is a complex of cultures – in the sense of languages, religions, ideologies – but this complex is not haphazard. There exists a *Weltanschauung* of imperium, albeit one with several variants, and there exist cultures of resistance to this imperium.

The major social institutions of the capitalist world-economy – the states, the classes, the "peoples," and the households – are all shaped (even created) by the ongoing workings of the world-economy. None of them are primordial, in the sense of being permanent, pre-existing, relatively fixed structures to which the workings of the capitalist world-economy are exogenous.

The capitalist world-economy is an *historical* social system. It came into existence, and its genesis must be explained. Its existence is defined by certain patterns – both cyclical rhythms and secular trends – which must be explicated. It is highly probable that it will one day go out of existence (become transformed into another type of historical social system), and we can therefore assess the historical alternatives that are before us.

2. The patterns of the world-economy

All historical structures constantly evolve. However, the use of any concept is a capturing in fixed form of some continuing pattern. We could not discern the world, interpret it, or consciously change it unless we used concepts, with all the limitations that any reification, however slight, implies.

The world-economy has a capitalist mode of production. This is an empirical statement. Although there have been other world-economies (as defined above) known in history, the modern one of which we are speaking is the only one which has survived over a long period of time without either disintegrating or being transformed into a world-empire (with a singular political structure). This modern one has had a capitalist mode of production – that is, its economy has been dominated by those who operate on the primacy of endless accumulation, such entrepreneurs (or controllers of production units) driving from the arena those who seek to operate on other premises. Since only one world-economy has survived over a long period of time, and since this one has been capitalist in form, we may suspect that the two phenomena are theoretically linked: that a world-economy to survive must have a capitalist mode of production, and inversely that capitalism cannot be the mode of production except in a system that has the form of a world-economy (a division of labor more extensive than any one political entity).

The capitalist world-economy has operated via a social relationship called capital/labor, in which the surplus created by direct producers has been appropriated by others either at the point of production or at the most immediate market-place, in either case by virtue of the fact that the appropriators control the "capital" and that their "rights" to the surplus are legally guaranteed. The extractors of surplus-value may in many cases be individuals, but they have tended increasingly to be collective entities (private or state corporations).

Once surplus-value has been extracted, it has yet to be "distributed" among a network of beneficiaries. The exchange processes of the "market" are one mode through which this redistribution occurs. In particular, the structure of the world-economy permits a (primarily trans-state) unequal exchange of goods and services, such that much of the surplus-value extracted in the peripheral zones of the world-economy is transferred to the core zones.

The exchange of products containing unequal amounts of social labor we may call the core/periphery relationship. This is pervasive, continuing, and constant. There tend to be geographical localizations of productive activities such that core-like production activities and periphery-like production activities tend each to be spatially grouped together. We can thus, for shorthand purposes, refer to some states as core states and others as peripheral states.

Insofar as some states function as loci of mixed kinds of production activities (some core-like, some periphery-like) we can speak of such states as semiperipheral. There always exist semiperipheral zones.

While the pattern of a spatial hierarchy of production processes within the capitalist world-economy is a constant, the position of any given state is not, since there have been regular partial relocations of core-like and periphery-like economic activities.

Since what makes a production process core-like or periphery-like is the degree to which it incorporates labor-value, is mechanized, and is highly profitable, and all these characteristics shift over time for any given product because of "product cycles," it follows that no product is inherently core-like or periphery-like but each has that characteristic for a given time. Nonetheless, there are always some products which are core-like and others which are periphery-like at any given time.

Because the imperatives of accumulation operate via the individual decisions of entrepreneurs, each seeking to maximize his profit – the so-called anarchy of production – there is an inherent tendency to the expansion of absolute volume of production in the world-economy. Profit can, however, be realized only if there is effective demand for the global product. But world effective demand is a function of the sum of political arrangements in the various states (the result of prior class struggles), which determine the real distribution of the global surplus. These arrangements are stable for intermediate periods of time. Consequently, world supply expands at a steady rate, while world demand remains relatively fixed for intermediate periods. Such a system must result, and historically has resulted, in recurring bottlenecks of accumulation, which are translated into periods of economic stagnation. The A-phases of expansion and the B-phases of stagnation seem to have occurred historically in cycles of forty to fifty-five years (sometimes called "Kondratieff cycles").

Each period of stagnation has created pressures to restructure the network of production processes and the social relations that underlie them in ways that would overcome the bottlenecks to accumulation. Among the mechanisms that have operated to renew expansion are:

(a)   reduction of production costs of former core-like products by further mechanization and/or relocation of these activities in lower-wage zones;

(b)   creation of new core-like activities ("innovation") which promise high initial rates of profit, thus encouraging new loci of investment;

(c)   an intensified class struggle both within the core states and between groups located in different states such that there may occur at the end of the process some political redistribution of world surplus to workers in core zones (often by means of fully proletarianizing hitherto semiproletarian households) and to bourgeois in semiperipheral and peripheral zones, thereby augmenting world effective demand;

(d)   expansion of the outer boundaries of the world-economy, thereby creating new pools of direct producers who can be involved in world production as semiproletarianized workers receiving wages below the cost of reproduction.

States in which core-like activities occur develop relatively strong state apparatuses which can advance the interests of their bourgeoisies, less by protection (a mechanism of the medium-strong seeking to be stronger) than by preventing other states from erecting political barriers to the profitability of these activities. In general, states seek to shape the world market in ways that will advance the interests of some entrepreneurs against those of others.

There seem to be cycles as well, albeit much longer ones, within the interstate system. On three separate occasions, one state has been able to achieve what may be called a hegemonic position in the world-economy: the United Provinces, 1620–50; the United Kingdom, 1815–73; the United States, 1945–67. When producers located within a given state can undersell producers located in other core states in the latter's "home market," they can transform this production advantage over time into one in the commercial arena and then into one in the financial arena. The combined advantages may be said to constitute hegemony and are reflected as well in a political–military advantage in the interstate system. Such hegemonies are relatively short-lived, since the production advantages cannot be sustained indefinitely and the mechanisms of the balance of power intrude to reduce the political advantage of the single most powerful state.

The core states in general, and the hegemonic state when one exists in particular, seek to reinforce the advantages of their producers and to legitimize their role in the interstate system by imposing their cultural dominance on the world. To some extent this occurs in the easily visible forms of language, religion, and mores, but more importantly it occurs in the form of seeking to impose modes of thought and analysis, including in particular the paradigms that inform philosophy and the sciences/social sciences.

3. The secular trends of the world-economy

The patterns of the world-economy may be at first glance cyclical in form, but they are not perfectly cyclical. The world-economy has an historical development which is structural and can be analyzed in terms of its secular trends.

The drive to accumulate leads to the constant deepening of the capitalist development. The search to reduce long-term costs of production leads to a steady increase in the degree to which production is mechanized. The search for the least expensive source of factors of production (including as an expense delays in time in acquiring access) leads to a steady increase in the degree to which these factors (land, labor, and goods) are commodified. The desire to reduce barriers to the process of accumulation leads to a steady increase in the degree to which economic transactions are contractualized. It is important to recognize two things about these processes of mechanization, commodification, and contractualization.

While there are regular increases in the world-economy taken as a whole of the degree of mechanization, commodification, and contractualization, the pattern is not linear but stepwise, each significant advance leading to overall expansion, and each overall stagnation leading to a restructuring of the world-economy such that there is further advance.

The capitalist development of the world-economy at the world level is far from complete in the twentieth century. These processes are still in full operation.

The recurring stagnations of the world-economy, which have led to the regular restructuring of this world-economy, have involved as part of this restructuring the expansion of the "outer" boundaries of the world-economy, a process, however, which has been nearly completed as of now. This expansion, which was central to the world history of the past several hundred years, gradually eliminated from the globe other kinds of historical social systems, creating the historically unique situation of there being, for all effects and purposes, a single social division of labor on the earth.

The steady but still incomplete commodification of labor, side by side with the now largely completed expansion of the outer boundaries of the world-economy, accounts for the shape of two of the major institutional structures of the capitalist world-economy: the classes and the households.

The commodification of labor ultimately means a structure in which direct producers have no access to the means of production except by selling their labor-power on a market; that is, they become proletarians. Although the percentage of direct producers who are full-life-time proletarians has been growing worldwide over time, nonetheless such proletarians are even today still probably no more than half the world's workforce.

The commodification of land and capital ultimately means a structure in which controllers of land or capital (including "human capital") have no access to the maintenance and reproduction of land and capital except by pursuing an active policy of maximizing the accumulation of capital; that is, they become bourgeois. In the twentieth century there are very few who control land or capital – directly (individually) or indirectly (collectively) – who are not bourgeois, that is, persons whose economic *raison d'être* is the accumulation of capital.

Hence, we have a situation in which *a part but not all* of direct producers are (full-life-time) proletarians (the other part we may designate as "semiproletarians"), but *most* of the controllers of land and capital are bourgeois.

The creation of two large worldwide classes has led to the molding of appropriate household structures as the member-units of these classes. We mean by household the unit which, over a longish (thirty- to fifty-year) period, pools the income of all its members, from whatever source and in whatever form.

The "semiproletarian" household, so extensive in peripheral zones of the world-economy, permits the wage-employment of some of its members for parts of their lives at wages below the proportionate cost of reproduction by pooling this wage-income with that received from subsistence, petty commodity, rental, and transfer income, which is what is meant by "super-exploitation" (since in this case the employer of the wage-labor is receiving not merely the surplus-value he/she is creating but that which other members of the household are creating).

The proletarian household, tending to receive wage-income approximating the real costs of reproduction (no less but also not much more), tends to move in the direction of a more "nucleated" household, sloughing off affines and others not defined as pulling their full weight.

The bourgeois household, seeking to maximize the use of capital, the direct control of which tends to increase by age, and utilizing the family structure as the primary mechanism of avoiding social redistribution, tends to take the form of extended, multilocal households.

The steady (now largely completed) expansion of the outer boundaries of the world-economy, combined with the continuing competition among bourgeois for advantage in the capitalist world-economy, accounts for the shape of the other two major institutional structures of the capitalist world-economy: the states and the peoples.

The drive of bourgeois for competitive advantage has led to increasing definition ("power") of the states as political structures and increasing emphasis on their constraint by the interstate system. This push for a "strong" state (strong both vis-à-vis other internal loci of power and vis-à-vis other states and external non-state forces) has been greatest and therefore most efficacious in those states with core-like production activities. The strong state has been the principal mechanism by which the bourgeois controlling these core-like production activities have been able (a) to limit and moderate the economic demands of their national workforces, (b) to shape the world market so as to compete effectively with bourgeoisies located in other states, and (c) to incorporate new zones into the world-economy, thus constantly re-creating new centers of peripheral production activities.

The increasing definition of state-structures has led to the shaping, reshaping, creation, destruction, revival of "peoples." To the extent that these "peoples" are defined by themselves (and by others) as controlling or having the "moral" right to control state-structures, these "peoples" become "nations." To the extent that a given "people" is not defined as having the right to control a state-structure, these people become "minorities" or "ethnic groups." Defining given states as nation-states is an aid in strengthening the state. Such a definition requires emphasizing one "people" and de-emphasizing, even destroying (conceptually or literally), others. This is particularly important for semiperipheral states seeking to transform their structural role in the world-economy. Various groups have interests supporting and opposing any particular nation-state definition. "Nationalism" is a mechanism both of imperium/integration and of resistance/liberation. The peoples are not haphazardly defined, but neither are they simple and unfixed derivations from an historical past. They are solidarity groupings whose boundaries are a matter of constant social transmittal/redefinition.

As the classes come to be defined vis-à-vis the developing division of labor in the world-economy and the peoples come to be defined vis-à-vis the increasingly rationalized interstate system, the locational concentration of various oppressed groups gives rise over time to antisystemic movements. These movements have organized in two main forms around two main themes: the social movement around "class" and the national movement around "nation" or people.

The seriously antisystemic (or revolutionary) forms of such move-ments first emerged in *organized* form in the nineteenth century. Their general objective – human equality – was by definition incompatible with the functioning of the capitalist world-economy, a hierarchical system based on uneven development, unequal exchange, and the appropriation of surplus-value. However, the political structure of the capitalist world-economy – the fact that it was not a single unit but a series of sovereign states – pressed the movements to seek the trans-formation of the world-system via the achievement of political power within separate states. The organization of these antisystemic move-ments at the state level had contradictory effects.

Organization at the state level for the social movement was ideo-logically confusing from the beginning, as it counterposed the logical and ideological necessity of worldwide struggle (proletarian inter-nationalism) against the immediate political need of achieving power within one state. Either the social movement resisted "nationalism" and was rendered inefficacious or it utilized nationalism and then faced ambiguously the so-called "national question" – that is, the "nationalisms" of the "minorities" within the boundaries of the state. Whatever the tactic of a given social movement, the achievement of partial or total state power involved power in a structure constrained by the interstate system, hence unable by itself to transform the system entirely (that is, to withdraw totally from the capitalist world-economy).

Organization at the state level created dilemmas for the national movements as well. The smaller the zone within which the national movement defined itself, the easier the access to state power but the less consequential. Hence, all national movements have oscillated in terms of the unit of definition, and the various "pan-" movements have had limited success. But defeats of "pan-" movements have tended to dilute the antisystemic thrust of particular national movements.

In general, both social and national movements have had a difficult time reconciling long-run antisystemic objectives and short-run "developmentalist" or "catching-up" objectives, which tend to reinforce rather than undermine the world-system. Nonetheless, the collective momentum of the social and national movements over time has been antisystemic in effect, despite the "reformism" or "revision-ism" of the various movements taken separately. Furthermore, the collective momentum of these movements has been such as to confound increasingly the social and national movements, which has in fact been a source of additional strength.

The unfolding of the institutional structures of the world-system – the classes, the states, the peoples, the households – has been reflected in the cultural mosaic of the world-system, whose pattern has been increasingly that of the tension between imperium and resistance.

As the axial division of labor became more pronounced and more unequal, the need to facilitate its operation through the allocation of workforces and the justification of inequality led to an ideology of racism which became the central organizing cultural theme of the world bourgeoisie. The existence of superior groups (whether in particular instances these groups were defined as Caucasians, or Anglo-Saxons, or other variants on this theme) became a method of simple *triage* in job and income allocation.

Whereas racism has served as a mechanism of worldwide control of direct producers, the bourgeoisie of strong core states (and particularly of the hegemonic power) sought also to direct the activities of the bourgeois of other states and various middle strata worldwide into channels that would maximize the close integration of production processes and the smooth operation of the interstate system such that the accumulation of capital was facilitated. This required the creation of a world bourgeois cultural framework that could be grafted onto "national" variations. This was particularly important in terms of science and technology, but quite important too in the realm of political ideas and of the social sciences.

The concept of a neutral "universal" culture to which the cadres of the world division of labor would be "assimilated" (the passive tense being important here) hence came to serve as one of the pillars of the world-system as it historically evolved. The exaltation of progress, and later of "modernization," summarized this set of ideas, which served less as true norms of social action than as status-symbols of obeisance and of participation in the world's upper strata.

Resistance to this cultural assimilationism was to be found among competitive bourgeois in semiperipheral and non-hegemonic core states and took the form of asserting the autonomy of "national" traditions and/or antipathy to structural generalizations in the domain of ideas. It also took the form of reinforcing alternative world linguistic groupings to the hegemonic one (in practice, English).

More fundamental cultural resistance on the part of antisystemic movements has come slowly to take the form of positing civilizational alternatives to dominant cultural forms. In particular, it has counter-distinguished civilizations (plural) to civilization (singular and imperial).

4. The system in crisis

A system which has cyclical patterns has recurring downturns, whatever we wish to call them. We have argued the regularity of world economic stagnations as one of the patterns of the capitalist world-economy. But insofar as there are also mechanisms which regularly bring these stagnations to an end and relaunch world economic expansion, we cannot count these cyclical downturns as crises, however much they are perceived as such by the individuals living through them.

Rather, a "crisis" is a situation in which the restitutive mechanisms of the system are no longer functioning well and therefore the system will either be transformed fundamentally or disintegrate. It is in this sense that we could talk for example of the "crisis of feudalism" in Europe in the period 1300–1450, a crisis whose resolution was the historic emergence of a capitalist world-economy located in that particular geographic arena. We may say that this capitalist world-economy in turn entered into a long "crisis" of a comparable nature in the twentieth century, a crisis in the midst of which we are living.

The causes of the crisis are internal to the system, the result of the contradictions built into the processes.

One of the mechanisms whereby the world-economy has overcome its downturn phases has been the expansion of the outer boundaries of the world-economy, but this is a process which has inbuilt limits, which are nearly reached.

Another of the mechanisms whereby the world-economy has overcome its downturn phases has been the expansion of world effective demand, in part through proletarianization of the direct producers, in part by redistribution of the surplus among the world bourgeoisie.

Proletarianization is also a process that has inbuilt limits. While they have hardly yet been reached, the process has been speeding up and one can foresee it reaching its asymptote within the coming century.

Redistribution of the surplus among the bourgeoisie is itself the result of bourgeoisification, which has entailed an increase of the total percentage of the world population who are bourgeois. If one distinguishes between the small group of bourgeois who control most of the fixed capital and the much larger group of bourgeois who control principally human capital, the growth and social concentration of the latter group has resulted in their acquisition of considerable political power in core states. As the price of their political support for the world-system as a system, they have been able to ensure that an increasing proportion of the appropriated surplus is redistributed to them, reducing over the long run the rate of profit to the holders of fixed capital.

Increasing proletarianization and the increasing constraint on individual mobility because of the degree to which definitions of peoples have been linked to position in the world-economy have led to the rise of the antisystemic movements. These movements have a cumulative effect which may be said to draw a logarithmic curve. We have entered into the phase of acute escalation.

The fact that we are in a systemic crisis and have been in one at least since the Russian Revolution – which was its symbolic detonator and has always been seen as such – does not mean that the capitalist development of the world-economy has come to an end. Quite the contrary. It is as vigorous as ever, perhaps more so. This is indeed the prime cause of the crisis. The very vigor of capitalist development has been and will continue to be the main factor that exacerbates the contradictions of the system.

It is therefore not the case that the crisis will be imminently resolved. A crisis of a system is a long, slow, difficult process, and for it to play itself out over a 150-year period is scarcely surprising. We have little perspective on it as we are amidst it, and we therefore tend to exaggerate each minor fork in the road. There is some constructive value in being overly optimistic in a short run, but the negative side of such exaggeration is the disillusionment it breeds. A crisis is best navigated by a cool, long-run strategy. It cannot, however, be totally planned, as the crisis itself gives rise to new possibilities of human action.

5. Prospectives

There are three different logics which are playing themselves out in the present world crisis. The outcome will be the result of their interaction.

There is the logic of socialism.

The capitalist development of the world-economy itself moves towards the socialization of the productive process. There is an *organizational* (as opposed to a political) imperative in which the full achievement of capitalist relations of production – through its emphasis on the increase of relative surplus-value and the maximum efficiency (free flow) of the factors of production – pushes towards a fully planned single productive organizational network in the world-economy.

Furthermore, the political logic of the appropriation of surplus by the few leads to the growth of the antisystemic movements and therefore towards the spread of socialist values among the world's direct producers.

Finally, the structure of the world-economy (multiple states within the division of labor) has created the possibility of socialist political movements coming to power in individual states, seeking to "construct socialism." Despite the fact that their continued location in the capitalist world-economy and the interstate system seriously constrains the kinds of transformations they can effectuate within the boundaries of a given state, their attempts to approximate in various ways a socialist order create additional institutional pressures on the world-system to move in the direction of socialism.

There is also the logic of domination.

Insofar as the powerful have, by definition, more power than the mass of the world population, and insofar as the process of transformation is slow and contradictory, it creates much opportunity for the ruling strata (the world bourgeoisie) to invent modes of continuity of power and privilege. The adoption of new social roles and new ideological clothing may be a route for existing dominant strata to perpetuate themselves in a new system. It is certainly the logic of domination that dominant groups seek to survive even a "crisis." As the land-owning hero of Lampedusa's *Il Gattopardo* says, "We must change everything in order that everything remain the same."

In the process of seeking to retain their power, the world bourgeoisie may engage in policies which lead to a nuclear world war. This could bring about a demise of the present system in a manner that destroys much of the forces of production and thereby make a socialist world order far less structurally feasible.

There is a logic of the civilizational project.

While the capitalist world-economy has been the first and only social system that has managed to eliminate from the earth all contemporaneous social systems, this has been historically true only for a very recent period of time. We could regard it as simply the conquest of the globe by western Europeans. In this case, in the long run of history, the political and technological supremacy of the West constitutes a short interval and, from the perspective of alternative "civilizational" centers, might be thought of as a transitory and aberrant interlude. There is thus a drive for a restored civilizational balance, which the very process of capitalist development of the world-economy makes more urgent and more realizable.

How a restored civilizational balance fits in with world socialism on the one hand and the drive of world ruling strata to survive on the other, however, is not at all clear.

We live facing real historical alternatives. It is clear that the capitalist world-economy cannot survive, and that it is in the process of being superseded as an historical social system. The forces at play are also clear, as are the secular trends. We can struggle for our preferences. We can analyze probabilities. But we cannot foretell, because we cannot yet know for certain how the conjuncture of forces at play will constrain the directions of change, and even less can we know what new possibilities of human liberation they will afford. The only thing of which we may be certain is that our present activity will be a major factor in the outcome of the crisis.

Part I

The states and the interstate system

---

3 ✦ The states in the institutional vortex of the capitalist world-economy

Words can be the enemy of understanding and analysis. We seek to capture a moving reality in our terminology. We thereby tend to forget that the reality changes as we encapsulate it, and by virtue of that fact. And we are even more likely to forget that others freeze reality in different ways, using however the very same words to do it. And we still cannot speak without words; indeed we cannot think without words.

Where then do we find the *via media*, the working compromise, the operational expression of a dialectical methodology? It seems to me it is most likely to be found by conceiving of provisional long-term, large-scale wholes within which concepts have meanings. These wholes must have some claim to relative space–time autonomy and integrity. They must be long enough and large enough to enable us to escape the Scylla of conceptual nominalism, but short enough and small enough to enable us to escape the Charybdis of ahistorical, universalizing abstraction. I would call such wholes "historical systems" – a name which captures their two essential qualities. It is a whole which is integrated, that is, composed of interrelated parts, therefore in some sense systematic and with comprehensible patterns. It is a system which has a history, that is, it has a genesis, an historical development, a close (a destruction, a disintegration, a transformation, an *Aufhebung*).

I contrast this concept of "historical system" with that of the more usual term of "society" (or of "social formation," which I believe is

27

used more or less synonymously). Of course, one may use the term "society" in the same sense I am using "historical system," and then the issue is simply the choice of formal symbol. But in fact the standard use of "society" is one which is applied indiscriminately to refer to modern states (and quasi-states), to ancient empires, to supposedly autonomous "tribes," and to all manner of other *political* (or cultural-aspiring-to-be-political) structures. And this lumping to-gether presumes what is to be demonstrated – that the political dimension is the one that unifies and delineates social action.

If boundaries drawn in every conceivable way – integrated pro-duction processes, exchange patterns, political jurisdiction, cultural coherence, ecology – were in fact always (or even usually) synonymous (or even highly overlapping), there would be little problem. But, as a matter of empirical fact, taking the last ten thousand years of human history, this is not at all the case. We must therefore choose among alternative criteria of defining our arenas of social action, our units of analysis. One can debate this in terms of philosophical *a priori* state-ments, and if so my own bias is a materialist one. But one can also approach this heuristically: which criterion will account for the largest percentage of social action, in the sense that changing its parameters will most immediately and most profoundly affect the operation of other parts of the whole?

I believe one can argue the case for integrated production processes as constituting this heuristic criterion, and I shall use it to draw the boundaries which circumscribe a concrete "historical system," by which I mean an empirical set of such production processes integrated according to some particular set of rules, the human agents of which interact in some "organic" way, such that changes in the functions of any group or changes in the boundaries of the historical system must follow certain rules if the entity's survival is not to be threatened. This is what we mean by such other terms as a social economy, or a specific social division of labor. To suggest that an historical system is organic is not to suggest that it is a frictionless machine. Quite the contrary: historical systems are beset by contradictions, and contain within them the seeds of processes that eventually destroy the system. But this, too, is very consonant with the "organic" metaphor.

This is a long preface to a coherent analysis of the role of states in the modern world. I think much of our collective discussion has been a prisoner of the word "state," which we have used transhistorically to mean any political structure which had some authority network (a leading person or group or groups, with intermediate cadres enforcing the will of this leading entity). Not only do we assume that what we are designating as "states" in the twentieth century are in the same universe of discourse as what we designate as "states" in, say, the tenth century, but even more fantastically, we frequently attempt to draw lines of historical continuity between two such "states" – of the same name, or found in the same general location in terms of longitude and latitude – said to be continuous because scholars can argue affinities of the languages that are spoken, or the cosmologies that are professed, or the genes that are pooled.

The capitalist world-economy constitutes one such historical system. It came into existence, in my view, in Europe in the sixteenth century. The capitalist world-economy is a system based on the drive to accumulate capital, the political conditioning of price levels (of capital, commodities and labor), and the steady polarization of classes and regions (core/periphery) over time. This system has developed and expanded to englobe the whole earth in the subsequent centuries. It has today reached a point where, as a result of its contradictory developments, the system is in a long crisis.[1]

The development of the capitalist world-economy has involved the creation of all the major institutions of the modern world: classes, ethnic/national groups, households – and the "states." All of these structures postdate, not antedate capitalism; all are consequence, not cause. Furthermore, these various institutions, in fact, create each other. Classes, ethnic/national groups, and households are defined by the state, through the state, in relation to the state, and in turn create the state, shape the state, and transform the state. It is a structured maelstrom of constant movement, whose parameters are measurable through the repetitive regularities, while the detailed constellations are always unique.

What does it mean to say that a state comes into existence? Within a capitalist world-economy, the state is an institution whose existence is defined by its relation to other "states." Its boundaries are more or less clearly defined. Its degree of juridical sovereignty ranges from total to nil. Its real power to control the flows of capital, commodities, and labor across its frontiers is greater or less. The real ability of the central authorities to enforce decisions on groups operating within state frontiers is greater or less. The ability of the state authorities to impose their will in zones outside state frontiers is greater or less.

---

[1] These theses are developed at length in I. Wallerstein, *The modern world-system*, 2 vols. (New York and London: Academic Press, 1974–80); and *The capitalist world-economy* (Cambridge: Cambridge University Press, 1979).

Various groups located inside, outside, and across any given state's frontiers are constantly seeking to increase, maintain, or decrease the "power" of the state, in all the ways referred to above. These groups are seeking to change these power constellations because of some sense that such changes will improve the particular group's ability to profit, directly or indirectly, from the operations of the world market. The state is the most convenient institutional intermediary in the establishment of market constraints (quasi monopolies, in the broadest sense of the term) in favor of particular groups.

The historical development of the capitalist world-economy is that, beginning with relatively amorphous entities, more and more "states" operating within the interstate system have been created. Their boundaries and the definitions of their formal rights have been defined with increasing clarity (culminating in the contemporary United Nations structure of international law). The modalities and limits of group pressures in state structures have also been increasingly defined (in the sense both of the legal limits placed on such pressures, and of the rational organization by groups to transcend these limits). None the less, despite what might be called the "honing" of this institutional network, it is probably safe to say that the relative power continuum of stronger and weaker states has remained relatively unchanged over 400-odd years. That is not to say that the same "states" have remained "strong" and "weak." Rather, there has been at all moments a power hierarchy of such states, but also at no moment has there been any one state whose hegemony was totally unchallenged (although relative hegemony has occurred for limited periods).

Various objections have been made to such a view of the modern state, its genesis and its mode of functioning. There are four criticisms which seem to be the most frequent and worthy of discussion.

First, it is argued that this view is too instrumental a view of the state, that it makes the states into a mere conscious instrument of acting groups with no life and integrity of their own, with no base of social support in and for themselves.

It seems to me this counter-argument is based on a confusion about social institutions in general. Once created, all social institutions, including the states, have lives of their own in the sense that many different groups will use them, support them, exploit them for various (and even contradictory) motives. Furthermore, institutions large and structured enough to have permanent staffs thereby generate a group of persons – the bureaucracies of these institutions – who have a direct socio-economic stake in the persistence and flourishing of the institution as such, quite independent of the ideological premises on which the institution was created and the interests of the major social forces that sustain it.

None the less, the issue is not who has some say in the ongoing decisions of a state-machinery but who has decisive or critical say, and what are the key issues that are fought about in terms of state policy. We believe that these key issues are: (a) the rules governing the social relations of production, which critically affect the allocation of surplus-value; and (b) the rules governing the flow within and across frontiers of the factors of production – capital, commodities and labor – which critically affect the price structures of markets. If one changes the allocation of surplus-value and the price structures of markets, one is changing the relative competitivity of particular producers, and therefore their profit-levels.

It is the states that make these rules, and it is primarily the states that intervene in the process of other (weaker) states when the latter attempt to make the rules as they prefer them.

The second objection to this mode of analysis is that it ignores the reality of traditional continuities, as ensconced in the operative consciousnesses of groups. Such consciousnesses do indeed exist and are very powerful, but are the consciousnesses themselves continuous? I think not, and believe the merest glance at the empirical reality will confirm that. The history of nationalisms, which are one of the salient forms of such consciousnesses, shows that everywhere that nationalist movements emerge, they create consciousness, they revive (even partially invent) languages, they coin names and emphasize customary practices that come to distinguish their group from other groups. They do this in the name of what is claimed to have always been there, but frequently (if not usually) they must stretch the interpretation of the historical evidence in ways that disinterested observers would consider partisan. This is true not only of the so-called "new" nations of the twentieth century[2] but of the "old" nations as well.[3]

[2] In 1956, Thomas Hodgkin wrote in a "Letter" to Saburi Biobaku (*Odù*, no. 4 (1957), p. 42): "I was struck by your statement that the use of the term 'Yoruba' to refer to the whole range of peoples who would nowadays describe themselves as Yoruba (as contrasted with the Oyo peoples simply) was due largely to the influence of the Anglican Mission at Abeokuta, and its work in evolving a standard 'Yoruba' language, based on Oyo speech. This seems to me an extremely interesting example of the way in which Western influences have helped to stimulate a new kind of national sentiment. Everyone recognizes that the notion of 'being a Nigerian' is a new kind of conception. But it would seem that the notion of 'being a Yoruba' is not very much older. I take it from what you say that there is no evidence that those who owed allegiance to the kingdom of Oyo – or to the earlier State system based upon Ife? – used any common name to describe themselves, although it is possible that they may have done so?"
[3] George Bernard Shaw has the Nobleman in *Saint Joan* exclaim: "A Frenchman! Where did you

It is also clear that the successive ideological statements about a given name – what it encompasses, what constitutes its "tradition" – are discontinuous and different. Each successive version can be explained in terms of the politics of its time, but the fact that these versions vary so widely is itself a piece of evidence against taking the assertion of continuity as more than a claim of an interested group. It surely is shifting sand on which to base an analysis of the political functioning of states.

The third argument against this form of analysis is that it is said to ignore the underlying centrality of the class struggle, which is implicitly asserted to exist within some fixed entity called a society or a social formation, and which in turn accounts for the structure of the state.

If, however, "classes" is the term we use for groups deriving from positions in relation to the mode of production, then it is to the realities of the set of integrated production processes that we must look to determine who constitute our classes. The boundaries of these integrated production processes are in fact, of course, far wider than the individual states, and even sub-sets of production processes do not correlate very often with state boundaries. There is consequently no *a priori* reason to assume that classes are in some objective sense circumscribed by state boundaries.

Now, it may fairly be argued that class consciousnesses have tended historically to be national in form. This is so, for good reasons we shall discuss below. But the fact that this is so is no evidence that the analytic perception is correct. On the contrary, this fact of the national form of consciousness for trans-state classes becomes itself a major explicandum of the modern world.

Finally, it is said that this mode of analysis ignores the fact that the wealthiest states are not the strongest states, but tend indeed to be relatively weak. But this is to misperceive what constitutes the strength of state machineries. It is once again to take ideology for analytic reality.

Some state machineries preach the line of a strong state. They seek to limit opposition; they seek to impose decisions on internal groups; they are bellicose vis-à-vis external groups. But what is important is the success of the assertion of power, not its loudness. Oppositions only

pick up that expression? Are those Burgundians and Bretons and Picards and Gascons beginning to call themselves Frenchmen, just as our fellows are beginning to call themselves Englishmen? They actually talk of France and England as their countries. Theirs, if you please! What is to become of me and you if that way of thinking comes into fashion?"

need to be suppressed where they seriously exist. States that encompass relatively more homogeneous strata (because of the unevenness of allocation of class forces in the world-economy) may achieve via consensus what others strive (and perhaps fail) to achieve via the iron hand. Entrepreneurs who are economically strong in the market do not need state assistance to create monopoly privileges, though they may need state aid to oppose the creation by others, in other states, of monopoly privileges which would hurt these market-strong entrepreneurs.

The states are thus, we are arguing, created institutions reflecting the needs of class forces operating in the world-economy. They are not however created in a void, but within the framework of an interstate system. This interstate system is, in fact, the framework within which the states are defined. It is the fact that the states of the capitalist world-economy exist within the framework of an interstate system that is the *differentia specifica* of the modern state, distinguishing it from other bureaucratic polities. This interstate system constitutes a set of constraints which limit the abilities of individual state machineries, even the strongest among them, to make decisions. The ideology of this system is sovereign equality, but the states are in fact neither sovereign nor equal. In particular, the states impose on each other – not only the strong on the weak, but the strong on the strong – limitations on their modes of political (and therefore military) behavior, and even more strikingly limitations on their abilities to affect the law of value underlying capitalism. We are so used to observing all the things states do that constitute a defiance of other states that we do not stop to recognize how few these things are, rather than how many. We are so used to thinking of the interstate system as verging on anarchy that we fail to appreciate how rule-ridden it is. Of course, the "rules" are broken all the time, but we should look at the consequences – the mechanisms that come into play to force changes in the policies of the offending states. Again, we should look less at the obvious arena of political behavior, and more at the less observed arena of economic behavior. The story of states with communist parties in power in the twentieth-century interstate system is striking evidence of the efficaciousness of such pressures.

The production processes of the capitalist world-economy are built on a central relationship or antinomy: that of capital and labor. The ongoing operations of the system have the effect of increasingly circumscribing individuals (or rather households), forcing them to participate in the work process in one capacity or the other, as contributors of surplus-value or as receivers.

The states have played a central role in the polarization of the population into those living off appropriated surplus, the bourgeoisie, and those whose surplus-value is appropriated from them, the proletariat. For one thing, the states created the legal mechanisms which not merely permitted or even facilitated the appropriation of surplus-value, but protected the results of the appropriation by enacting property rights. They created institutions which ensured the socialization of children into the appropriate roles.

As the classes came into objective existence, in relation to each other, they sought to alter (or to maintain) the unequal bargaining power between them. To do this, they had to create appropriate institutions to affect state decisions, which largely turned out, over time, to be institutions created within the boundaries of the state, adding thereby to the worldwide definiteness of state structures.

This has led to deep ambivalences in their self-perception and consequently contradictory political behavior. Both the bourgeoisie and the proletariat are classes formed in a world-economy, and when we speak of objective class position, it is necessarily classes of this world-economy to which we refer. As, however, the bourgeoisie first began to become class-conscious and only later the proletariat, both classes found disadvantages as well as advantages to defining themselves as world classes.

The bourgeoisie, in pursuit of its class interest, the maximization of profit in order to accumulate capital, sought to engage in its economic activities as it saw fit without constraints on geographic location or political considerations. Thus, for example, in the sixteenth or seventeenth centuries, it was frequent for Dutch, English or French entrepreneurs to "trade with the enemy" in wartime, even in armaments. And it was frequent for entrepreneurs to change place of domicile and citizenship in pursuit of optimizing gain. The bourgeoisie then (as now) reflected this self-perception in tendencies toward a "world" cultural style – in consumption, in language, etc. However, it was also true then, and now, that, however much the bourgeoisie chafed under limitations placed by particular state authorities for particular reasons at one or another moment, the bourgeoisies also needed to utilize state machineries to strengthen their position in the market vis-à-vis competitors and to protect them vis-à-vis the working classes. And this meant that the many fractions of the world bourgeoisie had an interest in defining themselves as "national" bourgeoisies.

The same pattern held for the proletariat. On the one hand, as it became class-conscious, it recognized that a prime organizational objective has to be the unity of proletarians in their struggle. It is no accident that the *Communist manifesto* proclaimed: "Workers of the world, unite!" It was clear that precisely the fact that the bourgeoisie operated in the arena of a world-economy, and could (and would) transfer sites of production whenever it was to its advantage, meant that proletarian unity, if it were to be truly efficacious, could only be at the world level. And yet we know that world proletarian unity has never really been efficacious (most dramatically in the failure of the Second International to maintain an anti-nationalist stance during the First World War). This is so for a very simple reason. The mechanisms most readily available to improve the relative conditions of segments of the working classes are the state machineries, and the political organization of the proletariat has almost always taken the form of state-based organizations. Furthermore, this tendency has been reinforced, not weakened, by whatever successes these organizations have had in attaining partial or total state power.

We arrive thus at a curious anomaly: both the bourgeoisie and the proletariat express their consciousness at a level which does not reflect their objective economic role. Their interests are a function of the operations of a world-economy, and they seek to enhance their interests by affecting individual state machineries, which in fact have only limited power (albeit real power, none the less) to affect the operations of this world-economy.

It is this anomaly that constantly presses bourgeoisies and proletariats to define their interests in status-group terms. The most efficacious status-group in the modern world is the nation, since the nation lays claim to the moral right to control a particular state-structure. To the extent that a nation is not a state, we find the potential for a nationalist movement to arise and flourish. Of course, there is no essence that is a nation and that occasionally breeds a nationalist movement. Quite the contrary. It is a nationalist movement that creates an entity called a nation, or seeks to create it. Under the multiple circumstances in which nationalism is not available to serve class interests, status-group solidarities may crystallize around substitute poles: religion, race, language, or other particular cultural patterns.

Status-group solidarities remove the anomaly of national class organization or consciousness from the forefront of visibility and hence
relax the strains inherent in contradictory structures. But, of course,
they may also obfuscate the class struggle. To the extent that particular
ethnic consciousnesses therefore lead to consequences which key
groups find intolerable, we see the re-emergence of overt class organizations, or if this creates too much strain, of redefined status-group
solidarities (drawing the boundaries differently). That particular segments of the world bourgeoisie or world proletariat might flit from, say,
pan-Turkic to pan-Islamic to national to class-based movements over a
period of decades reflects not the inconsistency of the struggle but the
difficulties of navigating a course that can bridge the antinomy:
objective classes of the world-economy/subjective classes of a state-
structure.

Finally, the atoms of the classes (and of the status-groups), the
income-pooling households, not only are shaped and constantly re-
shaped by the objective economic pressures of the ongoing dynamic of
the world-economy but also are regularly and deliberately manipula-
ted by the states that seek to determine (to alter) their boundaries in
terms of the needs of the labor-market, as well as to determine the flows
and forms of income that may in fact be pooled. The households in turn
may assert their own solidarities and priorities and resist the pressures,
less effectively by passive means, more effectively, when possible, by
creating the class and status-group solidarities we have just mentioned.

All these institutions together – the states, the classes, the ethnic/
national/status-groups, the households – form an institutional vortex
which is both the product and the moral life of the capitalist world-
economy. Far from being primordial and pre-existing essences, they
are dependent and coterminous existences. Far from being segregated
and separable, they are indissociably intertwined in complex and
contradictory ways. Far from one determining the other, they are in a
sense avatars of each other.

4 ✙ The three instances of hegemony in the history of the capitalist world-economy

When one is dealing with a complex, continuously evolving, large-scale historical system, concepts that are used as shorthand descriptions for structural patterns are useful only to the degree that one clearly lays out their purpose, circumscribes their applicability, and specifies the theoretical framework they presuppose and advance.

Let me therefore state some premises which I shall not argue at this point. If you are not willing to regard these premises as plausible, you will not find the way I elaborate and use the concept of hegemony very useful. I assume that there exists a concrete singular historical system which I shall call the "capitalist world-economy," whose temporal boundaries go from the long sixteenth century to the present. Its spatial boundaries originally included Europe (or most of it) plus Iberian America but they subsequently expanded to cover the entire globe. I assume this totality is a *system*, that is, that it has been relatively autonomous of external forces; or, to put it another way, that its patterns are explicable largely in terms of its internal dynamics. I assume that it is an *historical* system, that is, that it was born, has developed, and will one day cease to exist (through disintegration or fundamental transformation). I assume lastly that it is the dynamics of the system itself that explain its historically changing characteristics. Hence, insofar as it is a system, it has structures and these structures manifest themselves in cyclical rhythms, that is, mechanisms which reflect and ensure repetitious patterns. But insofar as this system is historical, no rhythmic movement ever returns the system to an equilibrium point but instead moves the system along various continua which may be called the secular trends of this system. These trends eventually must culminate in the impossibility of containing further reparations of the structured dislocations by restorative mechanisms. Hence the system undergoes what some call "bifurcating turbulence" and others the "transformation of quantity into quality."

To these methodological or metaphysical premises, I must add a few substantive ones about the operations of the capitalist world-economy. Its mode of production is capitalist; that is, it is predicated on the endless accumulation of capital. Its structure is that of an axial social division of labor exhibiting a core/periphery tension based on unequal exchange. The political superstructure of this system is that of a set of so-called sovereign states defined by and constrained by their membership in an interstate network or system. The operational guidelines of this interstate system include the so-called balance of power, a mechanism designed to ensure that no single state ever has the capacity to transform this interstate system into a single world-empire whose boundaries would match that of the axial division of labor. There have of course been repeated attempts throughout the history of the capitalist world-economy to transform it in the direction of a world-empire, but these attempts have all been frustrated. However, there have also been repeated and quite different attempts by given states to achieve hegemony in the interstate system, and these attempts have in fact succeeded on three occasions, if only for relatively brief periods.

The thrust of hegemony is quite different from the thrust to world-empire; indeed it is in many ways almost its opposite. I will therefore (1) spell out what I mean by hegemony, (2) describe the analogies in the three purported instances, (3) seek to decipher the roots of the thrust to hegemony and suggest why the thrust to hegemony has succeeded three times but never lasted too long, and (4) draw inferences about what we may expect in the proximate future. The point of doing all this is not to erect a Procrustean category into which to fit complex historical reality but to illuminate what I believe to be one of the central processes of the modern world-system.

1

Hegemony in the interstate system refers to that situation in which the ongoing rivalry between the so-called "great powers" is so unbalanced that one power is truly *primus inter pares*; that is, one power can largely impose its rules and its wishes (at the very least by effective veto power) in the economic, political, military, diplomatic, and even cultural arenas. The material base of such power lies in the ability of enterprises domiciled in that power to operate more efficiently in all three major economic arenas – agro-industrial production, commerce, and finance. The edge in efficiency of which we are speaking is one so great that these enterprises can not only outbid enterprises domiciled in other great powers in the world market in general, but quite specifically in very many instances within the home markets of the rival powers themselves.

I mean this to be a relatively restrictive definition. It is not enough for one power's enterprises simply to have a larger share of the world market than any other or simply to have the most powerful military forces or the largest political role. I mean hegemony only to refer to situations in which the edge is so significant that allied major powers are *de facto* client states and opposed major powers feel relatively frustrated and highly defensive vis-à-vis the hegemonic power. And yet while I want to restrict my definition to instances where the margin or power differential is really great, I do not mean to suggest that there is ever any moment when a hegemonic power is omnipotent and capable of doing anything it wants. Omnipotence does not exist within the interstate system.

Hegemony therefore is not a state of being but rather one end of a fluid continuum which describes the rivalry relations of great powers to each other. At one end of this continuum is an almost even balance, a situation in which many powers exist, all somewhat equal in strength, and with no clear or continuous groupings. This is rare and unstable. In the great middle of this continuum, many powers exist, grouped more or less into two camps, but with several neutral or swing elements, and with neither side (nor *a fortiori* any single state) being able to impose its will on others. This is the statistically normal situation of rivalry within the interstate system. And at the other end lies the situation of hegemony, also rare and unstable.

At this point, you may see what it is I am describing but may wonder why I am bothering to give it a name and thereby focus attention upon it. It is because I suspect hegemony is not the result of a random reshuffling of the cards but is a phenomenon that emerges in specifiable circumstances and plays a significant role in the historical development of the capitalist world-economy.

2

Using this restrictive definition, the only three instances of hegemony would be the United Provinces in the mid-seventeenth century, the

United Kingdom in the mid-nineteenth, and the United States in the mid-twentieth. If one insists on dates, I would tentatively suggest as maximal bounding points 1620–72, 1815–73, 1945–67. But of course, it would be a mistake to try to be too precise when our measuring instruments are both so complex and so crude.

I will suggest four areas in which it seems to me what happened in the three instances was analogous. To be sure, analogies are limited. And to be sure, since the capitalist world-economy is in my usage a single continuously evolving entity, it follows by definition that the overall structure was different at each of the three points in time. The differences were real, the outcome of the secular trends of the world-system. But the structural analogies were real as well, the reflection of the cyclical rhythms of this same system.

The first analogy has to do with the sequencing of achievement and loss of relative efficiencies in each of the three economic domains. What I believe occurred was that in each instance enterprises domiciled in the given power in question achieved their edge first in agro-industrial production, then in commerce, and then in finance.[1] I believe they lost their edge in this sequence as well (this process having begun but not

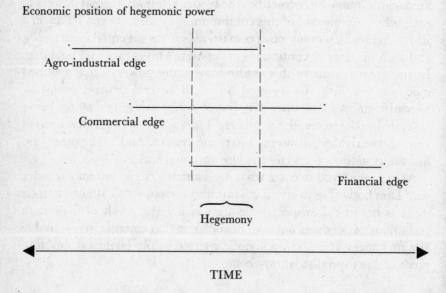

Economic position of hegemonic power

Agro-industrial edge

Commercial edge

Financial edge

Hegemony

TIME

---

[1] I have described this in empirical detail for the first instance in Immanuel Wallerstein, *The modern world-system*, vol. II: *Mercantilism and the consolidation of the European world-economy, 1600–1750* (New York and London: Academic Press, 1980), ch. 2.

yet having been completed in the third instance). Hegemony thus refers to that short interval in which there is *simultaneous* advantage in all three economic domains.

The second analogy has to do with the ideology and policy of the hegemonic power. Hegemonic powers during the period of their hegemony tended to be advocates of global "liberalism." They came forward as defenders of the principle of the free flow of the factors of production (goods, capital, and labor) throughout the world-economy. They were hostile in general to mercantilist restrictions on trade, including the existence of overseas colonies for the stronger countries. They extended this liberalism to a generalized endorsement of liberal parliamentary institutions (and a concurrent distaste for political change by violent means), political restraints on the arbitrariness of bureaucratic power, and civil liberties (and a concurrent open door to political exiles). They tended to provide a high standard of living for their national working classes, high by world standards of the time.

None of this should be exaggerated. Hegemonic powers regularly made exceptions to their anti-mercantilism, when it was in their interest to do so. Hegemonic powers regularly were willing to interfere with political processes in other states to ensure their own advantage. Hegemonic powers could be very repressive at home, if need be, to guarantee the national "consensus." The high working-class standard was steeply graded by internal ethnicity. Nevertheless, it is quite striking that liberalism as an ideology did flourish in these countries at precisely the moments of their hegemony, and to a significant extent only then and there.

The third analogy is in the pattern of global military power. Hegemonic powers were primarily sea (now sea/air) powers. In the long ascent to hegemony, they seemed very reluctant to develop their armies, discussing openly the potentially weakening drain on state revenues and manpower of becoming tied down in land wars. Yet each found finally that it had to develop a strong land army as well to face up to a major land-based rival which seemed to be trying to transform the world-economy into a world-empire.

In each case, the hegemony was secured by a thirty-year-long world war. By a world war, I shall mean (again somewhat restrictively) a land-based war that involves (not necessarily continuously) almost all the major military powers of the epoch in warfare that is very destructive of land and population. To each hegemony is attached one of these wars. World War Alpha was the Thirty Years' War from 1618 to 1648, where Dutch interests triumphed over Hapsburg in the world-economy. World War Beta was the Napoleonic Wars from 1792 to 1815, where British interests triumphed over French. World War Gamma was the long Euroasian wars from 1914 to 1945, where US interests triumphed over German.

While limited wars have been a constant of the operations of the interstate system of the capitalist world-economy (there having been scarcely any year when there was not some war somewhere within the system), world wars have been by contrast a rarity. In fact their rarity and the fact that the number and timing seems to have correlated with the achievement of hegemonic status by one power brings us to the fourth analogy.

If we look to those very long cycles that Rondo Cameron has dubbed "logistics," we can see that world wars and hegemony have been in fact related to them. There has been very little scholarly work done on these logistics. They have been most frequently discussed in the comparisons between the A–B sequences of 1100–1450 and 1450–1750. There are only a few discussions of the logistics that may exist after the latter point in time. But if we take the prime observation which has been used to define these logistics – secular inflation and deflation – the pattern seems in fact to have continued.

It therefore might be plausible to argue the existence of such (price) logistics up to today using the following dates: 1450–1730, with 1600–50 as a flat peak; 1730–1897, with 1810–17 as a peak; and 1897–?, with an as yet uncertain peak. If there are such logistics, it turns out that the world war and the (subsequent) hegemonic era are located somewhere around (just before and after) the peak of the logistic. That is to say, these processes seem to be the product of the long competitive expansion which seemed to have resulted in a particular concentration of economic and political power.

The outcome of each world war included a major restructuring of the interstate system (Westphalia; the Concert of Europe; the UN and Bretton Woods) in a form consonant with the need for relative stability of the now hegemonic power. Furthermore, once the hegemonic position was eroded economically (the loss of the efficiency edge in agro-industrial production), and therefore hegemonic decline set in, one consequence seemed to be the erosion of the alliance network which the hegemonic power had created patiently, and ultimately a serious reshuffling of alliances.

In the long period following the era of hegemony, two powers seemed eventually to emerge as the "contenders for the succession" – England

and France after Dutch hegemony; the US and Germany after British; and now Japan and western Europe after US. Furthermore, the eventual winner of the contending pair seemed to use as a conscious part of its strategy the gentle turning of the old hegemonic power into its "junior partner" – the English vis-à-vis the Dutch, the US vis-à-vis Great Britain ... and now?

3

Thus far I have been primarily descriptive. I realize that this description is vulnerable to technical criticism. My coding of the data may not agree with everyone else's. I think nonetheless that as an initial effort this coding is defensible and that I have therefore outlined a broad repetitive pattern in the functioning of the interstate question. The question now is how to interpret it. What is there in the functioning of a capitalist world-economy that gives rise to such a cyclical pattern in the interstate system?

I believe this pattern of the rise, temporary ascendancy, and fall of hegemonic powers in the interstate system is merely one aspect of the central role of the political machinery in the functioning of capitalism as a mode of production.

There are two myths about capitalism put forward by its central ideologues (and strangely largely accepted by its nineteenth-century critics). One is that it is defined by the free flow of the factors of production. The second is that it is defined by the non-interference of the political machinery in the "market." In fact, capitalism is defined by the *partially* free flow of the factors of production and by the *selective* interference of the political machinery in the "market." Hegemony is an instance of the latter.

What defines capitalism most fundamentally is the drive for the endless accumulation of capital. The interferences that are "selected" are those which advance this process of accumulation. There are however two problems about "interference." It has a cost, and therefore the benefit of any interference is only a benefit to the extent it exceeds this cost. Where the benefits are available without any "interference," this is obviously desirable, as it minimizes the "deduction." And secondly, interference is always in favor of one set of accumulators as against another set, and the latter will always seek to counter the former. These two considerations circumscribe the politics of hegemony in the inter-state system.

The costs to a given entrepreneur of state "interference" are felt in two main ways. First, in financial terms, the state may levy direct taxes which affect the rate of profit by requiring the firm to make payments to the state, or indirect taxes, which may alter the rate of profit by affecting the competitivity of a product. Secondly, the state may enact rules which govern flows of capital, labor, or goods, or may set minimum and/or maximum prices. While direct taxes always represent a cost to the entrepreneur, calculations concerning indirect taxes and state regulations are more complex, since they represent costs both to the entrepreneur and to (some of) his competitors. The chief concern in terms of individual accumulation is not the absolute cost of these measures but the comparative cost. Costs, even if high, may be positively desirable from the standpoint of a given entrepreneur, if the state's actions involve still higher costs to some competitor. Absolute costs are of concern only if the loss to the entrepreneur is greater than the medium-run gain which is possible through greater competitivity brought about by such state actions. It follows that absolute cost is of greatest concern to those entrepreneurs who would do best in open-market competition in the absence of state interference.

In general, therefore, entrepreneurs are regularly seeking state interference in the market in multiple forms – subsidies, restraints of trade, tariffs (which are penalties for competitors of different nationality), guarantees, maxima for input prices and minima for output prices, etc. The intimidating effect of internal and external repression is also of direct economic benefit to entrepreneurs. To the extent that the ongoing process of competition and state interference leads to oligopolistic conditions within state boundaries, more and more attention is naturally paid to securing the same kind of oligopolistic conditions in the most important market, the world market.

The combination of the competitive thrust and constant state interference results in a continuing pressure towards the concentration of capital. The benefits of state interference inside and outside the state boundaries is cumulative. In political terms, this is reflected as expanding world power. The edge a rising power's economic enterprises have vis-à-vis those of a competitive rising power may be thin and therefore insecure. This is where the world wars come in. The thirty-year struggle may be very dramatic militarily and politically. But the profoundest effect may be economic. The winner's economic edge is expanded by the very process of the war itself, and the postwar interstate settlement is designed to encrust that greater edge and protect it against erosion.

A given state thus assumes its world "responsibilities" which are reflected in its diplomatic, military, political, ideological, and cultural stances. Everything conspires to reinforce the cooperative relationship of the entrepreneurial strata, the bureaucratic strata, and with some lag the working-class strata of the hegemonic power. This power may then be exercised in a "liberal" form – given the real diminution of political conflict within the state itself compared to earlier and later periods, and to the importance in the interstate arena of delegitimizing the efforts of other state machineries to act against the economic superiorities of the hegemonic power.

The problem is that global liberalism, which is rational and cost-effective, breeds its own demise. It makes it more difficult to retard the spread of technological expertise. Hence over time it is virtually inevitable that entrepreneurs coming along later will be able to enter the most profitable markets with the most advanced technologies and younger "plant," thus eating into the material base of the productivity edge of the hegemonic power.

Secondly, the internal political price of liberalism, needed to maintain uninterrupted production at a time of maximal global accumulation, is the creeping rise of real income of both the working strata and the cadres located in the hegemonic power. Over time, this must reduce the competitivity of the enterprises located in this state.

Once the clear productivity edge is lost, the structure cracks. As long as there is a hegemonic power, it can coordinate more or less the political responses of all states with core-like economic activities to all peripheral states, maximizing thereby the differentials of unequal exchange. But when hegemony is eroded, and especially when the world-economy is in a Kondratieff downturn, a scramble arises among the leading powers for the smaller pie, which undermines their collective ability to extract surplus via unequal exchange. The rate of unequal exchange thereby diminishes (but never to zero) and creates further incentive to a reshuffling of alliance systems.

In the period leading to the peak of a logistic, which leads towards the creation of the momentary era of hegemony, the governing parable is that of the tortoise and the hare. It is not the state that leaps ahead politically and especially militarily that wins the race, but the one that plods along improving inch by inch its long-term competitivity. This requires a firm but discrete and intelligent organization of the entrepreneurial effort by the state-machinery. Wars may be left to others, until the climactic world war when the hegemonic power must at last invest its resources to clinch its victory. Thereupon comes "world responsibility" with its benefits but also its (growing) costs. Thus the hegemony is sweet but brief.

4

The inferences for today are obvious. We are in the immediate post-hegemonic phase of this third logistic of the capitalist world-economy. The US has lost its productive edge but not yet its commercial and financial superiorities; its military and political power edge is no longer so overwhelming. Its abilities to dictate to its allies (western Europe and Japan), intimidate its foes, and overwhelm the weak (compare the Dominican Republic in 1965 with El Salvador today) are vastly impaired. We are in the beginnings of a major reshuffling of alliances.[2] Yet, of course, we are only at the beginning of all this. Great Britain began to decline in 1873, but it was only in 1982 that it could be openly challenged by Argentina.

The major question is whether this third logistic will act itself out along the lines of the previous ones. The great difference is the degree to which the fact that the capitalist world-economy has entered into a structural crisis as an historical system will obliterate these cyclical processes. I do not believe it will obliterate them but rather that it will work itself out in part through them.[3]

We should not invest more in the concept of hegemony than is there. It is a way of organizing our perception of process, not an "essence" whose traits are to be described and whose eternal recurrences are to be demonstrated and then anticipated. A processual concept alerts us to the forces at play in the system and the likely nodes of conflict. It does not do more. But it also does not do less. The capitalist world-economy is not comprehensible unless we analyze clearly what are the political forms which it has engendered and how these forms relate to other realities. The interstate system is not some exogenous, God-given variable which mysteriously restrains and interacts with the capitalist drive for the endless accumulation of capital. It is its expression at the level of the political arena.

[2] See I. Wallerstein, "North Atlanticism in decline," *SAIS Review*, no. 4 (Summer 1982), pp. 21–6.
[3] For a debate about this, see the "Conclusion" in S. Amin, G. Arrighi, A. G. Frank and I. Wallerstein, *Dynamics of global crisis* (New York: Monthly Review Press, 1982).

5 ❧ The withering away of the states

When ultimately [the state] becomes really representative of society as a whole, it makes itself superfluous. As soon as there is no longer any class of society to be held in subjection, as soon as, along with class domination and the struggle for individual existence based on the former anarchy of production, the collisions and excesses arising from these have also been abolished, there is nothing more to be repressed which would make a special repressive force, a state, necessary. The first act in which the state really comes forward as the representative of society as a whole – the taking possession of the means of production in the name of society – is at the same time its last independent act as a state ... The state is not "abolished," it *withers away*.

Frederick Engels[1]

This famous statement of Engels summarizes the nineteenth-century perception of the state by socialists. No matter who controlled the state, it was the enemy of the working classes. It existed to repress them; it did repress them. Socialism had to be its antithesis; therefore, socialism involved the absence of the state.

With the extension of the suffrage in Europe and the creation of socialist parties, the workers' movement nonetheless had to decide what its attitude was to participation in the parliamentary political process of the existing states. Revisionism was in essence the belief that the workers could vote themselves into power and thereby tame the state. But even for the revisionists, the existing state remained the enemy – not only in theory, but in fact in praxis.

The situation changed radically with the Russian Revolution. On the eve of the Revolution, Lenin denounced in *State and revolution* those who would "emasculate" Engels' argument, "so singularly rich in

[1] Frederick Engels, "Socialism: utopian and scientific" in V. Adoratsky (ed.), *Karl Marx: selected works I* (New York: International Publishers, 1933).

ideas," by alleging that the term "withering away" of the state meant something *different from* the "doctrine of the 'abolition' of the state," on the ground that this latter doctrine was "Anarchist."[2] Lenin insisted that "withering away" did indeed mean "abolition." He said, however, that the correct interpretation of "abolition" was to see it as a process with two stages:

> The replacement of the bourgeois by the proletarian state is impossible without a violent revolution. The abolition of the proletarian state, i.e., of all states, is only possible through "withering away,"[3]

Thus the Bolshevik party, when it came to power in the Soviet Union, asserted it had established a "dictatorship of the proletariat" which existed to destroy the bourgeoisie inside and outside the boundaries of the USSR, a first stage in the process of creating a communist society. The later stage would result presumably from the withering away of the proletarian state.

It was not long before critics began to observe that the state apparatus in the USSR, far from withering away, seemed in fact far stronger than it had been in Imperial Russia. For many of the critics, the Soviet state was one governed by a "bureaucratic" stratum who were a new and, for some, a worse ruling class than the previous one.[4] In the wake of the Soviet experience, the concept of the "withering away of the state" fell into the background, even into disuse, except by acerbic critics who cited it to mock Marxism in general. The concept was frequently offered up as a good example of unfulfilled predictions.

I should like to suggest we take today another look at this concept, in the light of the realities of the twentieth century. The first and most fundamental reality is the contradictory fact that the capitalist world-economy, the system in which we live, has become much stronger as a system and much weaker simultaneously, and as a result of the very same processes.

This concurrent strengthening and weakening of the system as a whole has been brought about jointly by the principal forces interested

---

[2] V. I. Lenin, *State and revolution* (New York: International Publishers, 1932), p. 16.

[3] Lenin, *State and revolution*, p. 20.

[4] This criticism was in fact foreshadowed by Bakunin, who wrote in 1869: "The State has always been the patrimony of some privileged class, whether sacerdotal, noble, or bourgeois, and, in the end, when all the other classes have been used up, of a bureaucratic class ... It is absolutely necessary for its welfare that there be some privileged class interested in its existence. And it is precisely the solitary interest of this privileged class that we call patriotism." A. Fried and R. Sanders (eds.), *Socialist thought: a documentary history* (Garden City, N.Y.: Anchor Books, 1964), pp. 343–4.

in sustaining the system (private capitalist enterprises and entrepreneurs) and the principal forces interested in transforming the
system (the antisystemic movements). Both sets of forces have in
specific ways undermined *and* reinforced state-structures and the interstate system. In order properly to appreciate the particular dialectics of
the twentieth century, we must view the process in terms of tendencies
inherent in the functioning of the modern world-system from the outset,
which tendencies have culminated in the acute contradictions of today.

If we use the word "state" loosely, simply to mean a centralized
authority with some minimal bureaucracy, then of course states have
existed for thousands of years. But there has long been a school of
thought which insists that what we usually mean by the "state" in the
contemporary world did not in fact exist before the sixteenth century.
Alongside this debate about the moment of origin of the "state," there
has been a second discussion, often curiously kept separate from the
first, about the moment of origin of the modern "states system." Most
frequently the latter is dated as beginning in 1648, with the Treaty of
Westphalia,[5] but some insist that 1494, with the start of the Franco-
Spanish struggle over Italy, is the crucial date.[6] This seems a somewhat
scholastic debate, especially when we bear in mind Martin Wight's
reminder that a third conventional date (in addition to 1494 and 1648)
for "the beginning of modern international history" is 1492.[7] Wight's

[5] "Westphalia became the legal basis of the states system. Subsequent peace treaties, down at
least to Teschen in 1779, expressly confirmed Westphalia and were codicils thereto ... In
retrospect, Westphalia was believed to mark the transition from religious to secular politics,
from 'Christendom' to 'Europe,' the exclusion from international politics of the Holy See, the
effective end of the Holy Roman Empire by the virtual recognition of the sovereignty of its
members, the formal admission of the United Provinces and the Swiss Confederation to the
family of independent nations, and the beginning of the system of the balance of power. The
prestige of Westphalia was buttressed by that of Grotius, whose reputation as father of
international law was due to a work prompted by the same general war that Westphalia
ended. It seems to have been Grotius, incidentally, who brought the word 'system' into the
vocabulary of international politics, though not yet in the sense of the whole diplomatic
community." M. Wight, *Systems of states* (Leicester: Leicester University Press, 1977), p. 113;
see also M. Keens-Soper, "The practice of a states system" in M. Donelan (ed.), *The reason of
state* (London: George Allen & Unwin, 1978), p. 28.

[6] "The rise of the new system of states was the result of a complicated process of erosion of the
medieval structure spread over hundreds of years. Nevertheless, the new structure came into
existence at a quite definite moment, the beginning of the struggle among the great powers
over Italy in 1494. In much the same way, water gathers in the basin of a fountain until, at a
particular moment, the basin is filled and the water overflows into a second, surrounding
basin; then the process begins all over again." L. Dehio, *The precarious balance* (New York:
Vintage Books, 1962), p. 23. Martin Wight spends a whole chapter mulling over the merits of
the alternative dates and concludes in favor of 1494: "At Westphalia the states system does not
come into existence; it comes of age." Wight, *Systems of states*, p. 152.

[7] Wight, *Systems of states*, p. 114.

implication, which I share, is that the creation of this "states system" is in fact linked to the processes underlying the so-called expansion of Europe.

The point is really very simple. What distinguishes the modern state from any earlier "state" is that the modern state is *defined* by its participation in an interstate system; and what distinguishes the modern interstate system is that it was the first interstate system not to have been transformed over time into a world-empire.[8] Our interstate system evolved as the political superstructure of the capitalist world-economy, and it is this fact which explains the specifics of both the modern state and the modern interstate system, and which accounts for the fact that neither Charles V nor any of his spiritual descendants was able to create a universal empire.[9] The boundaries of the interstate system and the world-economy have thus been more or less synonymous, if both fuzzy.[10]

Over time and unevenly, the individual states have almost all become stronger, but, despite the ideology of juridically equivalent sovereignty, the operation of the balance-of-power mechanism has ensured the maintenance of a hierarchy of unequal powers linked in an interstate system.[11] The states in which core economic activities occurred have become stronger as a result of the efforts of groups located inside these states to ensure that the state machinery could be used to shore up quasi-monopolistic privileges for their enterprises (or to prevent others elsewhere from creating such privileges to the detriment of their enterprises). The states in which peripheral activities were developed became initially either weaker or stronger, compared to their starting points at the time of incorporation. Subsequently, under the pressure of the strong (core) states and local cooperating groups, they have tended to be stabilized at a level of "state strength" too weak to impede the economic flows of the world-economy but strong enough to facilitate these same flows. Finally, in semiperipheral states, groups have often sought to strengthen the state machinery in order to alter the composition of the production processes within their borders and hence to change their relative position in the axial division of labor of the

[8] I. Wallerstein, *The capitalist world-economy* (Cambridge: Cambridge University Press, 1979), chs. 1 and 9; Wight, *Systems of states*, pp. 43–5.

[9] I. Wallerstein, *The modern world-system*, vol. I: *Capitalist agriculture and the origins of the European world-economy in the sixteenth century* (New York and London: Academic Press, 1974), ch. 4.

[10] Wallerstein, *Modern world-system*; Keens-Soper, "Practice of a states system," pp. 30–1.

[11] Y. Durand, "Les compétences de l'état à l'époque moderne," paper delivered at Fourteenth International Congress of Historical Sciences, San Francisco (22–9 August 1975).

world-economy. These attempts by various semiperipheral states and the counter-pressures of the core powers have been one of the continuing points of military tension in the interstate system. What has resulted is what might be called a moving equilibrium over time; all states have grown "stronger," but the degree of dispersion of strength has remained at the very least at a constant level, and most probably has widened considerably.

From the beginning, the attitude of large-scale entrepreneurs to state power has been ambivalent. They have wanted states to help them both in their immediate objectives of economic gain and in their longer-run objectives of maintaining the political stability of the system. The longer-run objectives have of course frequently conflicted with the shorter-run ones. In such cases, the attitude of particular firms has varied. They have often fought their own state machineries, even to the point of selling weapons to enemy states in times of war, but they have usually manifested a kind of Schumpeterian wisdom, understanding (in practice if not explicitly) the necessity of making short-run economic concessions to maintain the long-run political superstructure of the system.

In the nineteenth century, the rise of antisystemic movements created a similarly ambiguous force. The socialist movements found themselves caught in a parallel short-run/long-run dilemma. It was however the obverse of that of the large-scale enterprises. While the enterprises often wanted a weaker state in the short run but saw the long-run necessity of a stronger state (and/or interstate system) to maintain the world capitalist system, the socialist movements wanted to destroy the state in the long run, but saw the necessity of a stronger state in the short run in order to preserve the movement and to make it possible eventually to destroy the world capitalist system.

In the nineteenth century, this dilemma of socialist movements took the form of debating merely whether or not to participate in a parliamentary system. After 1917, it took the form of deciding what to do about state power itself. For here we come to the crucial aspect of the state (singular) within a capitalist world-economy organized politically in an interstate system. The state (singular) is not in fact a "total" institution. No state (not even that of a hegemonic power) can do quite as it wishes. Hence no group which gains power in a given state is free to transform processes within its boundaries as it sees fit. Every state machinery is *constrained* by the operations of the world-economy (and the interstate system) to observe certain limits or to pay certain penalties exacted by other states (being forced to change policies, boundaries, or regime).

What we have discovered is that the Soviet experience – the anti-systemic movement coming to power and strengthening markedly the state machinery – is not an aberration but the result of deep structural forces operating on the social movements themselves. Indeed, Lenin himself saw this, if not most Leninists. The evidence is his parenthetical phrase which I quoted: "The abolition of the proletarian state, *i.e.*, *of all states*, is only possible through 'withering away.'"

The question is not nor has ever been "can, or will, a state wither away?" but "can or will the system of states, or all states, wither away?" That is the question we have been ignoring and should in fact be addressing. It is central to how we envisage the world's historic transition of capitalism to socialism. Allow me to deal with the issues of this transition as three successive questions: "Why is there presently a 'crisis' in the world-system?" "What form do the contradictory pressures take during the period of the crisis?" "What are the probable outcomes of the crisis?"

Let me start by suggesting what I mean by a "crisis." A crisis is not a mere economic downturn or a phase of acute political struggle, even worldwide. There have been many such since the capitalist world-economy came into being as an historical system some five hundred years ago. I have argued that the capitalist world-economy arose in Europe as a result of the "crisis of feudalism," which I date as roughly 1300–1450. This crisis can be distinguished from the economic stagnation (but not crisis) of the seventeenth century.[12] There is now, in my view, a similar "crisis of capitalism" which we have been living in for most of the twentieth century and will probably continue to live in for at least another century. By a crisis, I mean a turning point from one *longue durée* to another, which comes about when the mechanisms of adjustment within a system begin to fail because of the operation of the system itself. In such circumstances, more than a reshuffling of privileges occurs. Either the whole system must be fundamentally restructured or, as a social system, it collapses. A crisis means that the maintenance of the system as such is not in fact a viable historical option.

[12] Wallerstein, *Modern world-system*, ch. 1; Wallerstein, "Underdevelopment and Phase B; effect of the seventeenth-century stagnation on core and periphery of the European world-economy" in W. L. Goldfrank (ed.), *The world system of capitalism: past and present* (London: Sage, 1979), pp. 73–83; Wallerstein, "Y a-t-il une crise du XVIIe siècle?", *Annales ESC*, 34:1 (Jan.-Feb. 1979), pp. 126–44.

The reason why the existing capitalist world-system has come to be in a crisis is that the mechanisms that have in fact operated to deal with the periodic stagnations of the world-economy, and thus to reinvigorate the expansionary tendencies of the system so necessary for the accumulation of capital, involve movements toward asymptotes. Since I have dealt with this elsewhere[13] let me resume my views in a very brief form. The periodic stagnation of the world-economy, manifested by a deficiency of world effective demand, has been regularly resolved by a triple process: technological change, proletarianization, and the incorporations of new zones into the world-economy. They have provided respectively new sources of high-profit products (via the new leading sectors), new pools of monetary demand (via the increase of money income to workers receiving a larger proportion of total income through wage income), and new pools of low-cost labor (via the creation of new households engaged in part-time wage-labor). Of the three mechanisms, only technological change may continue for an indefinite future. The other two mechanisms move toward limits; hence the structural underpinnings of the "crisis." This basic economic constraint within the accumulation process has its political counterpart in the growing strength of antisystemic movements, both the social movements and the national movements, which have *collectively* grown considerably stronger in the twentieth century, however much particular movements have failed, and despite the fact that each individual movement has eventually been co-opted to one degree or another.[14] Let me address now how the contradictory pressures operate within the framework of this systemic crisis.

The collective strength of the antisystemic movements has begun to constrain significantly the worldwide freedom of action of the strong private enterprises of the core areas, which we have come to call (somewhat misleadingly) multinational corporations (MNCs). The calculations underlying political strategies to optimize capital accumulation have changed. The long-run economic costs to MNCs of interventionist actions in their behalf by core states in weaker states have risen considerably, and relatively more than the costs of co-optative strategies, although these too have risen. The change now makes the latter strategy more often than not the attractive one for the enterprises. The costs of the co-optative strategy would however rise

[13] Wallerstein, *Capitalist world-economy*, ch. 17 ("An historical perspective on the emergence of the new international order: economic, political, cultural aspects"), *passim*, esp. pp. 278–80.
[14] Immanuel Wallerstein, "The future of the world-economy," chapter 10 in this volume.

precipitately and render it "uneconomic," were the interventionist strategy not to be considered a credible alternative. This has led to a zigzag pattern of the real foreign policies of core states in so far as they respond to the pressures of the MNCs. The zigzag pattern itself has led to uncertainties, which have stimulated testing mechanisms, which thereby have increased the costs of *both* the interventionist and the co-optative strategies.

The rising costs of co-option have necessarily pushed enterprises to seek "weak points" in the political positions acquired by various strata of the world's working classes in the course of prior antisystemic battles. Such weak points are not restricted to peripheral zones, but are increasingly found in core areas as well, particularly during periods of economic stagnation. Thus in places where prior antisystemic movements have been thoroughly tamed, there exists the risk of reopening active political conflict. The regimes of the core states will have to take cognizance of this potential, and will not be as rapidly responsive to the needs of the business classes as previously. This will lead to a situation where the MNCs will be torn between the economic advantages of being tied to one state machinery as a protective force, and the economic advantages of moving between core states. As Ford contemplates Chrysler and its own future, one tactic is to try to pay workers less in Brazil and the USA; another is to transfer gradually its *base* of operations to Europe (where however the military backup is less credible); a third is to work out cooperative production arrangements with the USSR. The important point to note is that whichever choice is best in some short-run perspective, all of them are constrictive of accumulation in the long run.

At the same time, the antisystemic movements are caught in comparable dilemmas. The realities of the existing mode of functioning of the world-economy, and the weakness of any single state-structure vis-à-vis the totality of the forces operating, mean that the short-run costs in well-being and in the possibility of expanding the forces of production, occasioned by an effort to withdraw fully from the world-economy, are higher than any regime is politically capable of sustaining. The consequence is that there is enormous social pressure from within the antisystemic movements, when they obtain political power, to operate a state-level "catching-up" strategy. The catching up of a given state to the economic levels of well-being of the currently more "developed" states necessarily involves the accumulation of capital through the expropriation of surplus value, the proletarianization of labor, and the further commodification of all aspects of production and exchange not yet so commodified. Catching up, in short, means the triumph of the law of value in all corners previously resistant to its dominance.

On the one hand, this is eventually viewed by many supporters of these antisystemic movements as a frustration, if not an outright betrayal, of their goals. The historical succession of disillusionments affects the global ability of antisystemic movements to operate successfully. On the other hand, to the degree that these movements survive in however compromised a form, they provide social space and often resources for other movements in other places, and thus nonetheless contribute to the growing collective strength of antisystemic movements worldwide.

What may we expect? The increasing concentration of capital, and constraints on the global rate of profit, will push towards an ever greater state role everywhere in enterprises. In this sense, the right-wing slogan of "creeping socialism" is indoubtedly correct, if by that one means the trend toward one form or another of "nationalizing" the enterprises. We may expect too that everywhere outside the core, the ideology of "catching up" will spread and probably prevail. In that sense, the slogan of "convergence" is essentially correct, if one remembers that what is in fact happening is the completion of the logic of world capitalist development. In perhaps fifty years, and *for the first time*, the world-economy may *fully* operate according to the laws of value as outlined in Volume I of *Capital*.

But the full triumph of capitalist values is a sign, indeed *the* sign, of the crisis of capitalism as a system. Capitalism has never historically operated in the mode its ideology dictates, because it cannot. Among other things, if *everyone* were a wage slave, the ability of a few to extract surplus-value from the many would be almost impossible. The universalization of the law of value is precisely what will make it finally impossible to maintain the "mystical veil" of commodities,[15] what will complete the process of the "destruction of the protecting strata."[16] This will happen because the contradictory processes of the current phase of the capitalist world-economy will have so thoroughly demystified the techniques of domination that they will render them politically untenable.

So, I project what is in some senses a strange scenario: the efforts of

[15] K. Marx, "The fetishism of commodities and the secret thereof", *Capital*, Vol. I, ch. 1, section 4 (London: Lawrence and Wishart, 1972).

[16] J. A. Schumpeter, *Capitalism, socialism and democracy*, part 2, ch. 12, section 2 (London: George Allen & Unwin, 1943).

the entrepreneurs lead in the direction of the growing nationalization of enterprises, while the efforts of the revolutionaries provide the means by which the law of value will finally become pervasive. Yet of course this is not the whole story, because the entrepreneurs may still be presumed to be governed by the search for profit, while the antisystemic movements may still be presumed to be governed by the effort to replace the system based on the law of value with an egalitarian structure based on production for use. Both groups will therefore seek constantly to break out of the constraints under which they find they are operating.

As the possibilities for extracting surplus-value in the immediate sphere of production tighten, large-scale entrepreneurs may concentrate more and more on the interstices of the world-economy, the linkages among increasingly state-controlled production systems. This will "globalize" their base in ways and to a degree not known up to now, and may push them away from tight linkages with particular core state machineries. Their survival may come to depend on the fact that their political alliances are precisely spread out throughout the interstate system – ethereal "gnomes of Zurich" offering services too essential to be permitted to lodge in the hands of enterprises run by particular states.

Simultaneously, antisystemic movements, as more and more of them come to power, may go through a metamorphosis. They may return to their initial view that the states are their enemy, and they may move therefore toward the creation of structures which are neither national nor international but transnational. Though this can only happen when a tipping point is reached, and enough of the present variety of movements come to state power, we see the gestation of such trends already.

These processes will be supported by what has been called the "civilizational quest."[17] One of the fundamental expressions of anti-systemic sentiment has been the rejection of the veil of universalism under which the extraction of surplus-value and the political domination encrusted in the interstate system has proceeded. Thus we have today the multiple forms of the search for "endogenous intellectual creativity." These forms are all in some sense "nationalist," but they are by no means necessarily or enduringly "statist." Even a cursory look at Iran since the overthrow of the Shah should make this very clear.

The basic tensions of the world class struggles thus are coming to be

---

[17] A. Abdel-Malek, "East Wind," *Review*, 1:1 (1977), p. 64.

expressed in the tension between the state-based logics and the global logics. World politics may come to be played with three main groups of actors: the large sectors in power in the core states along with the smaller but significant sectors in power in the peripheral and semi-peripheral states; the tiny but still very powerful "globalized, private" entrepreneurial groups; the new "globalized" antisystemic move-ments, who will represent and may in fact include the majority of the world's population. If the latter two groups prove more powerful than the first, and I think they eventually will prove so to be, we shall see the completion of the transition from capitalism to socialism with a "withering away" of the states and the interstate system. The forms of a socialist world order – how the economy will be politically coordinated and culturally expressed – are very unclear, and it seems to me futile to predict.

However, I can envisage an alternative scenario. I said previously that by a crisis I mean a situation in which the whole system must be fundamentally restructured or it will collapse. Collapse is of course a real alternative to the "withering away of the states." The "state-based logics" may prove sufficiently strong in this period of transition to slow down the progress of the "global logics" – both that of the entre-preneurial strata and that of the antisystemic movements. In this case, a "time of troubles" of cumulative destructiveness could ensue in an acute struggle over resources seen to be too scarce (or made to be too scarce).

Note well what I have been suggesting in this new look at a now scorned concept. The socialist revolution in which we are living is not Armageddon. It may in fact be the only alternative to Armageddon. Nuclear war between the great powers, resulting in enormous destruc-tion of populations and productive forces, is entirely credible. But it is also entirely credible that the state, that is the states, may wither away, in the creation of a socialist world order.

6 ✈ Friends as foes

The year 1980 marks the midpoint in a global process: the steady erosion of the hegemonic position of the United States in the world-economy. The political keystone of this hegemony has been a strong alliance with western Europe and Japan. Until 1967 the United States dominated the world military arena and political economy – including the markets of other industrialized countries – and western Europe and Japan followed US leadership willingly and completely. By 1990 the former allies will have parted company with the United States.

This process is not fortuitous, mysterious, or reversible. Roughly comparable declines in the capitalist world-economy have taken place twice before: Great Britain from 1873 to 1896; and, although this is less well known, the United Provinces (the modern-day Netherlands) from 1650 to 1672. In each case, a nation of unquestioned supremacy fell to the lesser status of a very powerful state defending very central economic interests in the world-economy, but nonetheless one state amid several. And, in each case, in the decades following the loss of hegemony, the former predominant power continued to decline as a center of political–military strength and of high-profit enterprise, to the advantage of other states within the world-economy.

Such cyclical patterns – the rise and decline of hegemonic powers and the more frequent expansion and stagnation of the world-economy – exist within the framework of long-term secular trends that have been leading to a systemic crisis that transcend the immediate difficulties of the moment. These trends, characteristic of a capitalist world-economy, may be seen in the constant development of the division of labor in the world-economy as a whole and in the continued development of the interstate system.

For four hundred years the development of the division of labor has involved a steady increase in the degree to which production has been mechanized, land and labor made into commodities purchasable on the market, and social relations regulated by contracts rather than by customary rules. This secular division of labor has proceeded in a step-like fashion that alternates twenty- to thirty-year periods of expansion with similar periods of contraction (sometimes called Kondratieff cycles, or A-phases and B-phases). Each A-phase of expansion has culminated in a major blockage of the world accumulation process, resulting in stagnation. And each B-phase of stagnation has been overcome by the further concentration of capital, the launching of new product cycles, the expansion of outer boundaries of the world-economy, and the expansion of effective demand – in short, by the spreading and deepening of the capitalist world-economy and the further polarization of distribution as measured globally and not within individual states.

The development of the interstate system has involved the elaboration and institutionalization of power in each of the member states, within the constraints of interstate rules that have become increasingly explicit. As the roles of the state machineries have become more prominent the state has become even more the focus of antisystemic forces – social movements opposed to the basic mode of operation of the world-system – that have sought power in the name of socialist and nationalist ideologies. The strengthening of capitalist forces and the development of the world-economy itself have bred these antisystemic forces, whose own strength has increased significantly in the twentieth century.

A Mature Liberalism

This is the context within which the United States became the political center of global economic forces between 1945 and 1967. During the great postwar boom, despite the paranoia of American leaders and the constant clamor about national danger, there was no serious opposition in the world to US hegemony. In the late 1950s, it was the communist world (with destalinization) and not the West that was undergoing political crisis. The Soviet Union was easily contained; indeed, it was struggling to hold its own politically and economically, while it sought to rebuild militarily. Western Europe and Japan, the main beneficiaries of a massive creation of effective demand via US economic aid and military support, operated as virtual client states during the 1950s. Decolonization in Asia and Africa went smoothly, largely to the political advantage of the United States. And at home, the anticommunist political repression of the 1940s and 1950s (from President Truman's loyalty oaths to McCarthyism) seemed to stifle the dangerous social tensions of earlier periods.

The one major exception to complete US hegemony was China, where the accession to power of the Communist party represented an effective overthrow of foreign domination and a radical alteration of China's position in the world-system.

For the most part, a generalized self-congratulatory contentment pervaded the United States during the Kennedy administration, evincing the liberalism of a mature hegemonic power and encouraging the growth of its offshoots – the Peace Corps, civil rights, and détente.

This liberal self-confidence explains the tremendous psychological shock experienced by US political and business leaders in response to the events of 1967–68: the currency and gold crises that marked the fall of the US dollar from its pedestal; the Tet offensive against South Vietnam that revealed that a small Third World people could hold US military power in check; the student–worker rebellions – such as those at Columbia University and in France – that showed that internal struggles within Western states were once again on the agenda.

In retrospect, the sudden explosions of 1967–68 should not have been so surprising. The economic reconstruction of western Europe and Japan created centers of competition with US-based firms and contributed to the global overexpansion of world production. By concentrating on the military sphere, the Soviet Union had increased its military strength relative to that of the United States. At the same time, direct US military intervention had severe financial and economic consequences for the United States. The steady decolonization of the world could not possibly remain a controlled and formal process; it would inevitably become more radical and spread to the Western industrialized, or core, countries themselves (to the "Third World within"). And the liberalism of the mature hegemonic power would retreat once its largess was rejected by oppressed groups asserting demands on their own terms.

All of a sudden, in 1967 the United States found itself in a B-period, a period of decelerated growth. In the world-economy, the most significant result of this period of relative economic stagnation has been a striking decline in the competitiveness of US-based production organizations compared with those located in Japan and western Europe, excluding Great Britain. This relative decline is evident upon comparing growth rates, standards of living, capital investments as a percentage of gross national product, growth in productivity, capital–labor ratios, share in the world market, and research and development expenditures. The decline is also reflected in the relative strengths of currencies and in the rates of inflation and unemployment.

A second striking result of this B-phase has been the relocation of industry. On a world scale, this relocation involved the rise of the newly industrializing countries and the opening of the free trade zones – the creation of the so-called new international division of labor. In general, the bargaining power of large semiperipheral countries such as Brazil and countries with key commodities such as the Organization of Petroleum Exporting Countries (OPEC) bloc has been greatly strengthened.

Acquiescence or Collusion

With respect to the changing world-economy, it is the OPEC price rises that have caught everyone's attention and that politicians and the press have transformed from consequence into cause. Two things should be noted about the oil price rises. First, they began in 1973, not in 1963 or 1953. The oil-producing countries did not suddenly become avaricious. Rather, in 1973 oil price rises became, for the first time, economically and politically possible in large part because the global rise of industrial production entailed a vast increase in demand for current energy production. This overproduction in turn promoted competition among the core powers, thereby limiting their economic and military bargaining power. OPEC simply capitalized on this situation.

Second, the oil price rises met little opposition from the core states. This cannot be written off to political lassitude resulting from economic stagnation. There probably also existed US acquiescence, even collusion. It is hard otherwise to account for the crucial support in 1973 for this policy by the Saudi and Iranian governments, without which there would have been no OPEC price rise. James Akins, former US ambassador to Saudi Arabia, reported that the Saudis went along with the price rise only when they could not persuade the United States to put pressure on Iranian price demands.

The United States could have seen two short-run advantages in the

1973 oil price rise: a competitive boost relative to western Europe and Japan because of their greater dependence in 1973 on imported oil; and the creation of financial bases for the Shah and to a lesser extent the Saudis so they could serve as proconsuls for the United States, relieving in part the US political and financial burden.

There are also long-run advantages for the core powers collectively in the oil price rises – advantages that probably outweigh any disruptive effects. In a situation of global stagnation, one key problem concerns possibilities for new industrial complexes of high-profit growth. One such complex could involve new energy sources and energy-saving devices. The first advantage, then, is that the higher cost of petroleum created a major incentive for this kind of complex. Former Secretary of State Henry Kissinger after all did talk of a floor for petroleum prices and not of a ceiling.

The second major advantage is that inflation itself can in fact lead to a considerable decline in the real wage bill of the core countries, redistributing surplus to owners in a form that is far more manageable than the bread lines of 1933.

German Chancellor Helmut Schmidt has spoken of the struggle for the world product, emphasizing only interstate allocations. This might better be called the world class struggle in which reallocations are being made within as well as between states. For example, if the oil-producing states have gained considerably in the last decade, it is scarcely the large oil multinationals that have lost. It is, rather, the middle and lower strata in both core and peripheral countries.

The decline of US hegemony has had major effects on the interstate system as well. Alliances that emerged after World War II are collapsing. The Sino-Soviet split, begun in the 1950s but consecrated in the 1960s, did not necessarily serve the interests of the United States as a global power. The split made it impossible to consolidate stability through a political deal with the USSR and muddied irremediably ideological waters. And when the United States came to terms with China, western Europe and Japan could not simply maintain their old alliance with the United States, but were forced to reconsider all the options.

The Sino-Soviet split was liberating for national movements in the Third World. The split closed the books on the Communist International and forced liberation groups to move where they were under pressure to move anyway – to action that was autonomous of the world alliance system. Despite US–Soviet détente, a de facto US–Chinese alliance, and socialist wars in southeast Asia, the 1970s saw a steady acceleration of revolutionary movements (southern Africa, Central America and the Caribbean, and the Middle East) rather than the reverse.

The West–West Conflict

The most difficult issues, however, that confront US policy-makers in the coming decades are neither East–West issues (notwithstanding Afghanistan) nor North–South issues (notwithstanding Iran). Rather they are West–West issues that are based on the great economic and therefore political threat of the two significant US rivals, western Europe and Japan. President Carter's handling of the crises in Afghanistan and Iran as well as his decision to develop the MX missile could be viewed as attempts to maintain US political leadership in the West and regain economic supremacy via ideological pressure on US allies. Indeed, the effort to constrain US allies bids fair to become the priority concern of US foreign policy.

What are the real problems facing the United States in this growing West–West conflict? There is the immediate problem of fending off the worst aspects of the economic decline of the 1980s. There is the more important, long-run concern of trying to profit maximally from the probable renewed economic expansion of the 1990s.

Because there will have to be major contraction in some centers of world production, the basic issue for the 1980s is who will export unemployment to whom. Thus far inflation has masked this issue, at least politically; but should a dramatic fall in world prices occur, minimizing the resultant economic damage will become a matter of survival for regimes throughout the West.

In the short run, the United States has two major mechanisms at its disposal. It can prop up technologically doomed industries (the Chrysler handout), which reduces unemployment in one sector at the expense of others and also diminishes the capital available for investment in industries that will make America competitive in the 1990s. In addition, it can increase military expenditures, also at the expense of long-run development.

For the 1990s the basic policy issue is who will gain the competitive edge in the new technologies of microelectronics, biotechnology, and energy resources. Success will be determined by an interlocking triplet of research and development innovations; reduction of real costs of production; and increased access to markets for the older sectors of production – formerly high-profit sectors, now medium-profit sectors – such as electronics, automobiles, and even computers.

What is happening today in industries such as steel, automobiles, and electronics is a double process. First, west European and Japanese firms are undercutting US-based firms, even in the US home market. Second, production processes are being broken up. Large parts of production chains are being moved to semiperipheral countries, including socialist countries, and the chains themselves are more likely to end in western Europe and Japan rather than in the United States.

The structural causes of this massive shift in production centers outside the United States – a shift that is likely to accelerate sharply in the 1980s – are twofold. On the one hand, given large and older US industrial hardware, there are the higher costs of amortization of the overall plant. On the other, there is the higher US wage bill. The real difference between US costs of production and those of western Europe and Japan does not lie in the wages paid a skilled mechanic. The political bargaining strength of workers is basically the same in all parts of the West. The real difference in costs – paid in part directly by companies, in part indirectly through government expenditures – lies in the salaries of the well-to-do middle stratum (i.e., professionals and executives).

It is not that the individual incomes of US executives or professionals exceed those of their allied counterparts. In many cases, the opposite is true. Rather, it is that in the United States the well-to-do middle stratum is a significantly larger percentage of the total population. Hence, the social bill of the US middle class is dramatically higher, and it is impossible for either the government or the large corporations to do anything about it.

An attack on these expenditures of a magnitude sufficient enough to make US-based industry cost-competitive again would entail higher political costs than anyone dares pay, especially because American political structures are heavily dominated by precisely those people whose incomes would have to be cut. It is therefore far easier for a multinational corporation to consider shifting its sites of production and research and eventually even its headquarters than to try to reduce costs directly. This has already begun to occur.

The process of disinvestment in the old industries will affect the research and development expenditures on the new ones by reducing both the US tax and profit bases of US-based companies. The markets for the new industries will be located primarily in the core countries themselves, but the markets for the older industries will be more worldwide. It will be important for producers to find fresh markets – zones whose expansion depends upon the products of these older industries. Such zones encompass the semiperipheral countries that are industrializing and that, even if they have their own plants and production sites, will need advanced machinery and hardware. The European Economic Community countries are up front in this effort in terms of their economic partnership with developing countries covered by the Lomé Convention. The largest likely market of the 1980s and, to an even greater extent, of the 1990s will comprise the socialist countries. Behind the Sino-Soviet controversy lies a struggle to be this market in the most advantageous way possible. This is called catching up or modernizing.

European–Soviet Cooperation

Within this economic reality – this B-phase of stagnation – lie the bases for the realignment of alliances in the interstate system. In a sense, China jumped the gun by its dramatic and successful attempt to make an arrangement with the United States. It is no accident that this diplomatic turnabout was done with Richard Nixon, who represented those US forces whose deep anticommunist ideology was not tightly linked to a commitment to a North Atlantic Treaty Organization alliance structure.

Japan, no doubt miffed by its exclusion from the very first diplomatic steps, quickly allowed its true interests to prevail in the Sino-Japanese reconciliation. Because of the strong, complementary economic interests of the two countries and the fundamental link of civilization (still a major factor in policy-making), the reconciliation is even more important than the joint US–Chinese Shanghai communiqué.

If the United States has moved in the direction of China, it is because such movement makes geopolitical, strategic sense. And given that during the 1970s the economic fruits of détente with the Soviet Union were clearly being garnered by western Europe rather than by the United States, these strategic considerations seemed worth the risk.

In terms of the political economy of the world-system, western Europe and the USSR have much to offer each other, both positively and negatively. Were the two sides to move slowly toward a *de facto* structure of cooperation that need not involve anything affirmative in the sphere of military alliances, the USSR could obtain the capital equipment it needs to improve its long-term relative position in the world-economy, thus meeting the most pressing demand of its own cadres. Of course, the Soviet Union would also thereby obtain security against the dangers (real or imagined) implied by the US–Chinese structure of cooperation.

In conjunction with western Europe – and probably not without it – the Soviet Union could also effectuate a significant breakthrough in economic links with the Middle East. This presumes that the USSR and western Europe would be able to complete the Camp David process by an arrangement between Israel and the Palestine Liberation Organization. In addition, a Middle East agreement might partially defuse the Soviet Union's greatest internal danger point, the potentially higher consciousness of the Central Asian Moslem peoples.

Moreover, an arrangement of this sort between the Soviet Union and western Europe – in which the German Social Democratic Party would have to play a large part – could also discourage the revolt of eastern Europe against the USSR. The uprisings in Prague during spring 1968 threatened the USSR in two ways. The idea of liberalization might spread eastward particularly to the Ukraine. And Czechoslovakia might move out of the Soviet orbit, especially in economic terms, and into that of West Germany. In the context of west European–Soviet cooperation, the latter fear would become less relevant.

Such an arrangement could look equally attractive to western Europe. The Soviet market would be opened in some meaningful sense to western-Europe-based industries. The resources of the Soviet Union would become available, at least over a crucial twenty- to thirty-year period. And the USSR and east European countries could serve as geographically convenient and politically constrained reservoirs of relatively cheap labor for participation in western Europe's chains of production.

Furthermore, a solution to the east European question from the Soviet perspective is also a solution from the viewpoint of western Europe. Cooperation would permit the reintegration of Europe – culturally, economically, and eventually politically – a development that has up to now been barred by Soviet military strength. In particular, cooperation would permit, at a minimum, the two Germanies to move closer together.

An amicable working relationship with the Soviet Union would even have political advantages for western Europe. Just as the USSR might not gain a breakthrough in the Middle East without western Europe, so might the reverse be true. In addition, by guaranteeing a relatively strong position to west European firms during the difficult years of the 1980s, a structure of cooperation would ensure the continuance of the high degree of social peace that western Europe is currently enjoying. On the ideological front, it would also contain in part the USSR.

A New Hegemony?

Needless to say, the ideological sentiments on both sides remain very strong – but not unswerving. In the cast of West Germany, ideological commitments have not changed, but their role has: in the 1950s and 1960s, West Germany's economic interests were served by emphasizing ideological commitments, whereas in the 1970s and the 1980s, these same economic interests are being advanced by playing down political beliefs.

Should this kind of realignment come about, the most indecisive power will be Great Britain, which faces difficulty no matter which way it turns. But in any West–West split, Britain will probably have to stay with the United States, if only because in the very important geo-political struggle over southern Africa, British and American interests are closely linked. And in a world in which British markets are declining everywhere, southern Africa might be one of the last secure trading partners.

In this picture of potential realignments, what happens to the North–South struggle? At one level, a realignment of the Northern powers along the lines suggested would create incredible ideological confusion in the South. At another level, it might lead to an ideological clarification. The process of disintegration of the world-system, brought about by the cumulative strength of the world's antisystemic forces, cannot be controlled by the United States or the Soviet Union. Revolutions in, say, Honduras, Tunisia, Kenya, or Thailand are not primarily a function of geopolitical arrangements among the great powers. What realignments may bring about is a greater disillusion-ment among these revolutionary movements regarding the efficacy of achieving power via the control of individual state-structures. After a century of detour, the emphasis may return to the importance of creating real worldwide inter-movement links – ones that would cut across North–South and East–West boundaries. This is what is meant by ideological clarification.

And this is why even if the world-economy takes a major upturn in the 1990s and even if western Europe begins to play the role of a new ascending hegemonic power, the world is not entering merely another cyclical movement of the present system. It is in this sense that the underlying, long-run systemic crisis of world capitalism may be more meaningful over the next fifty years. In the middle run, world capitalism will seem to recuperate; in the long run, it will be transformed fundamentally.

In the short run, however, the biggest traumas will be felt by the United States. Americans have spent the past thirty years getting used to the benefits of a hegemonic position, and they will have to spend the next thirty years getting used to life without them. For the majority of the world, it may not make that big a difference. For that majority, the real question is not which nation is hegemonic in the present world-system, but whether and how that world-system will be transformed.

7 ✦ The USA in the world today

At the end of the Second World War, the United States was unquestionably the strongest power in the world. It was often remarked then that the US did not know how to "assume its responsibilities." What was meant by such remarks was that US leaders, and public opinion, seemed to lack the collective social psychology appropriate for the role of hegemonic power of the capitalist world-economy. There was no doubt a certain truth in this perception. Peoples are not born into social psychologies, any more than individuals are. They learn them, and there is always a lag in mentalities behind the changes in social structure. The lag does not usually last too long. In this case, one no longer heard such remarks by the late 1950s.

Today it might just as correctly be suggested that the US does not know how to adjust (yet) to its role as a post-hegemonic power. Perhaps it does not yet want to know how to adjust. One sign of this is the fact that Ronald Reagan somewhat surprisingly tried to imply that he was assuming the heritage of Franklin Delano Roosevelt, when in fact Reagan's presidency marks the end of the New Deal and the inauguration of the post-Roosevelt era.

The New Deal was the strategy of a hegemonic power, a strategy which the United States developed to ensure the solid internal social basis necessary to play this role. To understand the kind of social compromise which the New Deal represented, we must look at the problems the US faced at the time Roosevelt assumed office in 1933.

First of all, the end of the First World War represented far more a truce in a "thirty years' war" than a definitive victory for the Allies. Germany had lost a battle in its struggle with the US to be the successor hegemonic power to Great Britain; it had not yet lost the war. It set out, under Weimar, to reconstruct its position in preparation for a second round. It was the failure of the political leadership to do this effectively which created the political space for the Nazi movement. As we know, Hitler launched the second round in the form of the Second World War, and lost it definitively. In 1933, this outcome was far from sure.

Secondly, the struggle for world hegemony was enormously complicated by the Russian Revolution. On the one hand, the Soviet Union and the Third International represented the first truly serious political threat to its existence that the capitalist world-economy had ever faced. On the other hand, there were many indications that the USSR could be – and very much wanted to be – reincorporated into the interstate system, which continued to serve as the political superstructure of the capitalist world-economy.

Already tentatively considered during the time of Lenin, this putative reincorporation was the necessary complement of Stalin's "socialism in one country." But, if the USSR were fully reincorporated, what game would it play in the interstate struggle for world hegemony? There were many hints – from Brest-Litovsk to Rapallo – that it might find it more comfortable to be diplomatically close to Germany or closer than to the US. This might have been catastrophic for the US, and one of Roosevelt's first moves in power was to establish diplomatic relations with the USSR. In 1934, the USSR joined the League of Nations and preached therein "collective security," a doctrine clearly aimed at Germany and its future allies, Italy and Japan.

The world depression of 1929 placed both Germany and the United States in a very difficult internal situation. The political solution in Germany was Nazism. The Nazi program comprised five main elements: overt militarism; priority to links with other fascist or right-wing states; an internal welfare state; suppression of working-class organizations; extreme racism, which in Germany meant anti-Semitism. In some ways this was a "standard" right-wing program, but one designed for an aspiring hegemonic power (and hence including an internal welfare state).

The coming to power of the Nazis facilitated the development of the New Deal as an alternative type of political solution, one that was "centrist" rather than "rightist." Let us compare the New Deal program to the Nazi program on each of the five points.

(1) While Roosevelt clearly stood for US military preparedness, he had the greatest difficulty overcoming internal resistance to such a push. Indeed, the so-called isolationist–interventionist quarrel was the

central form of debate on foreign policy right up to US entry into the Second World War in 1941.

(2) The US gave priority to its alliance with western Europe's "democracies," that is to other "centrist" powers, but also left open the possibility, ultimately realized, of alliance with the USSR as well. This was one of the functions of Roosevelt's self-definition as "left of center." When Germany moved definitively "right" under the Nazis, it isolated itself diplomatically and allowed the US to construct the worldwide diplomatic "popular front" which would ultimately make possible final victory in the "thirty years' war" of 1914–45.

(3) Roosevelt also constructed an internal welfare state. This was a much more difficult task than in Germany, since in Germany the capitalist strata had a long political history, going back to Bismarck, of understanding the utility of the welfare state, whereas in the US such measures were considered more "radical." To this day, the US has the least comprehensive social security program of any major industrialized state. Furthermore, without remilitarization, as in Germany, Roosevelt accomplished very little in the effort to end unemployment, until the Second World War offered jobs for all.

(4) Far from suppressing working-class organizations, Roosevelt offered to facilitate and encourage trade unions which were promptly incorporated into the governing political machinery of the US. The thoroughness with which this was done forestalled the emergence of a socialist party, even of a labor party.

(5) Roosevelt took a "centrist" position on racism. Opposing it in rhetoric, he took only minimal steps against it in practice. In one sense, this was marvelously successful as a tactic, since he managed to secure the very strong support of oppressed groups without sacrificing the support (politically crucial at the time for him) of the Southern Democrats.

The end of the Second World War changed two of the fundamental givens of the previous period. First, in terms, of the interstate system, the US emerged as the uncontested hegemonic power. Furthermore there were no longer any significant "rightist" governments among the core states. On the world scene, the US quickly shifted therefore from being "left of center" to being the leader of a "free world" alliance against the world left, now dubbed "communist totalitarianism." The very concept "totalitarianism," which sought to put communist and fascist regimes in the same box, was an attempt to create a façade of diplomatic continuity over the reality of a significant realignment.

Secondly, in terms of the phases of the world-economy, 1945 marked the beginning of a long expansionary upswing, the sharpest Kondratieff A-phase ever seen hitherto. The problem was no longer how to overcome internal economic crisis but how to exploit maximally the possibilities of this new golden era.

The elimination of the need for a "popular front" alliance internationally ended all need for it internally in the US. Quite the contrary: the period after 1945 was one of sharp suppression of left forces in US society. McCarthyism was itself but the culmination of a process started under Truman (loyalty oaths, purges of Communists in the CIO, etc.).

In order to secure the home front for the imperial era, the government and the ruling strata had not merely to suppress the US left, but to neutralize its appeal to organized workers and the "minorities." This was easily done. Organized workers were offered their share of the imperial pie via increased real wages. The General Motors settlement of 1947 set the pattern which continued unabated for twenty-five years of "industrial peace" in the US. The higher wages did not come out of the profits of management but were passed on to "consumers" – largely to the nonunionized workers in the US and to customers outside the US.

The unionized workers in the US did well by this arrangement. To be sure, they had to pay a "small" price – there would be no extension of the trade-union sector to other sectors of the US working class. The passage of the Taft–Hartley Act and the blocking of the postwar CIO organizing drive in the South were the decisive events. If therefore US workers were offered a share of the imperial pie, it was an offer made only to *some* workers, not to *all* workers. It would be discovered in the next twenty years that the segments of the working class that benefited from this arrangement were, by some curious accident, primarily "white" workers.

The "minorities" – again *some* "minorities" – would also get their share. Significant upward mobility was offered to the traditional "Catholic ethnics" – that is, to the Irish, Italians, Slavs (and similarly to the Orthodox Slavs and Greeks). Their children entered the universities, eventually even the best ones. They obtained major political office – the Presidency with John F. Kennedy, the Vice-Presidency (and were it not for Watergate, probably the Presidency) with Spiro T. Agnew. Even those who remained workers found themselves in the unionized, privileged sector.

Jews similarly benefited. The universities and the professions were opened up to them as well as political office (though not yet the highest), and even major corporations lowered their barriers to access to executive positions. In twenty-five years, the Jewish working class virtually disappeared, leaving US Jews overwhelmingly in middle- (even upper-middle-) class positions. Both anti-Catholicism and anti-Semitism became widely illegitimate and reduced to an unofficial murmur, even in polite society.

Blacks did not do nearly as well, but nonetheless even they benefited. From the integration of the US armed forces by Truman in 1947 to the Supreme Court decision making segregation unconstitutional in 1954 to the passage of the Civil Rights Act in 1965, a legal transformation occurred. No doubt the social reality was much less advanced than the new legal order. This disparity resulted in the massive political organization of Black protest in the 1960s. Still the incorporation of US Blacks into some, if not all, of the privileges of the US social order was widespread and clearly, even explicitly, linked to US foreign-policy needs.

The New Deal program, which continued in force from Roosevelt to Carter – even Nixon, let us remember, proclaimed himself a Keynesian – provided a very strong social cement at home, at least at first. By offering visible improvements in their standard of living and social status to large sectors of the US working class as well as by offering them the chauvinistic rewards of participating in the glories of world power, the US government and ruling strata were left free of internal turmoil the better to concentrate on controlling the world-system.

Cracks appeared nonetheless in the social cement, as we well know. First of all, the fierce opposition of oppressed peoples in peripheral areas of the world-economy, their readiness to struggle against great odds, was to affect directly the US internal situation. The extraordinary achievement of the Vietnamese in resisting US military might led to a prolonged war that was costly to the US politically, economically, and in terms of the collective social psychology in the US. Vietnam not merely accounts for the antiwar movement and student uprisings of the late 1960s but also directly to Watergate and its unmaskings of the hypocrisies of those in power, with the seeming inevitability of a Greek tragedy.

Secondly, the internal welfare state began to reach its limits because the world-economy began to shift from an expansionary phase to a stagnation phase. Times began to get tight. Further accretions of welfare were threatened in the late 1960s, ruled out in the 1970s, and are beginning to be reversed in the 1980s. The frustration of those who had never really made it inside the secure nest – particularly Blacks and Hispanics – was matched by the fears of backsliding of those who had managed to achieve significant material and social gains under the New Deal – the Catholic "ethnics," the Jews, organized trade unionists.

The combination of these two factors led to the explosions, major but still "controlled," that went on for six years or so, from Columbia University in 1968, to the massive nationwide protests about the invasion of Cambodia in 1970, to the deposition of Nixon in 1974. The most significant consequence of this period was the shattering of the dominance of the centrist ideology which underlay the New Deal and which had, since 1945 at least, reigned supreme in all major US institutions – the three branches of government, the press, the universities, the health and welfare structures, the corporations.

What was shattered was not centrist ideology *per se* but its unquestioning supremacy in the institutional arenas of US life. 1968–74 marks the resurgence both of left-wing and right-wing language in US life. In the universities, in the foundations, in the press, voices of the left and the right were heard again and, for the first time in twenty-five years, considered in some sense "legitimate" or plausible, even if still those of a minority. This constituted a major threat to the simple reproduction of the system as it had been operating. It was to keep the situation from deteriorating further that the US political elites combined eventually to remove Nixon from office.

The period 1974–80 was a period of marking time internally while the US ruling strata tried to find an alternative strategy, internally and externally, to replace the now clearly outmoded New Deal. We must never lose from sight the major objective constraint on the decision-makers. This was the reversal of phases in the world-economy which I would date as of 1967, and which was accompanied by (in part caused by) a serious decline in US economic competitivity vis-à-vis western Europe and Japan in the world market. By 1980, the material base for hegemony had disappeared. The US had now become simply one strong core state – no doubt still the strongest – among others. The struggle among these core powers led to a marked decline in the global rate of profit. The so-called energy crisis of 1973 was merely the most visible symbol of an enormous economic reshuffle that was in process.

The objective economic weakening of US economic strength meant that the pie was no longer expanding. The New Deal social compromise was no longer economically viable. Something needed to be done. The first reflex was patchwork. Both Ford and Carter (that is, Kissinger and Brzezinski) tried to slow down the frittering away of the international position of the United States through "trilateralism" – which simply meant an appeal to the Japanese and the west Europeans to continue playing the game as it had been played since 1945, under US leadership. It became quite clear by 1980 that neither the west Europeans nor the Japanese were buying this line – diplomatically, militarily, or most importantly economically. Poor Jimmy Carter paid the price of being accused of weak leadership, as though bombast and/or firmness was what mattered.

Patchwork having failed, the US took a more significant turn – to Reaganism. If we wish to appreciate this new post-New Deal strategy, we must ignore some of the rhetoric for a cooler appreciation of what is at stake. It will be most clear if we compare Reaganism on each of the five points we enumerated as the New Deal strategy.

(1) Militarism is in. Its function will be the same as in Germany in the 1930s – to provide jobs and profits, to canalize frustrations against outside enemies. While the New Deal era involved the creation of an incredible military–industrial complex (to use the phrase coined, let us recall, by none other than Dwight David Eisenhower), the US was in this period an imperial power, not a militarist one. It dealt from strength and therefore never took, never needed to take, the risks of a nuclear war. In the post-New Deal era, one can no longer be sure of the same kind of self-interested self-restraint.

(2) The US is moving toward new international alliances. Soviet–American détente is dead, but so largely is NATO. Already under Nixon, the US began to implement a "Pacific Rim" strategy – an alliance primarily with Japan and China. In the next decade, we may expect the logical conclusion of this, the break with western Europe (Germany and France) and the rapprochement of western Europe and the USSR. The ideological justification for such a realignment has still to be created.

(3) The welfare state will be contracted. It is quite obvious why this must be so. If one combines economic stagnation and increased military expenditures, something must give. That something is welfare, not merely in terms of US government expenditures on social services but in terms of the real incomes of the US working class.

(4) Whereas the New Deal involved the incorporation of working-

class organizations into political machinery and social consensus of US life and thereby their neutralization, Reaganism involves the incorporation of all the "small" middle strata – the small businessmen, aspiring bureaucrats and provincial professionals, nonunionized artisans – into social legitimacy. It is not that, under Reagan, the "moral majority" has taken power. Quite the contrary. Reagan and his team are harnessing their energy but buying only limited parts of their program. Reaganism seeks to create not a right-wing coalition but a "right of center" one. The "moral majority" is quite correct to fear that the prominence of "trilateralist" Bush, and Haig, and Weinberger provide the proof that Reagan's presidency represents an adjustment of US strategy which is important but scarcely revolutionary.

The fifth element of the New Deal strategy was the weak but steady attempt to incorporate the "minorities." Regretfully, the Reaganites are going to drop this one. Not that they really want to. After all, what does it matter to them if a few more Blacks and Hispanics achieve social advancement? But somebody has to pay the social costs of the new strategy, designed for times of global economic difficulties. It surely can't be the big corporations. Nor, for the Reaganites, can it be the social strata that make up the "moral majority." It could be organized workers, but they are still strongly entrenched. Ah well, it will have to be the Blacks and the Hispanics primarily. Sorry, fellas, come back in 1995 and we'll see what we can do for you then!

What we all must recognize is that there has now emerged a new Establishment ideology in the United States. The days of "mature global liberalism" are over. Carter's human-rights thematics were not its highpoint but its swan song. It has now been replaced by a defensive conservatism – muscular, arrogant, spastic, not at all generous, and above all vigorous. Its sudden emergence and long-term prospects have, let us admit it, caught the US left unawares and a bit perplexed as to how to react. It will not do to use images of the 1930s ("fascism") or images of the 1950s (the "cold war mentality" of John Foster Dulles) to categorize it, and this because the *world* political *rapport de forces* is entirely different.

The decline of US power relative to that of other states is at one and the same time a great constraint on the US left and a great liberating force. It is a great constraint because it means reactionary and racist social forces can play on fears of loss of status and income by American workers which are acutely felt and not without objective basis, in a situation where it may in fact be true that a reactionary and racist politics would slow down, *in the short run*, the rate of relative decline.

But it is also very liberating. It means that the US left can at last shed, not the heritage of the New Deal insofar as the New Deal was the result of mass popular pressure for greater freedom and equality, but the albatross of the New Deal insofar as it tied the American working class and the "minorities" into an alliance, nationally and internationally, with the sophisticated conservatives of the transnational corporations. The legitimation offered to sophisticated conservatives by the political alliance with the trade unions and the major organizations representing "minority" groups is what has permitted these sophisticated conservatives to dominate *de facto* since the Second World War all the major "liberal" institutions in the United States – the Democratic Party, the judiciary, the media, the universities.

Of course, fear of the "moral majority" may tempt many on the left to try to "reconstruct" the New Deal "coalition." But this has all the promise of warming up a fried egg. The social realities within the United States and within the world-system as a whole are profoundly different today from what they were in 1933. It follows that an intelligent agenda for the left, both in the United States and the world, must be different.

I have already indicated one enormous difference. In 1933, the United States was about to enter its moment of hegemonic dominance. In 1984, it is entering the post-hegemonic era. In 1933, the left was about to enter a world political alliance with centrist forces against the very real threat of world fascism. In 1984, the emerging restructuring of the interstate system has no clear ideological base. If, as I have suggested, in the next decade, a Washington–Tokyo–Beijing axis faces a Bonn–Paris–Moscow axis, there is no *a priori* reason why left forces should automatically line up with either side. This does not mean that tactically, in particular instances, one or the other of these axes may not be cooperating with progressive forces. This does mean that the trajectory of the world antisystemic movement will not necessarily be tied, as it has been for most of the twentieth century, to the military and economic struggles of the great powers.

I cannot here and now resume this trajectory, made up of countless national and social revolutions from Mexico and Russia at the beginning of the century to El Salvador and South Africa today. This trajectory is at once stirring (even intoxicating) and disappointing. The deceptions, the mistakes, the disasters have been many, and not a few of them are our own doing. There are however two facts about this trajectory I want to underline. The cumulative effect of the mass mobilizations and struggles has been a collective accretion of political power by the world's antisystemic movements, taken as a whole, such that the defenders of the world status quo are running scared. And there has been enough recuperation of these movements and enough reinforcement by them of the very capitalist world-system they are presumably dedicated to overthrow, that we are today perhaps ready – and if so for the first time – to reanalyze the very bases of our theoretical analyses and worldwide strategy, both derived from the limited vision of our nineteenth-century forerunners.

For the moment, I will confine my suggestions to the priorities I see for those antisystemic forces which are operating within the United States.

(1) In this period of stagnation, capitalists are going to try to cut costs heavily through reduction of labor costs – by relocating industries from higher-wage to lower-wage countries, by technological advances which will increase the capital–labor ratio of various industries, and by direct attack on high wages within the United States through a combination of methods: union-busting, inflation with its wage-lag, reduction of welfare transfer payments, and internal industrial relo-cation (including revival of putting-out systems). The same people who will do all these things will turn around and try to convince the US worker that he can save himself by advocating "protectionism" – against other nations, against the Third World within. Priority number one therefore is to argue the case that the middle-run "protec-tion" of the wages of the US working class necessarily includes steps towards increasing real wage levels elsewhere – in other states, among the Third World within. Greater egalitarianism in world wage levels undermines the ability of transnational corporations to play off one set of world workers against another.

(2) The "minorities" are no longer so few in number in the US. As these groups are socially defined today, and given demographic trends, they are moving towards being perhaps one-half of the US *working class*. It is inevitable that this group will intensify the expression of their class interests in "racial" or "ethnic–cultural" clothing. In addition, the civil war in South Africa will come increasingly to the fore of US consciousness. Hence the social turmoil of the United States in the 1980s – and there will be much turmoil – will be increasingly perceived by the media and by many of its participants as a "race war." It is our

task to turn this perception around, not by some stupid insistence on the priority of class analysis or some blind refusal to recognize the existential centrality of the reassertion of cultural specifics, but by a clear analysis of the ways in which and the degree to which social movements can bring together antisystemic thrusts taking on quite different formal expressions (both the terminology of class and the terminology of race, caste, and culture). We must make central to our analyses how the *creation* of race and nation has itself been one of the many mechanisms of organizing the world's labor force hierarchically. In the US, we have to link systematically our internal struggle for unity on the left with our struggle to support comparable movements in the peripheral regions of the world-economy.

(3) We must, as our third priority, rethink our whole relationship to all the socialist states. The game of labels – the good ones, the bad ones; the revolutionary, revisionist, and in-between ones – diverts us from the central reality which is that these states are still within the world-system and that therefore there is an internal and unending class struggle inside these states which is part and parcel of the single global struggle. These states are no more politically inert than any others, and we must therefore devise ways of effective trans-state alliances of movements which include the movements within these states (which latter movements we may predict will become increasingly numerous and variegated).

(4) We must weigh with full seriousness the impact of the womens' movement. This is in many ways the hardest phenomenon for the left to handle, because it requires the most rethinking in the most different spheres of human activity. On the other hand, this is the strength of the womens' movement. Precisely because it opens up the question not merely of equal access to the workplace, but of the very structure of the workplace, of the very patterns of consumption, of the very workings of the family (which, the conservatives are right, is a fundamental institution of social life), of the very organization of the everyday reproduction of material life – precisely because it raises all these questions simultaneously, in what seems a torrent of questioning and protest, the womens' movement forces us to face up to what will be the true social content of a socialist world, one based on production for use, one egalitarian in reality.

8 ❧ The world-economy and the state-structures in peripheral and dependent countries (the so-called Third World)

We have been oppressed a great deal, we have been exploited a great deal, and we have been disregarded a great deal. It is our weakness that has led to our being oppressed, exploited, and disregarded. Now we want a revolution – a revolution which brings to an end our weakness so that we are never again exploited, oppressed and humiliated.

Arusha Declaration, TANU, Tanzania, January 1967

The capitalist world-economy which came into existence in Europe in the sixteenth century is a network of integrated production processes united in a single division of labor. Its basic economic imperative is the ceaseless accumulation of capital, made possible by the continuous appropriation of surplus-value, which is centralized via primitive accumulation, the concentration of capital, and the mechanisms of unequal exchange. Its political superstructure is the interstate system composed of "states," some sovereign, some colonial. The zones under the jurisdiction of these states in this interstate system have never been economically autonomous, since they have always been integrated in a larger division of labor, that of the world-economy.

As the world-economy has expanded over historical time in consequence of its internal needs, it has "incorporated" new zones into the world-economy's division of labor. These zones that were being incorporated had of course very different kinds of political structures at the moment of incorporation. These ranged from previously self-sufficient world-empires with strong centralized administrations and long historical heritages at one extreme to "stateless" bands of hunters and gatherers at the other. There were all manner of variations in between.

From the point of view of dominant forces in the capitalist world-economy, the optimal state-structure of a newly incorporated zone was one that (1) was not strong enough to interfere with the flows of commodities, capital, and labor between this zone and the rest of the capitalist world-economy, but (2) *was* strong enough to facilitate these same flows. This meant that incorporation involved in some cases weakening the pre-existing state-structures, in other cases strengthening them or creating new ones – in *all* cases, restructuring them.

Restructuring involved not merely reshaping the effective tools of power of these state-structures but also almost always redrawing the boundaries of their domain. In the case of the previously centralized politics, the pressure was usually to divide them up into smaller entities. In the case of the previously "weak" state-structures, the pressure was usually to group them into one new larger entity, or to attach them to some larger pre-existing entity.

When large and relatively strong structures such as the Russian Empire, the Ottoman Empire, Persia, and China were incorporated, the outside forces sought to weaken the powers of these state-structures and contract their boundaries. Eventually those newly incorporated state-structures became what Lenin and others called "semi-colonies." In zones like the Caribbean, North America, or Australia, the indigenous polities (and large parts of the population) were destroyed upon incorporation, and new colonial states were established, often with the help of European settler populations. Finally, there were a large number of zones, such as the Indian subcontinent and many parts of southeast Asia and Africa, where there were located some fairly strong political structures surrounded by other weaker ones. Typically, these areas were invaded and reduced to colonial status, but without the intrusion of European settlers. These colonies were thereupon governed by a mixture of "indirect" and "direct" rule.

When the dust settled, a set of boundary lines had been created which served to delineate entities which became the participants in the interstate system. The various peripheral (or dependent) zones enjoyed for the most part colonial status at the high point of the expansion of the world-economy (circa 1900). That is, each was under the formal, direct political jurisdiction of a European power. The non-colonized states in the periphery were typically "weak" states, which however participated in the interstate system as formally sovereign entities. Their "sovereign" status was of course encroached upon by arrangements such as the "concessions" in China; and military intervention by the European states occurred whenever European powers thought the local state was either too assertive or too inefficacious. European intervention in China after the so-called Boxer Rebellion was a typical instance.

Once these states were integrated into the interstate system, the system operated to facilitate the peripheralization of the production processes in the region and the flows of surplus to core regions via unequal exchange. Popular resistance to the initial imposition of this system was a constant, but historically this initial resistance for the most part failed, as we know. The new or restructured state-structures in the periphery were either overtly in the hands of the imperialist powers (formal colonialism) or subordinate to them and controlled by collaborationist elements. Hence the rise of the post-incorporation movements of resistance was directed always first of all against the European imperialists (as the most clear political expression of world capitalist forces), but almost always equally against the local tenants of political power, even those who were directing technically independent states. The Iranian Revolution against the United States and the Shah is merely one recent instance of a long-standing trend in all these countries.

In colonial territories, the demand of these movements was for national independence; and in technically sovereign states the demand was for a strong state that was "nationalist" in orientation. In most countries, the movements organized to achieve what they perceived as radical political change. They proposed "revolution." Whether this revolution was to be "national" or "social" in form was less of a difference than theorists have sometimes claimed. The two types of revolution were frequently conflated, and the varying emphases were often more the consequence of the formal status of the country (colony or not) than of some fundamental difference in the nature of the movement.

As nationalist movements organized and grew strong, they came more and more to take the form of, or be succeeded by, national liberation (or socialist) movements. Obviously, this was neither simple nor clearcut. Nationalist movements were coalitions of elements who were truly antisystemic in interest and motivation and those who were merely seeking the advancement of their own stratum within the reward system of the capitalist world-economy. In the phase of mobilization, the unity of such a coalition usually depended less on the elements within the coalition than on the tactic of the power structures against which the coalition was fighting. To the extent that the local power structure was rigid and unremittingly reactionary, the coalition found it easy to maintain a united front. To the extent that the local power structure was flexible and sophisticated, the coalition forming the movement often split over tactics, reflecting the underlying internal tension between the antisystemic elements and the others. What *all* elements in the coalition could agree upon, however, under all conditions, was that the immediate political objective of the movement had to be obtaining power in the local state-structure. This was always seen by everyone as the key to obtaining the changes they desired, however they defined these changes.

In the twentieth century, one such movement after another has in fact come to power, by one means or another. Sometimes the route to power was the protracted armed struggle of a liberation movement. Sometimes the route to power was a relatively brief period of popular demonstrations accompanying the internal collapse of the old regime. Sometimes the route to power was a military coup d'état, often following upon popular demonstrations. Sometimes the route to power even involved a mere voting process within the previous constitutional framework.

Which road to power was utilized reflected particular historical circumstances that were the conjoint consequences of the conditions of the world-economy and the interstate system as a whole at a given moment, the position of the particular state in the whole system, and the existing distribution of class and other social forces within the particular state. Each country has had the revolution that was possible for it.

Revolutions, however, are not events but processes. Obviously the route to power of particular movements was very consequential in the changes such movements were in fact able to institute in the state-structures after their coming to power. To be sure, each such movement sought, once in power, to strengthen its own state-structure within the interstate system. But the quality of their subjective will and their objective opportunities varied. Suffice it to say that no movement has succeeded, when it came to power, in strengthening its state-structure as much as it intended in the phase of mobilization. But some have succeeded more than others.

One of the realities that all movements discovered, once in power, is that state power is not merely an opportunity; it is also a constraint. A group in power seeks to remain in power in order to carry out its objectives, and remaining in power in a state within an interstate system means being subject to the continuing pressure of the other states to observe certain very real *de facto* limitations on sovereignty. A given state can verbally assert its *total* autonomy from all outside forces, but no single state has in fact the effective power to act on this assertion.

A state can become stronger; it cannot become totally autonomous. This is so for two reasons. Other states will not let any individual state be totally autonomous and will intrude directly and indirectly, politically and militarily if necessary. But this is not the only reason. The main reason is that elements within the movement itself work against this total autonomy. Total autonomy is only meaningful in a closed economy. And the existing strength of the forces of production in the capitalist world-economy means that *total* economic withdrawal of any peripheral or dependent state involves a major economic sacrifice for all their lifetime of, first of all, the very cadres of the revolutionary movement. Their objective class interests work against such self-abnegation.

This is why the revolutionary movements, once in power, have all *without exception* been beset by internal strains, and have all without exception made major compromises in terms of their long-run anti-systemic ideals. The conflict should be posed neither as that of the pure versus the impure (this is the path of infantile leftism) nor as that of the realists versus the utopians (this is the path of rightward ending of the revolutionary thrust). The issue is rather how to maintain for each movement the constant pendulum between new mobilizing thrusts and the rational recognition of existing limits of possibility. It is a problem for the antisystemic movements as a worldwide collectivity of movements of their strategy not only vis-à-vis the power centers of the capitalist world-economy as a whole on the one hand but also vis-à-vis all the states in which all the many revolutionary, antisystemic (national and social) movements have taken power on the other.

A Manichean view of the world, any Manichean view, will paralyze our collective efforts worldwide ultimately to transform the capitalist world-economy into a socialist world order. For the forces at work are contradictory, and none more contradictory than those of the anti-systemic movements themselves. They have achieved much. In the twentieth century, these movements have fundamentally shaken the political structures of the capitalist world-economy and the self-confidence of the world bourgeoisie. But, in their very success, their partial success, these movements have simultaneously strengthened the capitalist world-economy and its political superstructure, the interstate system.

Our task is to take account of these contradictory realities, and within the framework of the objective state of the world-economy, organize where we can, mobilize where we can, and constantly push against the weak points of the existing world order (which are to be found everywhere). The strategy is easy to lay out; it is the tactics that are difficult. It would therefore be wise if we all recognized that the tactical decisions of each movement are difficult and ambiguous, and if we empathized with each other a bit before we condemned each other. Condemnations are sometimes necessary; but they should not be hasty.

The capitalist world-economy is in one of its periodic economic stagnations. This period of stagnation is also a period of the renewed rivalry of the stronger states, a period of the slow decline of the former hegemonic power (the USA). Interstate alliances are being reconstructed. And the revolutionary movements are finding themselves at odds with each other. It is not at all clear yet along what lines the interstate system will restabilize in the next decade.

Whatever the pattern of interstate alliances, the worldwide collectivity of antisystemic movements (old and new) will continue to organize to transform the system as such. The cutting edge of this worldwide collectivity constantly shifts locus. The newer movements are always less inhibited than the older ones. If the movements remember the states are structures which they may utilize but which also hamper them, if the movements bear in mind that the object of their revolutionary thrusts is not the reinforcement of their separate state-structures (linked necessarily in the interstate system) but the transformation of a capitalist world-economy into a socialist world order, then the movement may be able, collectively, to surmount some of the contradictions of their own inevitable participation in the existing system. We should not be seeking to "develop" our separate states; this is the lure and the trap of the capitalist system. We should be seeking to transform the system as a whole, which requires recognizing our own states as both agents in this transformation and barriers to it. "Social life is essentially *practical*. All mysteries which mislead theory to mysticism find their rational solution in human practice and in the comprehension of this practice."[1]

[1] Karl Marx, *Theses on Feuerbach*, VIII.

9 ⤳ Socialist states: mercantilist strategies and revolutionary objectives

The revolutionary strategy of the world socialist movement before 1917 was based on two main premises. First, since communism was a historical stage that was supposed to follow capitalism, the political objective of revolutionaries was to bring about a change from one system to the other. There was no suggestion that there was to be some long intermediate stage between the two systems with some structure peculiar to it.

Secondly, it was believed, insofar as the matter was thought about, that to the degree the various states made the transition separately, the "first" revolutions would occur in the most advanced states. In theory, this should have meant that Great Britain was candidate number one, and at one point Marx suggested something along this line. But if we look at real expectations, at first hopes were pinned upon France (in the revolutionary lead, so to speak, from 1789 to 1870) and then in the early twentieth century upon Germany. The latter expectation was based on the political strength of the German socialist movement, and not on some derivation from an analysis of the forces and relations of production in Germany. This was a first inconsistency which should have elicited some collective self-questioning or major internal debate, but as far as I know there was nothing of the sort anywhere.

Instead, there did occur a different debate about revolutionary strategy in, of all places, Russia. The Menshevik–Bolshevik debate, it should be underlined, is not the first but the second great debate of the world socialist movement, *lato sensu*. The first great debate had been the Anarchist–Marxist debate of the First International. It revolved around the strategic question whether or not the way to achieve communism was to create an *organized* movement which would seek to achieve state power. The Marxists said this was the essential first step and basically they carried the day by the 1880s. The creation of the Second International was based on this strategic premise, which has ever since governed the world socialist movement (once again and throughout defined in a broad and encompassing sense).[1]

Both Mensheviks and Bolsheviks agreed upon this strategy. What they disagreed about was which kind of organized movement was in fact likely to achieve state power, a mass working-class party or a cadre party of "professional revolutionaries." If this debate emerged in Russia, and not either in western Europe or in what later came to be called the Third World, it was precisely because Russia was one of the few countries where the answer to this second strategic choice did not seem obvious to the militants. In western Europe, long before 1914, legal mass working-class parties already existed within state-structures with wide suffrages and regular electoral processes. To have adopted a Bolshevik strategy in these countries before 1917 would have involved dismantling a functioning and rising organizational structure. It was simply never seriously considered. In the colonial and semi-colonial world of Asia and Africa (and of most of Latin America), on the other hand, the political conditions were such that organized workers' movements barely existed. Russia was one of the few places that had both a large group of urban workers (in absolute numbers, even if the percentage were small) and embryonic workers' organizations, which however were subject to acute political suppression (no routinized electoral system, limitations on legal organizing, etc.). The Russian workers' movement thus faced a real political choice – hence the debate. As we know, the Bolshevik option historically prevailed.

Recently, in discussing the differences in view between Marx and Lenin on the role of the party, Ralph Miliband concluded:

I think that, although Marx did not reject all forms of organization, he nevertheless greatly underestimated how much organization a socialist movement – let alone a socialist revolution – required; and that Lenin, for his part, altogether underestimated the problems that the organization which he wanted and brought into being must in all circumstances produce.[2]

It is of these difficulties engendered by organization, and in particular by organizations which assume state power, that I wish to speak.

The early history of the Russian Revolution in broad outline is

---

[1] I have developed this theme of the importance of the decision to organize, and its implications for contemporary parties in western Europe, in "Eurocommunism: its roots in European working-class history," chapter 11 in this volume.

[2] Ralph Miliband, "Kolakowski's Anti-Marx", *Political Studies*, 29:1 (Mar. 1981), p. 120.

familiar. The Bolsheviks came to power through insurrection in the wake of the collapse of the Czarist state-structure. The party leadership believed that a revolution in Germany was imminent and that further-more such a revolution was essential to secure the political seizure of power in Russia. The new Russian revolutionary government was immediately assailed by an invasion by hostile foreign forces who supported internal counter-revolutionaries. It was subject as well to a partial economic boycott which has in a sense never been lifted since. The expected revolution in Germany was aborted. Within a few years, the CPSU made the decision that it could only survive if it built a relatively autarkic economy. It set about doing this under the ideo-logical slogan of "socialism in one country." In a sense, this objective has never been completely dropped.

Survival in a hostile world has been the leitmotiv of the Bolsheviks in power. This necessity, and the subjective appreciation of this necessity, dictated a series of priorities which became institutionalized. I do not say these priorities were the only possible choice. But they were one rational option in terms of survival.

Priority number one was to secure the party's power against internal opposition. This involved the creation of a one-party state, the strengthening of the state bureaucracy in general and of the police apparatus in particular, and the control of the dissemination of information.

Priority number two was to secure the state as such against foreign enemies. This required strengthening the state's military and eco-nomic bases. It involved rapid industrialization and its historical concomitant, the expropriation of the peasantry. It also involved the creation of a military machine capable of neutralizing at least enemy military forces.

But there was another side to this coin. One can enhance the neutralization of enemies by political/diplomatic as well as by military means. The political/diplomatic thrust was twofold. The first element was the structuring by the CPSU of allied political forces in other countries into a formal network. These forces were the communist parties brought together under the Draconian discipline of the 21 Points within the Third International. These parties were thereby enjoined to place "the defense of the Soviet Union" at the top of their list of tactical considerations, which was very useful for the CPSU but less useful for the other parties in the Third International.

The second element of the political/diplomatic thrust was the insistent demand by the government of the USSR that it be admitted as a full-fledged participant in, indeed as a member of, the inner circle of the interstate system. From Locarno to the League of Nations, from Yalta to détente, the USSR has been the postulant. Re-entry offered greater power and security for the socialist state, but it was bought at the price of muting revolutionary forces elsewhere which, from China in the 1920s to Spain in the 1930s to Greece in the 1940s to today, the USSR has always been willing to do, provided the other great powers would make it worth its while.

Priority number three was to evolve a theoretical model which would make the survival of the CPSU compatible with the general aspirations of the world socialist movement. Without this kind of ideological bridge, the CPSU would not be able to maintain the internal coherence of the party and above all the world network of allied forces so critical to the strategy. This theoretical model involved the invention of an intermediate stage between capitalism and communism, the so-called stage of "socialism," which was defined as a stage of the development of each separate state, all of which were said to be on parallel but not synchronous historical paths going from primitive communism to real communism via human history.

This intervening stage of "socialism" was not reached immediately after the assumption of political power by a communist party. For example it was only in 1936 that the USSR was proclaimed to be a socialist state and, if not a classless society, at least a society without class contradictions. What had been achieved by 1936 which made this proclamation possible was presumably three main things: the collectivization of all the basic means of production; the elimination of all internal hostile political organizations; the creation of a stable and reliable state-structure under the effective control of the party. What then remained to be done in order to proceed from the stage of socialism to the stage of communism? Presumably one thing and one thing only: the full development of the forces of production to some level not hitherto achieved even in the most "advanced" capitalist states. In effect, the CPSU now put forward in Marxist clothing a mercantilist strategy of "catching up" and "surpassing" rival states. Khrushchev cried: 'We will bury you." Thus accumulation was to be the mainspring of the socialist stage. Of course, it would be socialist and not capitalist accumulation, and this because the beneficiaries would be the collectivity (via the state) and not individuals or private organizations. And because the beneficiaries were intended to be collective and not individual, it was asserted that there would occur, more or less automatically, a transformation of collective psychology (the creation of "socialist man").

It may be argued that the Second World War was the testing-ground of the rationality of this strategy. It worked: that is, the CPSU survived the most serious attempt to destroy it that had ever been attempted since the initial foreign invasions. The CPSU not only survived but it emerged enormously strengthened: internally, externally, and ideologically.

There emerged however an unexpected problem, in significant part deriving from the military and diplomatic successes of the USSR. By 1949 there were eleven other states (eight in Europe and three in Asia), all more or less bordering the USSR, which had governments controlled by communist parties, and there would be more later in zones geographically more remote from the USSR. Most of them adopted substantially the same strategy as had the USSR—establishment of tight internal controls, request (even demand) of full re-entry into the interstate system (a request which has had only middling success), adoption of the concept that there was an intermediate stage between capitalism and communism, emphasis on the rapid development of the national forces of production.

One problem was, however, necessarily new. Both the USSR and the post-1945 communist governments faced the issue of the nature of interstate relations among these socialist states. The CPSU had a simple answer. They proposed the same relationship as that which already existed between the parties, that is, the political primacy of the CPSU/USSR. As we know, several of these states rebelled against this great-power–satellite format. Yugoslavia and China were the most striking instances but they were by no means the only ones. As these rebellions began to occur in sequence, the CPSU developed a new doctrine, that there now existed a socialist community of nations with a socialist division of labor and within which there was a right of intervention to maintain in power governments following parallel strategies. This right was not hypothetical: it was invoked most notably in Hungary in 1956, in Czechoslovakia in 1968, and in Afghanistan in 1979.

There have been two major attempts to develop a strikingly different strategy from that of the CPSU: China during the Cultural Revolution, and Kampuchea under Pol Pot.[3]

In the case of China, Mao Zedong saw clearly two of the difficulties

[3] I do not consider that Yugoslavia or Albania or Korea have made more than marginal alterations in the basic mercantilist strategy as outlined here, although of course in each case their interstate relations with the USSR were not of a kind that pleased the CPSU.

that had been faced by the CPSU. He saw first of all the dilemma suggested by Miliband: that organization is central to revolution but creates problems for revolution. If an organization has state power, there tends to emerge a privileged stratum in the party and in the state-structure, who develop interests that are not identical with those who are direct producers. He saw, second of all, that the concept of an intermediate socialist stage within which there were no contradictory classes could and did serve as ideological protection for this privileged stratum.

Mao Zedong's solution to these problems was twofold. First of all, he reconceptualized the socialist stage, insisting that there persisted contradictory *classes* and consequently a continuing class struggle during this stage. Hence he talked of "capitalist roaders" and "socialist roaders"; he even argued that these two groups were to be found side by side within the very highest ranks not only of the state but even of the party itself. Since, however, the different classes did not now find expression in separate parties (as they had in Marxist theory and political reality before, say, 1917) but were in fact located inside the single legal party, the Communist Party, the question was posed as to how class struggle could be waged organizationally? The answer Mao Zedong offered was that proletarian class struggle could now be waged via a "Cultural Revolution" which took the organizational form of pseudo- or semi-autonomous groups – Red Guards, revolutionary committees, etc. – who would "storm" the citadels of capitalism defended, among others, by the then President of the country and the then Secretary-General of the Communist Party.

The Cultural Revolution was a political failure in that the Chinese government and Communist Party have since reverted to the basic strategy that prevails in the other socialist states. This is not to say that the internal structures of say China and the USSR in 1981 are identical. Samir Amin insists that there remains the crucial difference that the Chinese strategy is founded on a "peasant–worker alliance" whereas the Soviet model is based on "a massive extraction [of surplus] by the state from the countryside."[4] That may be so, but it remains the case that the "construction of socialism" in China remains wedded today to a mercantilist vision: it is by the development of the forces of production within China that China will one day move on from the stage of socialism to the stage of communism.[5]

---

[4] Samir Amin, "Quelques reflexions sur le étapes du développement de la construction socialiste en Chine," manuscript 1980, p. 12.

[5] It is true that in the late 1950s, in the course of their ideological quarrel with the CPSU, the CCP took the position that the transition from socialism to communism would occur not in each

Nor is China less wedded than the USSR to the assumption that the starting point of political analysis for a communist party in power is the need to assure its survival in a hostile world. The fact that the Chinese today believe that the greatest hostility to them comes from the USSR and not from the USA does not alter the basic analytic framework. If the attempt of the Cultural Revolution to institutionalize class struggle within a socialist state and its governing communist party did not succeed, this may be because such an attempt is in contradiction to the need to assure survival of this same party in a hostile world.

The attempt of Kampuchea under Pol Pot to break with a mercantilist strategy was basically quite different from that of China during the Cultural Revolution. Paradoxically, it can be interpreted as the adoption of a supermercantilism in order to be anti-mercantilist. The policy was supermercantilist in that it involved the most extreme economic withdrawal from the world-economy and even from the interstate system that has been attempted in the twentieth century. It was nonetheless anti-mercantilist in that the objective of "catching up" in terms of the forces of production was abjured and the social division of labor was minimized. Economically, the regime seemed to be pushing towards the consolidation of an agriculturally self-sufficient, basically rural social order.

The Kampuchea of Pol Pot is no more for several reasons. The economic policies were so objectionable to so many that they could only be enforced by a repression so heavy that it was counterproductive (not to speak of being morally objectionable). Total withdrawal from the world-economy and the interstate system was not feasible because other states refused to permit it, as the Vietnamese invasion demonstrated. And once again the primacy of the political objective of survival was what led to the particular tactics (internally and vis-à-vis its neighbors) that account for the overthrow of the regime.

It may sound as if I thought survival were somehow not a legitimate objective. It is both legitimate, rational, and normal as an organizational goal. The question is the degree to which the survival of a socialist party in power pursuing a mercantilist strategy serves the revolutionary objectives of the world socialist movement. Let me say right off that I do not believe there is a simple or easy answer to this question. I merely wish to explore the alternatives that are available in

state separately (the Soviet position), but throughout the world simultaneously. To my knowledge, this theme is no longer stressed in Chinese analyses.

the light of some sixty years of experience with such movements in power in various states.

It is quite clear that all these movements in power have been acting within constraints that were not of their making nor within their control. They obtained state power, it may be fairly assumed, with the intent of furthering the long-run transformation of the world into a communist society. That they may have had other more short-run or middle-run objectives (abolition of specific oppressive institutions, removal of particular groups from power and privilege, restoration of national dignity, etc.) takes nothing away from the basic intent to pursue a social (that is, a socialist) revolution.

To the extent they were revolutionary in intent and politically successful in terms of achieving state power, they of course were faced with counter-revolutionary forces within the state and, even more importantly, within the world-system as a whole. The coming to power of such movements by definition was antisystemic in effect as well as in intent, since it threatened the smooth functioning of the economic and political machinery of the world-system and encouraged by example and by deed other antisystemic movements.[6] Given this, such movements did not find it easy to remain in power and those who failed to mobilize energies for survival in a hostile world did not survive.

However – and this is the contradiction, which cannot be eliminated – organizational survival was bought at the price of accepting the rules of the system (after no doubt certain modifications were made of some of these rules). And accepting the rules, particularly improved (that is, in some sense "fairer") rules, constituted a reinforcement (and not a minor one) of the system.

The very objective of socialism in one country – what I have designated as the mercantilist strategy of "catching up" – involved the assumption by socialist parties of what was once upon a time thought to be the "historic task" of the bourgeoisie – the primitive accumulation of capital, the destruction of the "feudal fetters," the total commodification of all the factors of production. It is an historic fact of the twentieth century that communist parties in power in socialist states have done at least as much as transnational corporations to extend the domain of the law of value.

It seems to me therefore that it is an exercise in futility to try to create

---

[6] See my discussion of the trajectory of antisystemic movements and the way in which the coming to power of particular movements affects the political *rapport de forces* in the world-system as a whole in "The future of the world-economy," chapter 10 in this volume.

a morphological category for these socialist states. Are they only socialist states as they themselves proclaim, and as many of their bitterest opponents accept? Or are they, in the version of one or another dissident left analysis, deformed workers' states, state capitalist states, states dominated by a "new class," states that are neither capitalist nor socialist but some unnamed (and unnameable?) third form?[7]

Any morphology assumes that the units to be thus described are the states and that these states have modes of production. Almost inevitably, a morphology based on such an assumption leads to defining such a state as being in some "transitional" stage. To define an entity as transitional is to define it not in terms of what it is (and was) but in terms of what it will be, when in fact what it will be is a function of forces far longer than those controlled by the "transitional" entity. This is a profoundly anti-empirical procedure.

Before the assumption of power by communist parties in the socialist states, these states were located within the social division of labor of the capitalist world-economy and its political superstructure, the interstate system. The burden of proof is upon those who contend that this is no longer so. For my part, I remain unconvinced, since it seems to me that the steady extension of the law of value within the boundaries of these very states and the unremitting attempts of these states to strengthen the interstate system (which they call the "struggle for peace") is evidence that runs strongly in the opposite direction.

So much for categorizing the states. But what of the movements? Before the assumption of power by communist parties in the socialist states, these parties were part of the assemblage of world antisystemic movements. Did they remain so? Here the answer must be far more nuanced. It depends on which movement and which moment of time. Obviously, state power is a tool these movements can use in the furtherance of antisystemic objectives, but it is also a constraint on the degree to which these movements can be antisystemic, as we have argued.

Does perhaps the balance turn systematically towards greater constraint of revolutionary objectives the longer a communist party retains state power (in a state which continues, willy-nilly, to be part of a singular world-system)? Can survival in state power be, after a certain point, counterproductive – counterproductive, that is, for revolu-

[7] See a brief and instructive review of these categorizations in Philip Corrigan *et al.*, "Bolshevism and the USSR," *New Left Review*, no. 125 (Jan.–Feb. 1981), pp. 45–60. The authors point out that in all these categorizations there lie – sometimes overtly, sometimes in latent form – the themes of betrayal and backwardness.

tionary objectives? I hesitate, to be honest, to put forward such a heretical notion, since hitherto the concept of alternance in state power has been linked to the adoption of a reformist, antirevolutionary, prosystemic stance. But may this not be the way to make a cultural revolution work – not from within state power, as Mao Zedong tried and failed, but from without? Should not Polish Communists locate themselves inside the Gdańsk shipyards in the name of the struggle for socialism rather than on the outside? No doubt the putative loss of state power would involve enormous risks for a revolutionary movement. But is it not the case that sometimes – not at every moment or in every place – the retention of state power holds greater risks? Must the leadership of popular forces in socialist states be handed over to the ideologues of the traditional right and the disillusioned ex-revolutionaries on a silver platter? Should revolutionaries put themselves in the position where they fear revolutionary upheavals?

These are not moral questions but questions of strategy. They are at least worth discussing at a time when there is a widespread sense that socialist movements in power have not fulfilled their collective promise, have not discharged *their* presumed "historic task," the overthrow of the world capitalist system. The moment is not for reproach, though many reproaches are to be made. The moment is one for reflection on the possibilities and modalities of structural change.

In 1941, Isaac Deutscher wrote about the USSR:

Whether we want it or not, socialism (regardless of its shade and tendency) bears the responsibility, in the eyes of the working class, for the outcome of the Soviet experiment. This truth is unaffected by the fact that the Soviet regime is only the bastard offspring – or prodigal child – of socialism.[8]

The albatross that world antisystemic movements bear is today all the heavier. The responsibility they bear is for *all* the many movements now in power. The only way we can remove the albatross is by a reassessment of revolutionary strategy.

The movements in power are a political reality reflecting the form and nature of the world class struggle heretofore. The regimes they have created are neither transitional societies not previews of the future but institutions of the presently existing world-system. Movements cannot afford to be bound hand and foot to institutions. As for the socialism of the future, towards which the world-system *as a whole* is in

---

[8] Isaac Deutscher, "22 June 1941," *New Left Review*, no. 124 (Nov.–Dec. 1980), p. 92. From this Deutscher concluded that "the democratization of the Soviet regime would prove salutary not only for the Soviet Union itself, but would act as a powerful impulse for the development of socialism elsewhere."

transition, it will be what we make it to be through our collective expression, the family of world antisystemic movements. Edward Thompson has thundered with his usual passion:

> ... if we look towards any future described as "socialist," there is no error more disabling and actively dangerous to the practice of any human freedom than the notion that there is some "socialist" mode of production ... within which some "socialist" relations of production are *given*, which will afford a categorical guarantee that some immanent socialist society ... will *unfold itself*: not perhaps instantly, ... but in good time, out of the womb of the mode of production itself. This is wholly untrue: every choice and every institution is still to be made ...[9]

This statement perhaps overstates the voluntarist possibilities – it should perhaps be balanced by Hobsbawm's reminder that "hope and prediction, though inseparable, are not the same"[10] – but Thompson's enjoinders are nonetheless salutary.

Nothing in this paper should be taken, I repeat, as a suggestion that the achievement of state power is not an appropriate, desirable, or important goal for an antisystemic movement. But perhaps the seizure of state power should be considered a tactical rather than a strategic opinion. This was, let me remind you, the original conclusion in the nineteenth century about participating in the electoral and parliamentary processes in the first place. Revolutionaries warned this could be a lure, but said it may be useful to play the game *up to a point*. Perhaps the seizure of state power is equally a lure, although it may be useful to play the game *up to a point*. If, however, the world antisystemic movements are to consider seriously such a basic reorientation, they shall have to *invent* a plausible alternative strategy. There isn't one out there simply waiting for us.

[9] E. P. Thompson, *The poverty of theory* (London: Merlin Press, 1978), pp. 353–4.
[10] Eric J. Hobsbawm, "Looking forward: history and the future," *New Left Review*, no. 125 (Jan.–Feb. 1981), p. 18.

Part II

Antisystemic movements

---

10 ✢ The future of the world-economy

We are fond of temporal contrasts (the future and the past, the new and the old) as well as temporal disjunctures (the present, the crisis, the transition). But time is a social reality, not a physical one. And our visions of time (or rather of space–time) both reflect the social system of which they are part, and in a very basic way are constitutive of those systems.

We cannot discuss what we think to be the future of the modern world-system unless we come to some agreement about which past it is to which we are referring. For me, the answer has become increasingly clear. The modern world is a capitalist world-economy, and this capitalist world-economy came into existence in Europe somewhere between 1450 and 1550 as a mode of resolving the "crisis of feudalism" that had shaken this same Europe in the period 1300–1450.

It came into existence as a mode of repressing the increasingly successful ability that the European workforce had demonstrated, during the period of crisis, to withhold surplus from the seigniorial and urban patriarchal strata who had appropriated it under the feudal system. From this perspective, the capitalist system that replaced the feudal system proved marvelously adept. The period from 1450 to 1600 registered a dramatic fall in the real income of Europe's direct producers and, with the constant widening of the geographic scope of the world-economy, this process of polarization (and therefore, in the old-fashioned phrase, of absolute immiserization) has never ceased to expand since. This can be empirically demonstrated, *provided* one measures the polarization in terms of the world-economy as a whole and not in terms of particular states.

In order to appreciate the real changes which are occurring today and which may occur in the future, we must assess what are the structural mechanisms by which the system has up to now reproduced itself, and what are the structural contradictions by which it has up to now undermined itself. I shall however do this somewhat briefly, as I wish to concentrate on the organizational responses of the oppressed strata, the politics of the antisystemic movements that have grown up in the course of the historical development of the capitalist world-economy. For it is these movements which themselves represent a principal nexus of both the undermining and the reproduction of the system.

All systems are both structure and change, have both cycles and trends. Intelligent analysis must always be wary of emphasizing the one at the expense of the other – of seeing only repetitive patterns, of discovering always what is "new." For much of the "new" has always been there, and the repetitions, such as they are, are spiral in character.

The basic economic mechanisms of the capitalist world-economy derive from the fact that the absence of an overarching political structure renders it likely that those producers who seek to operate on the imperative of ceaseless accumulation of capital will drive from competition, over the long run, those who would operate economic enterprises on any other normative principle. This means that producers/entrepreneurs tend to make their production and investment decisions in terms of what will optimize the medium-run likelihood of individual profit.

The basic contradiction of the capitalist system is found in the disjuncture of what determines supply and what determines demand. World production decisions are made on an individual basis. The sum of the activities of the individual producers/entrepreneurs constantly increases world production, which means that continued profitability for all is necessarily a function of an *expanding* world demand. However, expanding world demand is not a function of the decisions of the individual producers/entrepreneurs. If anything, the sum of their individual decisions, insofar as they press individually to reduce costs of their factors of production (and hence to reduce labor costs), serves actually to diminish world demand. World demand is fundamentally determined by a set of pre-existing political compromises within the various states that are part of the world-economy, and which more or less fix for medium-run periods (circa fifty years) the modal distribution of income to various participants in the circuit of capital. This phenomenon is often discussed under such names as the existence of different "historic levels of wages." Wage-levels are indeed based on historic factors, but they are far from unchanging on that account.

An economic system in which world supply expands more or less continuously but world demand remains relatively fixed for medium periods of time is bound to create a cyclical pattern of production. Empirically the capitalist world-economy has in fact known such cycles of expansion and contraction since its beginning (that is, for at least five hundred years). The most important of these cycles seems to be the expansion–stagnation cycle of, forty to fifty-five years that is often called the Kondratieff cycle.

In the stagnation phase of the cycle, precipitated by the excess of world production over world demand, individual entrepreneurs seek to maintain their own relative share of profit (or even expand it) either by expanding production, or by reducing costs (through reducing wages or through technological advance that increases productivity), or by reducing competition, or by some combination of these three methods. One of the many ways of reducing costs is to shift the locus of production to lower-wage zones (from city to country, or from core to peripheral zone both within states and within the world as a whole). Along with this goes pressure to redirect global flows of labor ("outward" from core towards periphery, rather than "inward" from periphery toward core, as occurs in expansion phases).

While individual entrepreneurs and individual geographic areas may benefit precisely because of stagnation, globally the effect is perceived as a squeeze, one felt on the one hand by weaker entrepreneurs (who face bankruptcy amidst the concentration of capital), and on the other hand by those segments of the world labor force previously steadily employed as wage workers. This latter group is unevenly distributed worldwide. Wherever wage workers are found in sufficient numbers, acute class struggles become the visible outgrowth of the stagnation phase. Wherever segments of the petty bourgeoisie are dispossessed because of the effects of stagnation, they join in the acute social conflict.

Over the period of this stagnation phase, the acute class struggles in the various states usually lead to a reopening of the previous historic compromises that had resulted in the existing distributions of appropriated surplus. In addition, semiperipheral zones are able to achieve either higher prices for their goods or a higher proportion of the world market, and thus retain larger segments of world surplus.

There results a redistribution of surplus – more to the bourgeoisie of semiperipheral zones, and more to parts of the labor force of core areas – which effectively expands world monetary demand enough to revive the inherent expansionist tendencies of the capitalist world-economy.

However, as a result of this redistribution of surplus, the world bourgeoisie, and particularly that segment located in the old core areas, is faced with a diminution of its share of world surplus, unless it takes two kinds of crucial countermeasures: technological advances which lead to temporary (but significant) superprofits deriving from temporary monopolies; and expansion of the outer boundaries of the world-economy to incorporate new zones of low-cost, not fully proletarianized, workers.

In this cyclical mechanism, we can see the pressures that lead to the creation and reinforcement of the four basic institutions of the capitalist world-economy: the states; classes; ethno/national status-groups; households. We shall briefly indicate the function of each.

It is by reinforcing and utilizing the state machineries of the states in which they are domiciled that entrepreneurs/producers can best increase their ability to profit, both vis-à-vis other entrepreneurs and vis-à-vis the working classes. The consequent pressure to strengthen the efficacity of state machineries is not countered by working-class pressure in an opposite direction. Far from being antistate *per se*, the working classes of a given state in their struggle with the bourgeoisie of that state equally seek to strengthen the particular state machinery (whether their tactics are reformist or revolutionary), however much they are politically opposed to the domination of the existing regime by bourgeois elements. Hence, over time, and particularly in periods of stagnation, state machineries in *all* parts of the world have in fact been systematically articulated and strengthened. This does not mean, however, that the initial difference between the greater state strength of core areas and the lesser state strength of peripheral zones has been diminished. Quite the contrary, despite the fact that all states have grown stronger in relation to internal forces and that there has been an overall trend to the ever-clearer institutionalization of a well-defined interstate system (which has reached its ideological culmination in the formation of the United Nations based on the formal insistence on sovereign equality), there has nonetheless also been an ever-increasing polarization of the strength of states.

The states are not the only institutions thus created by the operations of the world-economy. Classes are also created. Indeed, Marx's original insight that the operation of the capitalist system created two clear and polarized classes is in fact affirmed and not disconfirmed by the evidence. Whereas, originally, the multiplicity of social arrangements meant that the vast majority of households were in part of their activities the appropriated, and in another part the appropriators, hence both "proletarian" and "bourgeois," the slow but steady commodification of the workforce as well as of the managerial sectors has in fact diminished the "social veil" that blurred class structure. Most households today fall clearly into either a category which is receiving *all* segments of its total income less than the social product it is creating (and hence is objectively proletarian) or into a category which is receiving a part of the global surplus product in all segments of its total income (and hence is objectively bourgeois).

What is important for our purposes is to note two things. This objective clarification, or lifting of the social veil, is in fact the product of the periodic stagnation phases and the consequent pressures on both entrepreneurs and workers. And the needs of both groups, especially insofar as they have wanted to manipulate state-structures, have led to increasing class consciousness at both the state and the world level, initially historically of the bourgeoisie and then later of the proletariat.

The creation of classes is matched by the creation and re-creation of the multitude of status-groups (whether the lines are national, ethnic, racial, religious, or linguistic) as a mode by which sectors of the bourgeoisie and of the proletariat assert short-run interest amidst the cyclical rhythms of the world-economy. In the times of economic squeezes (the B-phases) groups seek extraeconomic legitimation for monopolistic hoarding of privileges (such as employment, education, etc.). In the times of expansion (the A-phases), upper- and middle-status groups seek to preclude the potential decline of market advantage by encrusting access to position through legislating cultural specifications of rights; or lower-status groups pursue class objectives in status-group garb in those situations in which working-class terminology has been pre-empted by middle-status groups. In all these instances, a renewed emphasis on status-group distinctions helps advance the interests of specific segments of the world-economy. When all is said and done, status-group formation, like state activity, serves as a mode of constraining and constricting both market and class forces in favor of some group or groups who would otherwise lose out in the medium run.

Finally, we should not ignore the fact that the capitalist world-economy has organized its bourgeoisie and its proletariat into income-pooling households of particular kinds. Despite the vaunted individualism of capitalist ideology, the members of classes and status-groups are not individuals but these households. And these households too are creations of the world-economy in that the boundaries of the real economic units are the result of pressures upon kin and coresident-ial groups to expand and contract their boundaries in specific ways in order to produce the necessary labor force at appropriate wage-levels in specific zones of the world-economy.

In particular, the so-called "extended family," which is often in fact not a purely kin group, is a created structure that optimizes the furnishing of part-life-time wage labor at below the minimum wage, by attaching such laborers to income pools fed by surplus-value created by other members of the pool (or by themselves at other moments of time) to the benefit of the employer of the wage laborer. Conversely, the so-called "nuclear family," which may also be not a purely kin group, optimizes the creation of monetary demand, by reducing the propor-tion of consumption goods not obtained via the market. The contra-dictory pressures of the world economic forces create a cyclical pattern wherein household structures vary according to economic zone and to expansion–stagnation phases.

The periodic cyclical stagnations of the world-economy have been essentially resolved by a combination of three mechanisms. First, some producers have utilized advances in technology to create new and/or more efficiently produced commodities which would enable them to successfully challenge other producers who had previously dominated particular commodity markets. This provided new, so-called "dynamic" sectors of production. Secondly, some segment of house-holds which were previously "extended" and receiving only a small proportion of their life-time income from wage sources have found themselves dislocated, expropriated, or otherwise forced to become "proletarianized," that is, to become more fully dependent on the wage-labor market for life-time household income. For those that survived the process of forced transition, this in fact has meant an increase in money income (if not at all necessarily an increase in real income). Thirdly, new direct producers have been incorporated into the world-economy, on its former "frontiers." These newly incorporated direct producers formed new pools of low-cost, part-time wage labor; they were of course also productive of new supplies of raw materials for world industrial production necessary for the new expansion phase of the world-economy.

Of the three mechanisms – technological change, proletarianization, incorporation – most writers refer to the first one as the most linear of all processes in the capitalist world-economy. In fact, the contrary is true, if one analyzes technology not as an autonomous process but in terms of its impact on the structure of the world-system as such. More than other mechanisms, the impact of technological change is the most cyclical and the least secular. Let me explain. What technological advance has accomplished above all is that it has regularly permitted one set of entrepreneurs to compete successfully with other entrepreneurs. This has had two consequences. The specific nature of the high-profit, high-wage commodities has repeatedly changed in favor of those in which the new technology has been invested. Particular commodities that were previously in this category have shifted downward in terms of overall profitability, and consequently in the attached wage structures. Secondly, the physical locus of the most "dynamic" sectors has also regularly changed – both within state boundaries and across state boundaries.

Hence, both the list of commodities involved in unequal exchange and the geographical location of core and peripheral economic processes have constantly shifted over time, without however transforming to any significant extent the worldwide structure of unequal exchange based on the axial division of labor. At first, wheat was exchanged against textiles; later textiles against steel; today steel against computers *and wheat*. Once Venice was a core zone and England semiperipheral; later Britain was core and the northern states of the United States semiperipheral; still later the United States was a core zone and Russia or Japan or many others semiperipheral; and tomorrow? In this way, technological advance has created a situation of constant geopolitical restructuring of the world-system, but has it *directly* undermined its viability? I suspect not.

It is rather in the two other cyclical processes – the reorganization of household structures and the incorporation of new zones into the world-economy – that I find the working-out of the essential contradictions of capitalism as a world-system, contradictions that are bringing about the contemporary systemic crisis in which we are living. Each time a segment of world household structures has been reorganized, the relative number of what we may call proletarianized house-holds has grown as a proportion of the world labor force. Each time new zones have been incorporated into the ongoing production pro-cesses of the world-economy, the proportion of global land and popula-tion that is a real part of the operations of the capitalist world-economy has risen. But proportions inevitably have a limit. Their maximum is 100%. Ergo, these two mechanisms – proletarianization and incor-poration – which serve to permit the regular renewal of expansion of the capitalist system also are its own undoing. Their success renders less likely their future utility as renewal mechanisms. This is one way to translate operationally the concept of the contradictions of capitalism as a system. These secular trends result from the basic contradiction of combining the anarchy of production with the social determination of demand.

The growing economic constraints produced by the secular trends precisely generate at the political level the rise of the antisystemic movements who are acting as the crucial social intermediary of global systemic change. These antisystemic movements have taken two generic forms since their emergence as important forces in the nineteenth century. These two forms are the social movement and the national movement.

While rural-worker and urban-poor discontent have been a constant of the system, and have periodically resulted in jacqueries and food riots, it was not until the relative concentration of proletarianized households in the core countries of the capitalist world-economy in the nineteenth century that the social movement emerged in the form of labor unions, socialist parties, and other kinds of workers' organiz-ations. The social movement emphasized the growth of the polarity bourgeois/proletarian and called for a basic transformation of the system of inequality. *Ad interim*, however, the particular movements organized to obtain partial or total state power to advance the interests of the proletariat. The *Communist manifesto*, for example, clearly exemp-lified this dual approach: on the one hand, the call for fundamental restructuring; on the other, the pursuit of *ad interim* objectives en route.

While the search for weaker states for greater strength has also been a constant of the system, it was not until the reorganization of the interstate system that followed on the Napoleonic wars and the subse-quent Holy Alliance – with the increasing drive for culturo-linguistic as well as religious homogenization – that the peripheral and semi-peripheral zones of Europe took up the banner of nationalism. The national movement emphasized the growth of the polarity core/periphery and called for a basic transformation of the system of inequality. *Ad interim*, however, the particular movements called for a somewhat stronger national entity (shifting from being an assimilated zone to being an autonomous zone, from a colony to an independent entity, from a weak state to a stronger state). 1848 was the Springtime of the Nations as well as the year of the *Communist manifesto*.

Both the social movement and the national movement have had breathtaking careers since 1848. The social movement has spread from core to semiperiphery and periphery. Today there is hardly a corner of the earth that has not been touched by such movements. Conversely, the national movement, having swept the semiperipheral and peripheral zones of the world, has now reached the core, with the new explosion of political ethnicities in western Europe and North America.

In the process of the social movement spreading from core to periphery and the national movement from periphery to core, the two movements have in fact rallied each other in two ways. First, they began their history in the nineteenth century as ideological rivals. But today, there is scarcely a social movement which is not nationalist, and there are few national movements which are not socialist. The confluence is not perfect, but it is great enough to argue that a social movement that is not nationalist or a national movement that is not socialist is suspect as a fraud to large segments of the world population. Secondly, and even more fundamentally, the two world movements have followed a similar trajectory. The initial ambiguity – the search for equality on the one hand via fundamental transformation and on the other hand via *ad interim* solutions – has revealed itself as being not an ideological option subject to the change of individual or even collective will but as being the result of a structural pressure of the world-system as such.

The capitalist world-economy is precisely a system in which the basic economic processes are located in a zone far larger than that of any political authority, and hence these processes are not *totally* responsive to the set of political decisions of any state – even to those of a hegemonic state: *a fortiori* to those of a state in the periphery. Yet, the mechanisms that are most easily manipulable are these same state-structures of limited power, especially precisely for antisystemic movements. Hence both the social movement and the national movement almost necessarily have to seek medium-run gain via the control (or partial control) of a given state-structure. Yet to achieve this control, they strengthen these state-structures, which in turn reinforces the operations of the interstate system and thereby of capitalism as a world-system. The dilemma is not a minor one.

I should like to view this dilemma too as acting itself out historically in the form of a cycle and a trend. The cycle is very simple and has been widely observed, most often cynically. It is described in the following manner: The movements have emerged and asserted revolutionary objectives. They have succeeded and achieved power. Once in power, they have effectuated changes, which were however less fundamental than previously sought. Having compromised, they have thereupon been accused of "betrayal" or "revisionism." Finally, Thermidor has been imposed either by counter-revolution or by inner transformation of the movement. The adepts, such as survive, have been disillusioned, and for the next generation what had been revolutionary slogans have become ideological and oppressive myths.

Is this simple cycle what has in fact historically happened? Only partially. It is true of course that the social-democrats of nineteenth-century Europe seemed to have followed such a path when they came to (partial) power in the early twentieth century. It is true that one could make a similar case for the various communist parties, most prominently first that of the USSR, then that of China. And it is true that every anticolonial revolution has seemed to fit the pattern.

But are we telling the whole story? I think not. There has been first of all the impact of the initial mobilizations. Many particular movements were total failures, but those that succeeded did so because, over a period of time, they were able to create organizational structures of some kind that were able to mobilize their prospective audiences in three concentric circles of intensity: an inner circle of dedicated cadres, a middle circle of activists, an outer circle of sympathizers. The very process of creating these structures over time itself had major consequences for the political structure of the world-system, and first of all in terms of the political *rapport de forces* in the particular state in question.

For such movements to come to even partial power in given states represented a *conquest* of power, whose very achievement resulted not only in the specific reforms subsequently enacted but in shifts in collective mentality which were themselves continuing political facts. Nor are the "reforms" themselves to be lightly condemned. They may have seemed paltry next to the aspirations, but is this the appropriate measure? Should they not be seen rather as a mechanism, and a rather successful one, of slowing down the galloping polarization of the world-system as a whole, thereby preserving the material possibilities for antisystemic activity? From this point of view, such "revolutions" have in fact been neither "false" nor without effect. But they have to be sure been "recuperated" in the sense that the achievement of state power has forced the movements sooner or later to conform to the norms of the interstate system and, more than they wished, to the law of value underlying the operations of the capitalist world-economy.

The fact is that, however radical the reforms that have been initiated by any such movement, these movements have discovered that no single state-structure can enact a transformation either of the interstate system or of the world-economy, and there is no simple way in which the rest of the world can be wished away. A given state led by a given movement can attempt to "secede" from the politico-economic structures of the world-system. The Cambodia of Pol Pot has perhaps been the most dramatic example of such an attempt. But quite apart from whether this was at all a desirable tactic in terms of the results, it has become quite clear that it was not a feasible tactic, since the rest of the world-system was simply not prepared to let it happen – even for such a minor segment of the globe as Cambodia. Everywhere, the reality has been that the fact that a movement proclaims the unlinking of a state's productive processes from the integrated world-economy has never in fact accomplished the unlinking. It may have accomplished temporary withdrawal which, by strengthening internal production and political structures, enabled the state to improve its relative position in the world-economy. In this case, it has merely meant that, *de facto*, particular relative prices were imposed in fact on particular exchanges, such that – within the proclaiming state – some gained and some lost. But this is of course how the capitalist world-economy has always operated. Hence the logic of Mao Zedong's position on the continuing class struggle within states undergoing "socialist construction" is impeccable. The only issue is what to do about it.

Here we must return to the movements. The arrival at partial or total state power has meant always partial compromise. And in many cases, it has eventually meant total compromise, given movements having ceased altogether to be antisystemic movements. But we must view these movements historically. After the phase of mobilization came the phase of compromised power for an antisystemic movement. Compromised power was not at all the same as total abandonment of antisystemic objectives. It was this fact of a phase of compromised power that created the spiral effect, and turned what seemed to be a cyclical phenomenon into a secular trend of the world-system as a whole.

The achievement of power by given movements has had two important consequences beyond whatever reforms such movements were able to enact in particular states. These movements have, first of all, quite clearly served as inspiration and reinforcement for analogous neighboring movements, particularly at the very beginning of their phase of achieved power. One cannot imagine the political history of the twentieth century without taking into account this spread effect. Mobilization has bred mobilization, and the success of one has been the source of hope of the other. Secondly, the success of the one has created more political space for the other. Each time an antisystemic movement has come to partial or total power, it has altered the balance of power of the interstate system such that there has been more space for other antisystemic movements.

But if the coming to power of one movement gave both inspiration and space to others, should not the inevitable compromising in which movements in power engage have reduced both the inspiration and the space? Not at all, because the operations of the world-system are more complex than such a simple symmetry would suggest. The movements that have come later have not only been inspired; they have been instructed. They have learned that part of the world political struggle for them involves putting pressure on these movements in power, these movements who have compromised but whose internal strength depends in part on a maintenance of the continuity of ideology. The mobilizing movements have not hesitated to play upon this social reality and force these movements in power to "compromise" less than they would otherwise be inclined – extracting the space and even the inspiration they need from now reluctant partners.

Hence what seems like a simple upward–downward cycle of the political effect of antisystemic movements turns out on closer inspection to have been an upward–downward–upward thrust. If one cumulates such threefold thrusts across the world-economy and over time, one can quickly see that there would be, has been, a secular upward trend of the overall strength of antisystemic movements in the capitalist world-economy over the past 150 years, despite all the "recuperative" political mechanisms which exist within the system. This is why the prophets of doom are to be found not among antisystemic forces but rather among the defenders of the system. The importance of antisystemic movements is not in the reforms they achieve or in the regimes they establish. Many of these regimes are in fact parodies of their stated objectives. The importance of these movements is in terms of the changes they bring about in the world-system as a whole. They transform not primarily the economics but rather the politics of the capitalist world-economy. Joined with the more narrowly socioeconomic trends previously described, this secular increase of the strength of antisystemic movements undermines the viability of the world-system.

In the light of this analysis, let us look at the contemporary conjuncture. Worldwide, the downward turning point of the post-Second World War Kondratieff cycle was either 1967 or 1973. (It is hard to tell at such short historical distance.) If we take it at 1967, which for the moment seems to me the more plausible, we can see the accentuation of worldwide class struggle that occurred in the very early moments of this B-phase. The shakiness of world markets for the products of core countries (these products being essentially too numerous for world demand) was signaled by the end of the period where the US dollar anchored the world monetary system. All over the world, in various forms, there came to be a squeeze on total social expenditure – reflected both in household spending patterns and in state and other collective "fiscal crises."

Social unrest was immediately visible. In China, there was an acute internal struggle known as the Cultural Revolution. In Czechoslovakia, a social movement within the Communist Party led to the Dubček reforms, implying changes not only internally but in the whole relationship of eastern European states to the USSR. In the West, 1968–69 was the high point of the antiauthoritarian uprisings by students and workers, which was combined in many countries with an intensification of the political demands of the ethno-nationalist movements within them, as well as a new "nationalism" in the social movement (e.g., Eurocommunism).

The weakening of the financial solvency and political stability of the core states meant that the United States could no longer offer efficacious opposition in southeast Asia, or Portugal in Africa, to the persistent struggle of the nationalist movements in these areas. In 1973, the oil-producing states took advantage of the changed world economic situation to increase dramatically the price of their crucial product. The result of course was not only to reallocate distribution of world surplus, but to constrain world production. (It is for this reason that political opposition to OPEC in the core states has only been nominal.) In a number of peripheral areas, the world economic squeeze was felt in the form of acute famines, which cleared some rural zones of producers, forcing many of the survivors into a marginalized existence in urban areas. (This involves also a reduction in world agricultural production, to the benefit of the mechanized agrobusiness of certain core areas.)

This first outburst of political struggles in the current world stagnation seems to have been contained – reversal of the Cultural Revolution, the Soviet invasion of Czechoslovakia, the suppression of the various so-called radical movements in North America and western Europe, the "socialist wars" in southeast Asia, the pressures for "internal settlements" in southern Africa, the recycling of OPEC money. On the other hand, this B-phase is far from over. Relatively high unemployment rates, further fiscal crises, even perhaps an acute price crash are still to be expected throughout the 1980s.

One state in which further acute social unrest is likely is the United States, which must go through a widespread income readjustment as a result of its relative decline vis-à-vis other core states. Acute class struggles that will center on the demands of Blacks and Spanish-speakers will probably result. This will be especially true if the United States increases its support to white settler interests in southern Africa. We may perhaps see similar acute struggles within the USSR. The need to keep the lid on wages in order for Soviet products to compete in the world market may lead to migrations of Moslem/Asian populations to industrial zones and thus to accentuated *de facto* ethno-class stratification, which may in turn force class tensions there, as in the United States, to take on ethnic forms in the tight years ahead.

In the many semiperipheral zones in the world, the internal pressures created by the desire of each to profit from the conjuncture will lead many of them to have internal explosions. Wherever they occur, the explosion will of course eliminate that particular state from the race the semiperipheral states are conducting with each other, and in which there can only be one or two who gain substantially. Iran was the first such explosion, but explosions similar in effect if not in form are not to be ruled out in such diverse zones as China, India, South Africa, Brazil.

Finally, we are witnessing a major reshuffling in the interstate system. The reconciliation of China with the United States, and even more significantly with Japan, may be matched in the years to come by equally spectacular revisions of alliances. For example, I would not rule out a German–Soviet entente.

Finally, I expect the world-economy to take a marked upturn once again in the 1990s. The result of the turmoil and the realignments will in fact have been, as before, to increase world demand to a point high enough to stimulate a further expansion of world production. There will probably be significant cost-saving technological inventions, possibly centering on the provision of energy. There will be significant further "proletarianization," deriving on the one hand from the impact of the displacement of "traditional" industrial enterprises to semi-peripheral areas and on the other hand from the reinforcement of wage-income-dependent household structures in the core. This further change in core household structures will be effectuated by a vast increase in the tertiary sector, the continuing entry of women into the full-time wage-labor force, and the redefinition of social roles sought by the various antisexist and antiracist movements. We shall probably enter the year 2000 to the renewed hosannas of the rosy-eyed optimists of capitalist apologetics. This will be particularly true if we survive the critical 1980s without any serious interstate war.

And yet underneath, both the structural contradictions of capitalism and the antisystemic movements it has bred in such force will continue to eat away at the entrails of the system. The details are impossible to predict, but the broad pattern is clear. We are living in the historic world transition from capitalism to socialism. It will undoubtedly take a good 100–150 years yet to complete it, and of course the outcome is not inevitable. The system may yet see several periods of remission. There may come again moments where capitalism will seem to be in bloom. But in a comparison of life-cycles of social systems, the modern world-system can be seen to be in a late phase. What will replace it will surely not be utopia. But with the end of this peculiar moral aberration that capitalism has represented, a system in which the benefits for some have been matched by a greater exploitation for the many than in all the prior social systems, the slow construction of a relatively free and relatively egalitarian world may at last begin .This it seems to me, and only this, is likely to permit each individual and the species to realize their potential.

11 ❧ Eurocommunism: its roots in European working-class history

The earliest manifestations of workers' *movements* occurred in western Europe. This was natural. It was western Europe that was the locus of the expanded development of urban industrial centers in the late eighteenth and early nineteenth centuries. And it was western Europe that was the first locus of bourgeois revolutionary ideologies with their legitimation of antistate political activity, including ultimately the right to rebellion. Everyone knows this of course. But we occasionally forget that, despite these facts, the lot of working-class organizing was an extremely difficult one in western Europe, all the way up to the Second World War. It was not easy to organize a trade union, or a socialist party. The dominant parties and trade unions of today – both communist and social democrat – claim pride in and draw enormous strength from these class struggles of the past century.

Historically, the first battle was within the working class itself, among its activists and its sympathizers. The issue was whether or not to organize at all. There is nothing obvious about long-term organizing. Throughout history, oppressed groups have complained, demonstrated, risen up. But it was not until the nineteenth century that anyone took seriously the idea that they should create formal organizations which would collect and mobilize force over a long period of time in order to achieve political objectives. Nor was the idea immediately and wholeheartedly endorsed, even by politically conscious workers. Indeed, one might say that the great debates within the European social movement were precisely about the wisdom of this strategy. Some thought conspiratorial and rapid insurrection by a small elite was the correct strategy. Some thought withdrawal into ideal communities was the way. Some believed in terrorism via secret societies.

But against the multiple versions of individual or small-group voluntarism stood another tendency, of which Marx was a champion, which believed that only the organized efforts of the proletariat as a whole could bring capitalism to an end and create socialism. Both the Second and the Third Internationals were the heirs of this latter tendency.

It is well to remember that the most significant single attempt of workers to seize power in the nineteenth century, the Paris Commune, was *not* the consequence of prior organized activity. Henri Lefebvre has called it "the last popular festival," and the Commune was probably inspired more by Bakunin's ideas than by those of Marx, however much Marx hailed it.[1] The Commune indeed was the occasion of the final split between Bakunin and Marx at the Hague Congress of the International Workingmen's Association in 1872, at which Congress Marx's faction was outvoted.

However, by the time of the founding of the Second International in 1889, the Marxists had gained great ground against those who were now being labeled Anarchists, which, as James Joll has noted, "came to be a name to be applied to anybody who rejected the Marxist ideas of a disciplined political party with a rationalist 'scientific' philosophy."[2] Despite the growth of "Marxist" movements, "Anarchism" continued to have a significant following in a few countries – particularly, be it noted, in France, Spain and Italy. The first important legacy therefore of the three key "Eurocommunist" parties is their continuing struggle against the regularly reappearing "Anarchist" tendencies on the left in their respective countries – a struggle which came to the fore again in May 1968 in France and with the rise of the Red Brigades of the 1970s in Italy. It is not that such tendencies were unknown in other countries – say Germany or the Netherlands – but they have always been stronger in France, Italy and Spain than in northern Europe.

Nonetheless, with the founding of the Second International, the day was essentially won for those who believed in "organization." Everywhere in western Europe, the workers' movement took on the form of institutionalized mass parties, and once organized, these parties naturally sought to "survive" – against very great odds, as we have

---

[1] Lefebvre's essay "La Commune: dernière fête populaire" is in James A. Leith (ed.), *Images of the Commune* (Montreal: McGill–Queen's University Press, 1978), pp. 33–45. On Bakunin and the Commune, see, in the same collection, Arthur Lehning, "Michael Bakunin: theory and practice of anti-state federalism in 1870–1871," pp. 225–44. Of course the Blanquists also played a major role in the Commune, and were at that point on the same side as Marx.

[2] James Joll, *The Second International, 1889–1914* (New York: Harper Colophon, 1966), p. 24.

said. Nonetheless, the die was cast along certain lines which made more likely certain strategic choices of the future.

Among the "Marxists," a great internal debate now occurred, precisely about strategy. The fundamental issue was the position organized working-class movements should take vis-à-vis bourgeois parliamentary institutions. Two basic positions emerged, that of Bernstein and that of Lenin. This is sometimes termed the split between evolutionary and revolutionary roads to socialism. The issue was quite fundamental. It led to different positions on the structure of the party and on the role of violence in the revolutionary process, as crystallized in the debate in Russia between the Mensheviks and the Bolsheviks.

There was a third debate in the nineteenth century. It was the debate between socialists and nationalists, between those who argued the primacy of class factors and organization and those who sought to organize in terms of interclass alliances to achieve the political objective of creating a new state. Essentially, these two groups saw themselves as quite different and strongly opposed to each other. Despite some occasional ambivalence, nineteenth-century socialists saw themselves as *inter*nationalist ("workers of the world, unite!") and saw nationalism (even in eastern and southern Europe, even in oppressed and colonized areas) as a bourgeois ideology.

Again, as we all know, the internationalism of the Second International collapsed with the onset of the First World War. The various national workers' parties supported their (bourgeois) governments in the war. Why? A major clue is to be found in the minutes of the International Socialist Bureau meeting on 29–30 July 1914, on the eve of war. At that moment, the delegates believed that war was threatened between Austria and Serbia, but that France, Germany and Great Britain continued to be restraining forces. The Austrian delegate Victor Adler, deeply pessimistic about the ability of the Austrian party to prevent war, was very skeptical about the idea that a European general strike could in fact succeed:

Ideas of striking, etc., are mere fantasies. The matter is very serious and our only hope is that we alone will be the victims, that the war will not spread. Even if it remains localized the party is in a very sad position ... We hope that the Bureau believes us when we say that we could not have acted differently. *We want to save the party*.[3]

---

[3] Quoted in Georges Haupt, *Socialism and the Great War* (Oxford: Clarendon Press, 1972), p. 252. Italics added.

The same language was spoken by A. Nemec, representing the Bohemian party: "Together with the German socialists of Austria his comrades had considered the possibility of a general strike. Both parties had reached agreement. *Their organizations were at stake*."[4]

All the other delegates were said to have been disturbed, even outraged, by the Austrian pessimism. (No Serbian delegate attended.)[5] But behind their disturbance lay an optimism, not only about their own proletariats but about their own bourgeoisies, which turned out, a mere one week later, to have been totally misplaced. As long as the French and German socialists in particular thought that their (bourgeois) governments were seeking peace, they were ready to discuss militant international action by the European proletariat against war. But once their governments showed they were ready to wage war, the French and German parties (and all the others), realizing that *their organizations too were at stake*, adopted the very same attitude of the Austrians which had provoked their dismay one week earlier.

The only significant exception was the Bolshevik party. And why was this so? Here too a clue was given by the Russian representative (of the Mensheviks) at the Brussels meeting (the Bolshevik delegate having failed to come.) I. A. Rubanovich said of Adler's remarks: "The Russian situation is different from that in Austria. *We are a secret and unorganized party*. Our preoccupations therefore differ."[6] Precisely!

The Marxists advocated *organization* against anarchist individualism on the grounds that no serious revolution could occur without organization. This was unquestionably true. But the other side of organization was the fact that the organization's survival became the first priority, particularly where it was already a legal party. A strong organization became the primary weapon of revolution; it simultaneously served as a constraint on revolutionary activity. This primary contradiction explains much of the subsequent history of workers' parties.

The Russian Revolution seemed to break the impasse, but it did so in a very particular way. Like the Commune, the Russian Revolution was not primarily the result of prior organizational activity, whether above- or underground. Rather, it was largely spontaneous explosion due to

[4] Quoted in Haupt, *Socialism*, p. 253. Italics added. Nemec continued: "We in Prague are not afraid of the struggle, we are only afraid of the destruction of our party" (p. 254).

[5] See the detailed discussion in ch. 10 of Haupt, *Socialism*, pp. 195–215.

[6] Quoted in Haupt, *Socialism*, p. 261. Italics added. When he says the Russian party is "unorganized," he obviously means that it is not a legal structure operating in the conventional political arena. He does not mean that it is unstructured.

the collapse of the Czarist regime during the war. The difference with the Commune was that this time there was a structured underground group of cadres ready to exploit the situation and *seize* power once the disintegration of existing power had occurred. The October Revolution could be said to be the only serious example of the successful application of Blanquist ideas.[7] In this sense the Bolshevik route to power was profoundly different not only from that of the European parties of the Second International but also from that of the "long march" practiced by the national-liberation/socialist movements, as in China, Vietnam, Yugoslavia, Cuba and Mozambique. Each of the latter involved a *guerrilla* movement which mobilized popular support *over time* and a *protracted* armed struggle which *culminated* in the collapse of the regime, whereas in the Russian case it was the collapse of the regime which permitted the seizure of power by a party which had never engaged in serious guerrilla activity.

The Russian Revolution had two significant organizational consequences. First, there was created a Marxist regime in a major country that was immediately surrounded and beleaguered by the great (bourgeois) powers and which had to fight for its survival. This desperate struggle for survival placed the Bolshevik party/government in the same dilemma as had faced Victor Adler in 1914. On the one hand, the organization (now not only of the party, but of the regime) was seen as the primary tool of promoting revolution (both in Russia and the world); but on the other hand, the need of the

---

[8] Notice how much this description by G. D. H. Cole of Blanqui's ideas sound like a description of Bolshevik tactics:

> In 1848 Blanqui was prepared to uphold the Provisional Government, while subjecting it to continual pressure from the left-wing societies and the working-class groups. But this did not mean that he had given up the idea of further revolution – merely that he wished to bide his time. His idea continued to be that of a seizure of power by a *coup d'état*, organized by a minority of disciplined revolutionaries, trained in arms and prepared to use them. In his successive societies, he refused to accept all comers: he aimed at creating, not a mass party, but a relatively small revolutionary elite of picked men ...

> [Blanqui's] fundamental belief was in the efficacy of a small highly disciplined armed party organized for revolution and destined to establish a dictatorship which would control the education of the people with a view to the introduction of the new social system of Communism.

Socialist thought: The forerunners, 1789–1850 (New York: St. Martins, 1953), pp. 161, 164.

An official Comintern document of the 1920s speaks very favorably of Blanquism: "Blanqui's doctrine ... is very close to modern Marxism, and is the latter's direct precursor." A. Neuberg, *Armed insurrection* (London: New Left Books, 1970, originally published in German in 1928), p. 42. The document suggests merely that his theory was "immature" in that "Blanqui did not understand and could not understand that certain conditions were required before the insurrection could succeed."

USSR to survive became once again simultaneously a constraint on revolutionary activity throughout the world.

This dilemma, this contradiction, operated most explicitly via the second organizational consequence of the Russian Revolution, the creation of the Third International. The Third International was intended to operate at the international level just as the Bolshevik party did at the national level. Not anyone could join the Bolshevik party. It was a party of professional revolutionaries. Similarly, not any party could join the Third International. They had to meet the Twenty-One Conditions laid down in 1919, which required a total break with "reformism" and a commitment to defend all soviet republics. These demands led to internal divisions in most existing parties, the most significant case undoubtedly being that of France where, at the Congress of Tours in 1920, the Socialist Party split relatively evenly in two, a split which has remained up to today.[8]

From 1920 on, the west European communist parties found they had a two-fold commitment to survival: survival of their own party and survival of the USSR. It would not always be the case that these two objectives were entirely consonant one with the other. What became clear in the period from 1920 to 1945 was that, wherever a conflict was posed between these two objectives, the Comintern existed to enforce priority for the survival of the USSR, and even more narrowly for what Stalin believed was most likely to ensure the survival of the USSR, no matter what its consequences were for revolutionary activity in that particular country.[9] Those who disagreed were purged.

What policies did Stalin believe were most likely to ensure the survival of the USSR? At first, the Comintern advocated armed insurrection by communist parties as soon as it was feasible. In a manual compiled in 1928, under the direction of none other than Palmiro Togliatti, the position is unmistakably clear:

Armed insurrection ... at a determinate historical state ... is absolute, an inexorable necessity ... Denial of the inexorable necessity for armed insurrection ... means automatically denial of the class struggle as a whole ... All the other conceptions which strive to prove the possibility, and necessity, of a different path [from the dictatorship of the proletariat] – non-violent, i.e., non-revolutionary – from capitalism to socialism deny the historic role of the proletariat as the vanguard of society ...[10]

[8] See the detailed discussion of the split in the first seven chapters of Gérard Walter, *Histoire du Parti communiste français* (Paris: Aimery Somogy, 1948).

[9] For a good account of how this constraint operated, see Fernando Claudín, "Spain – the untimely revolution," *New Left Review*, no. 74 (July–Aug. 1972), pp. 3–32.

[10] Neuberg, *Armed insurrection*, p. 29.

But this book, published in the wake of the leftward turn of the sixth World Congress of the Communist International in 1928, turned out to be less a manual for the communist parties of western Europe than a last gasp of insurrectionary rhetoric.

It should be noted that all three communist parties – in Spain, Italy and France –conducted armed warfare in the twentieth century. But in Spain, it was not conducted to conquer power, but in defense of a bourgeois republic against a fascist insurrection militarily supported by two foreign powers, Germany and Italy. In Italy, armed struggle began in 1943, after the German occupation of northern Italy and the establishment of a puppet regime in Salo. In Italy, as in France, the armed struggle was not primarily against the bourgeoisie. It was primarily an anticolonial, anti-German Resistance. At no point, in the 1930s or later, did any communist party in western Europe seriously plan or even seriously contemplate an armed insurrection against its national bourgeoisie. In 1945, the French and Italian parties had significant armed units at their disposal. The US Army had gone home between 1945 and 1949. These parties were in as good a position as they ever had been or ever were likely to be again to engage in insurrection. If not then, it is probably never.

If they *de facto* renounced insurrectionary tactics, we must ask why. It seems to me the answer is simple: neither the Soviet nor the west European communist leadership ever really thought the situation permitted it. The three European parties that did engage in indigenous insurrection were all minuscule before World War II. They were the parties of Yugoslavia, Albania and Greece. Yugoslavia and Albania ended with communist regimes which both had subsequently spectacular breaks with the CPSU, which may have justified retrospectively to the Soviets their policies on insurrection. The Greek party's efforts were squelched by the USSR as much as by the US and Great Britain.[11]

The basic decision was made in the 1930s with the adoption of the

---

[11] On the non-insurrectionary politics of European parties, see in general Fernando Claudín, *The communist movement: from Comintern to Cominform* (New York: Monthly Review Press, 1975). On the squelching of Greek insurrectionary tendencies, see in particular Vol. II, pp. 309, 379–81, 416, 449. Claudín sums up his views as follows: "it is clear that, in the conditions of 1945, with the Red Army on the Elbe, the confirmation of the 'revolutionary possibility' created in France and Italy would have meant the victory of revolution in continental Europe and a radical change in the world balance of power, to the detriment of American imperialism, the only large capitalist state which had come out of the war strengthened. Correspondingly, it is impossible to exaggerate the negative effect of the frustration of this possibility on the further development of the world revolutionary movement. Without any exaggeration, it can be compared to the consequences of the defeat of the German revolution in 1918–19" (p. 316).

"Popular Front" strategy. The arguments for a Popular Front were very powerful ones. There was the threat of fascism. The noncommunist left has never ceased reproaching the German Communist Party for its failure to adopt Front tactics in the years immediately preceding 1933. The lesson has been well learned. And despite the tactical pendular shifts, which continue right up to today – in 1980, for example, the French Communist Party was in a distinctly non-Popular Front mood – the fact is that this strategy is now deeply anchored in the west European parties. The continuing fear of the far right, plus the need for organizational survival, are telling arguments, especially for parties, as in France and Italy, which can command 20 to 35% of the electorate, enough to make one recoil before adventurism, but not enough to win an election outright. This is the structural basis of a "Gramscian" strategy.

The Soviet Union, since at least the 1930s, has been clearly hostile to insurrections that were not under the wing of their own army – a policy that derived in part from interstate accommodationism, but in part from the fear of independent communist governments. There was thus no contrary pressure on the western European parties within the framework of the world communist movement. On the contrary, the leaders of the official communist parties were required to toe the line, whenever they were tempted by local circumstances to go astray. And yet, of course, so might it be thought were the leaders of the Chinese and Vietnamese parties. Nonetheless, later history reveals that these latter parties did organize a revolutionary army. There are three objective differences about the social structures of western Europe and those of Asian countries like China and Vietnam which are fundamental to an appreciation of the strategic options of the western European working-class movements. (1) The bourgeoisie (broadly defined) is demographically a significant proportion of the population in western Europe, and therefore politically stronger. (2) The proletariat (broadly defined) is deeply split politically in Europe, at least half being committed objectively and subjectively to a reformist ideology, which is simply not true in Asia. This split weakened the European proletariat in any class struggle. (3) Asia was colonized and oppressed nationally by western Europe, and not vice versa. Hence anti-imperialism and anti-capitalism had a natural congruence in Asia which they lacked in western Europe. This congruence strengthened revolutionary movements in Asia.

For all these reasons, contrary to what must now be seen as the naive tactical analyses of (all the factions of) the nineteenth-century workers' movement in Europe, there was and is far less popular support for armed struggle of the proletariat in western Europe than in Asia – and this must already have become clear by the 1930s to the leadership of the western European parties, even if they were not yet prepared to state it openly.

Far less support did not of course mean that there was no support. Ergo, at a verbal level, the leadership of western European communist parties did not abandon insurrection; they merely put off the day, in favor of a presumably interim tactic of survival and incrementalism. If the western European parties are to be accused of abandoning their "revolutionary" stance, the moment of decision was not the 1970s but the 1930s. Their justification, if one seeks to justify, lay in the assessment that even mere survival would not be easy. Lest we think this is pure rationalization, let us not forget that one of the strongest communist movements in the world, that of (West) Germany, is no more. It was laid low by Hitler and finished off by the postwar policies of the world bourgeoisie. It was thus not unreasonable for the French, Italian or Spanish communist leadership in the 1930s to have feared the same fate. Nor is it unreasonable to say that their policies helped them avoid that fate. One may of course take the (ultra-left?) line that survival in the forms in which they exist today was somehow not "worth" it.

The Second World War changed many things. For one thing, the USSR as a state and a regime did in fact survive and, despite massive physical destruction, emerged ultimately far stronger. Whereas up to 1939 it was plausible to argue that the very survival of the only communist government in power was still unsure and hence was the number one priority of the world communist movement, this ceased to be plausible with the emergence of a mighty Soviet military establishment on the one hand and the creation of other communist governments on the other.

Secondly, the century-long battle between nationalist and socialist movements was being replaced in one country after another by an overt or covert convergence of the two movements. This happened in Asia, in Africa, in Latin America – in Yugoslavia, in Albania and even in Canada. In a way it could even be said to have occurred (in a very centrist form) in Germany, Britain, Scandinavia and the US. The one part of the world where this didn't seem to be true was France, Italy and Spain. In this sense, the phenomenon of Eurocommunism (defined by Giuseppe Morosini as "national communism") may be interpreted as the attempt of the western European communist parties to catch up with the rest of the world. Marcel Padovani caught the spirit of this when he entitled his account of the history of the Italian Communist Party "the long march."[12] The fact is that no communist party has come to power, through insurrection or the ballot, if it did not incarnate the nationalist thrust. Because of the particular history of the western European parties in relation to the Comintern, these parties have been deeply marked as uncertain in their nationalist credentials. If today Georges Marchais proclaims "le socialisme aux couleurs de la France," it is in large part to expiate the fact that Maurice Thorez refused to support the Resistance during the period of the Soviet–German pact.

Eurocommunism involves, however, another kind of expiation as well. The Twentieth Party Congress of the CPSU transformed the organizational life of all communist parties. The psychological shock of the "revelations" about the Stalin era was immense, as all sorts of autobiographical documents attest. Once this had occurred, it was inevitable that, for the very survival of their organizations, the western European parties had to distance themselves from the USSR. The clarion call of Eurocommunism was undoubtedly Togliatti's vision of "polycentrism" in the world communist movement. He made this statement in 1956, in direct response to the Twentieth Party Congress. And yet, of course, the Eurocommunist parties cannot split irremediably from a strategic alliance with the CPSU in some form or another. For this too would threaten their organizational survival by removing all barriers from a complete, Atlanticized "Socialdemocratization," and hence inevitably a merger *into* the social democratic parties. Keeping distance from the USSR without breaking with it has been the continuing tactical dilemma of the Eurocommunist parties.

Destalinization was linked, let us also remember, with desatellization. 1956 was the year not only of Khrushchev's speech, but of workers' riots in Poznan and of the Hungarian uprising. Nationalist revolt there, too, but was it socialist? Only for some. This reassertion of nationalism in eastern Europe led almost inevitably to the Prague spring and then its suppression by Soviet troops in 1968. Poland in 1980 shows once again the power of blending social demands of ordinary workers with nationalist sentiments. Destalinization too has caused serious problems for the western European communist parties, but of a kind that has not gotten the attention it should. The suppression of the Dubček regime meant that the face of eastern European

[12] Giuseppe Morosini, "The European left and the Third World," *Contemporary Marxism*, no. 2 (Winter 1980), pp. 67–80; Marcel Padovani, *La longue marche* (Paris: Calmann–Lévy, 1976).

nationalism was likely to get less and less socialist. If nationalism once again reverted to being an exclusively right-wing force in eastern Europe, could nationalism acquire a left-wing face in western Europe? The Eurocommunist parties feared not. Hence, the continuing and openly expressed concern of these parties about Soviet policy in eastern Europe was not a question of liberal idealism; it was once again a question of national organizational survival.

We have thus argued that Eurocommunism, in the light of European working-class history, represents the dilemmas of national organiz-ation as the political weapon of the proletariat – both of organization at all, and then of organization at the level of the nation-state. The decisions of the Eurocommunist parties are the application to their concrete historical situation of the same fundamental option of the Soviet, Chinese, Vietnamese and Cuban parties. If we are to applaud, to condemn, or merely to discuss in a comradely fashion, we must recognize that we are raising questions about issues far larger than whether or not Eurocommunist parties are becoming like social demo-cratic parties. The questions concern the fundamental strategy of the workers' movement in Western Europe, as it has been shaped by two fundamental decisions – the decision in the 1880s to organize as legal, mass parties; the decision in the 1930s to seek power via a Popular Front. Eurocommunism is merely the logical culmination of these two decisions in the context of the history of the Third International. A "Gramscian" strategy may be logical; the question is whether it will be successful.

12 ✛ Nationalism and the world transition to socialism: is there a crisis?

While the capitalist world-economy has existed since the sixteenth century, it is only with the so-called classical era in the eighteenth century that thinkers began to conceptualize self-consciously the system in which they were living. The original conceptualizations were very optimistic and revolved around the idea of progress. Stated in simple terms, it was believed that capitalism meant science, rationality, education, and the eventual elimination of scarcity. The doctrine was melioristic and gradualist. For those who suffered, it preached hope tempered with patience.

In the nineteenth century, some who were hopeful became nonetheless impatient. Thus were born various movements to accelerate the social change which was thought to be "lagging" behind the technological evolution. Some of these movements furthermore began to incorporate directly into the model of inevitable progress the concept of physical conflict as one of the ingredients of the process. "Force," said Marx, "is the midwife of history."

Both the social movement and the national movement, as antisystemic movements, turned to revolution as the agent of progress – or at least major segments of these movements did so. And all segments believed in progress. Indeed, when there began to be the onset of doubt among European thinkers about the idea of progress – essentially as of the last third of the nineteenth century – it was within the bourgeoisie and among tenants of the status quo (or a status quo) that these doubts arose. Socialists (and also for the most part nationalists) still believed in progress, and the sentiment was if anything even stronger outside of Europe.

One way to trace the history of the world social movement is to trace the successive debates that have occurred. Each of these debates has left its mark. Each has split the movement. Even when the particular debate became submerged by a later one, it remained in the background (if less salient), emerging again at critical moments.

The first debate was whether the proletariat should *organize* – that is, form bureaucratized, non-governmental, secular structures – to achieve its objectives. It was not at all obvious at first that this should be done. It was a major innovation in world history. And it was the heart of the debate that divided the First International between "Anarchists" and "Marxists." This debate was won, in terms of the main thrust of the movement, by the Marxists, if only because those who "organize" have in the long run more staying power than those who emphasize conspiratorial and/or individual spontaneist action.

It is with the second debate that the issue of nationalism began to bedevil the social movement. Indeed, the second debate concerned precisely the attitude socialist movements should take to nationalist movements, in particular to movements of oppressed national groups. Within the framework of "internationalism," assumed by all Marxists to be a premise of proletarian class struggle, there seemed to emerge two major positions: (a) organize within the framework of existing states on a purely class basis, denouncing all "nationalisms" (that is, movements to create new states or establish sectional rights) as divisive of the working class; (b) recognize that under certain conditions nationalist demands were antisystemic and therefore should be supported, as part of the wider set of progressive demands by working-class movements. While this was a tactical debate of considerable importance and divisiveness, neither group challenged the strategic premise that "all history is the history of the class struggle," and hence that the ultimate objective was the triumph of the proletariat.

The third debate seemed at first to ignore nationalism. It was the debate over the position socialist movements should take vis-à-vis parliamentary activity, given the trend toward universal suffrage as of the late nineteenth century. This was the debate of evolution vs. revolution, Menshevism vs. Bolshevism, revisionism vs. orthodoxy. After 1919, this was the debate between the Second and Third Internationals. While on the surface the issues of nationalism were irrelevant here, the fact is that a social democratic option coincided well with an acceptance of state boundaries as they were. On the other side, both communist movements and movements of oppressed nationalities often found themselves in many parts of the world advocating parallel "revolutionary" efforts, and thus *de facto* a certain sympathy grew up between them. Lenin explicitly sought to theorize this *de facto* coalition. Eventually in some countries communist parties actually took the lead in the national movement. This was the case notably of China and of Vietnam.

The fourth debate that split the social movement concerned the way to conceive of the role of the USSR in the world movement to socialism. Stalin argued that it was possible to build "socialism in one country," provided that all other communist parties made the defense of this first beleaguered socialist state their primordial consideration. This had the paradoxical result that while the CPSU could utilize during the Second World War and afterwards strong nationalist appeals for the defense of the "Soviet homeland," communist parties elsewhere were trapped sporadically but regularly in anti-nationalist stances. While the Trotskyist split from the Third International was in the long run organizationally minor, the "revelations" of Khrushchev at the Twentieth Party Congress decisively shook the hegemony of the CPSU over other communist parties. This speech did as much as anything to launch what Togliatti advocated as "polycentric communism," which turned out to be adaptations or linkages to divers national realities, that is "national communisms."

Still in all these successive debates and splits, the idea of progress remained firm; only the details of the itinerary varied. While the 1960s was a period of considerable "disillusionment" in various parts of the world left with the USSR (and/or with "Stalinism"), many substituted other models of socialist development – principally China, Vietnam, Cuba. The 1970s has however been a period in which significant new sectors became disillusioned in turn with these other movements. The causes were many. The petering out/reversal of the Cultural Revolution and the socialist wars in southeast Asia were merely the most dramatic events in this second round of disillusionment.

What we are seeing now, and will probably see still more in the 1980s, is the beginning of a questioning as to whether these various revolutions were indeed revolutions. Of course, this is in one sense nothing new. Ever since the putting down of the Kronstadt rebellion, there has been such questioning. Indeed, there has been a long litany of ex-members about "the God that failed." But all of the successive critical analyses have had one of two basic thrusts. The critic renounced the movement and now asserted that the ideal of socialism was unfeasible or even undesirable. Or the critic attacked the movement's leadership as renegades, who had "betrayed" for personal gain the social movement. What I believe is new today is the assertion of the position that the social movements in question had never been social movements at all but in fact always were essentially national movements – that Mao Zedong or Ho Chi Minh or Fidel Castro, or even Vladimir Lenin, were simply variants on Kemal Atatürk or Gamal Abdel Nasser clothed in the language of the social movement.

Behind this suggestion lurks one that is perhaps even more serious – doubts about the idea of progress itself, and therefore about the high probability of a world transition to socialism. Already there are those who are suggesting that the true model of today's world is that of the decline of the Roman Empire. When an author suggests that the only hope for "capitalism" in Italy is the coming to power of the Italian Communist Party, this is seen as cynical wit, but many whisper to themselves that nevertheless it may be true.

There are two main "charges" made to sustain this new pessimism. It is said that "real existing socialism" has, *in each case*, involved internal repression and a highly politically (and economically) stratified regime. It is further argued that all these regimes have pursued policies vis-à-vis the states that represent strongholds of private capital (US, western Europe, Japan) of seeking accommodation and advantage for their elites, at the long-run expense both of their internal working classes and of neighboring countries.

If these allegations are in fact true – that is, if they are both correct and complete descriptions of the results of 150 years of revolutionary activity – it is indeed a somber picture. The crisis we would be in would not be a crisis of the capitalist world-economy but a crisis of the social movement and of the idea of socialism. I believe however that this is not a correct picture of what has happened because it is not a complete picture. It is however understandable that this picture is becoming widespread because of the misplaced emphases and incorrect historical analyses of the world social movement itself over all of its own history.

The first historical element we must appreciate is that the capitalist development of the capitalist world-economy has far from reached its climax. On the contrary, there is still a considerable distance to go in the working-out of the processes that have been instituted, that is, in the universalization of the law of value. For example, we have seldom taken into account the fact that, to the extent that Volume I of *Capital* was a correct description of the workings of the capitalist mode of production, it was a projection forward in time of an ideal-type which had *not yet* been realized and toward which we are *still today* moving. The analysis may have been wrong in many ways, but *not* because things have changed since the nineteenth century (the point of departure of almost all the "friendly" critics). Quite the contrary!

The three central structural secular trends of capitalism – mechanization, commodification, and contractualization – are at best only partially realized as of 1980 in the world-economy as a whole. And even if we were (illegitimately) to take only the most "advanced" states as our units of analysis, it would not be the case even then that these states are more than "halfway" in an approach toward the asymptote on some appropriate scale of measurement. As for the centralization of the world-economy as a whole, it has been proceeding steadily, but when all is said and done slowly.

While however the developmental thrust of capitalism is still proceeding, and proceeding energetically, its very development has engendered antisystemic forces within its bounds. These forces first appeared in Europe in the course of the nineteenth century and, from the beginning, in two forms, what we may generically call the social movement and the national movement. These two forms of antisystemic movement have always had a complicated, confused, and uncertain relationship one to the other.

In the twentieth century, both movements have become generalized and, as a worldwide collective force, extremely strong. The ongoing politics of the capitalist world-economy in the twentieth century can be seen as an overt, continuous struggle between the forces that sustain the system and those that seek to transform it. That there is such a struggle few would deny. It goes by many descriptive names, reflecting differing ideologies. But can it go by the name of a worldwide class struggle between the bourgeoisie and the proletariat? I believe it can, although I have the impression few (even on the left) would agree.

Class-*formation* is one of the central processes of capitalist development. The steady (even if slow) commodification of labor means the steady proletarianization of the workforce, that is, its increasing relative dependence on wages as the principal source of life-time household income. Since the process is continuous in reality, and not discontinuous as much of the literature perceives it, we can and should speak of degrees of proletarianization – for the workforce in the whole of the world-economy, for the workforce of particular zones, for individual worker households. This very fact means that the *political* lines between worker households with different degrees of proletarianization are far more blurred than we frequently assume, and more and more blurred as time goes on. Thus objectively *and* subjectively a world proletariat has been in the steady process of creation for a long time and comprises a far larger segment of the world workforce than its presumed "classical" model-group, industrial wage-workers.

If proletarianization is to some extent studied and analyzed, this is far less true of the parallel process, bourgeoisification. The process of commodification (and not only of labor) forces all those who are not direct producers to relate to the economy as bourgeois, that is, as appropriators of and sharers in the surplus-value and therefore (singly and collectively) as maximizers of the surplus-value that is extracted.

In this sense, the polarization of real income distributed is in fact, at the level of the world-economy as a whole, reflected in an emergent polarized class structure. There is however one important dissymmetry. The steady proletarianization of the world workforce has the effect of reducing social differentials among the workforce in the ways they relate to the work process, in the household structures in which they participate, and in the general cultural parameters of their existence. It tends to make the conditions of all workers responsive to the same cyclical patterns of the world-economy. While I am not seeking to be sanguine about remaining differentials of both life-styles and objective conditions, the trend is in the direction of uniformization of proletarian life rather than against it, and thus to that extent the trend is towards unification of political interests and hence eventually of political action.

Bourgeoisification has opposite consequences because the surplus-value off which the bourgeoisie lives is not merely extracted from the proletariat; it is also wrenched away from other competing bourgeois. Intra-bourgeois competition is the true zero-sum game. And bourgeois appetite for gain is structurally insatiable, since relaxing one's efforts is merely opening up the way to loss of position relative to other bourgeois.

Over time two things have been happening to the bourgeoisie. More and more of the upper strata – loosely defined – have been acting like bourgeois, and therefore discarding constraints on action deriving from other systems of values. This has had the net result of intensifying competition. Secondly, despite the concentration of capital, both the absolute number and the percentage of the world's population who are bourgeois have grown and will continue to grow. This growth has been the consequence essentially of the politics of co-optation. But the other side of the safety for the bourgeoisie as a class provided by demographic growth of the bourgeois sector has been the growing pressure of bourgeois who are weaker in the economic arena to use their numbers and access to the political arena to gain *redistribution* of surplus-value to them, a redistribution from other bourgeois. Hence, whereas proletarianization as a process tends to be unifying of the class, bourgeoisification tends to be divisive. The combined patterns constitute the real political Achilles' heel of capitalism as a world-system.

Parallel to the creation of classes in the development of capitalism has been the development of peoples. Peoples have, of course, in some sense always been there, but not really the peoples we know today. These latter peoples have been a political creation which has played a central role in the workings of capitalism as a world-system.

The creation of states within the constraints of an interstate system has meant the constitution and frequent reconstitution of boundary lines based on immediate (and long-run) economico-strategic considerations. From the point of view of the previous cultural history of the world, almost all state boundaries of the modern world are arbitrary, even irrational. This is widely recognized as true of contemporary Africa but it is equally true everywhere, including the *locus classicus* of the modern state, western Europe.

Once created, there has been a pressure to transform each state as defined by its boundaries into a nation-state, that is, one that is culturally homogeneous and culturally exclusive. From the point of view of those who control the state machinery at any given point, the creation of a "national society" co-extensive with the state has certain clear advantages: defense of territorial claims against both secession and aggrandizement of others; mobilization of popular energies behind state policies; deflection of criticisms of oppressed strata and often reduction of their capacity to organize. This is all well known. From the point of view of those who, for whatever reason, are hostile to the policies of those who control a given state machinery at a given point in time, it is very convenient to legitimize this opposition on the basis of a different perception of cultural, that is "national," entities. These counter-claims, made by groups internal to the state or external or both at the same time, are ultimately claims for either the reconstruction of state boundaries or claims to reduce the given state's strength vis-à-vis the world-economy.

These claims and counter-claims represent both bourgeois/proletarian struggles and intra-bourgeois struggles. Since there is no firm objective basis for the cultural claims because they reside in collective consciousnesses that are constantly in motion, there exist no clear results to centuries of claims and counter-claims. The perfect nation-state has never existed, but on the other hand there probably exists no state without some minimum claim of national loyalty on the part of some of its citizens. The tension consequently is perpetual. If nationalism looms so large in our readings of the political map of the world, it is in part because it is a central phenomenon. But only in part. We all exaggerate it, because it is like a taut spring in perpetual tremor. It attracts our constant attention even though quite often the tremors effect no structural change.

What I am suggesting is that we begin to distinguish between those rarer but very important moments when nationalism mobilizes significant antisystemic sentiment, and thereby affects the politics of the entire world-economy, and those more frequent moments when nationalism operates, to use another metaphor, as the nervous tic of capitalism as a world-system. To pursue that metaphor, a tic itself is only in minor ways a cause; it is in most ways a consequence.

Both the social movements (or workers) and the national movements have involved "organization." In many cases, in most of the successful cases, they have involved organizations with a long history prior to accession to state power. The basic dilemma of a revolutionary organization was long ago described by Michels. In order to change the world, we must organize in order to obtain power. But organizations require bureaucracies, and once created bureaucracies have interests which are not identical with the ostensible objectives of the organization.

Movements therefore are inherently a contradictory phenomenon – their own most efficacious enemy. Power may corrupt individuals but it corrupts most of all the leadership of movements. This has nothing to do with the psychology, the morality, or the ideological fervor of these leaders. It has only to do with their interests that derive from their social location. Because of this phenomenon, social movements have found it very difficult to remain essentially antisystemic once in power, and nationalist movements have found it virtually impossible. Thus, whereas Vietnamese nationalism had a deeply antisystemic thrust as of 1970, it had no such thrust as of 1980 (but then neither does Chinese or Kampuchean nationalism).

Still, one cannot draw from this the conclusion that movement activity is futile and has no significant political consequence. The antisystemic activities of individual movements (both social and national) are cumulative in their political effect on the operations of the world-economy and the interstate system. I have argued this in detail elsewhere and will not repeat this argument here.[1] What I would say here is that this universality of the "Michels effect" by no means implies that we are in a crisis of socialism, or that we are *not* in a crisis of the system. The roots of the systemic crisis are structural and the contradictions of the system are still expanding, which means the "crisis" will yet intensify.

What we perhaps need is to make our analyses more relevant by some reformulation of our vocabulary, by utilizing concepts that are more consonant with historical reality. In the early 1960s, Sukarno of Indonesia suggested a new locution to apply to world politics. He spoke of "the new emerging forces." It was a very murky concept, and those Sukarno included within its scope were chosen in function of various immediate foreign-policy concerns. But the essential underlying idea was to find an umbrella for all social and national movements that were antisystemic, for as long as they were. We need some such concept.

We need to put this concept together with the frutiful concept of Mao Zedong on the "continued class struggle" - continued, that is, in all those states where movements that had mobilized on antisystemic bases have achieved state power. I don't believe that the lesson of the 1970s is that Mao Zedong taught us how to conduct this continued class struggle – his methods have shown themselves inefficacious – but he did delineate the problem.

As we begin to draw an ever sharper, ever more sophisticated analysis of how the capitalist world-economy has operated over the past four hundred years and its likely paths of continued development, and as we begin to feed into this structural analysis of cyclical rhythms and secular trends the operations of the antisystemic movements themselves, we will move away from an emphasis on the importance of and expectations about regimes established by antisystemic movements and move toward an emphasis on the modes and sources of revitalization of the movements. In this way, we can feed our knowledge back into these movements and thus contribute to progress in the mode of operation of the movements themselves. In turn such a revitalization of the movements will itself play a major part in the political transformation of the system as a whole.

---

[1] See Immanuel Wallerstein, "The future of the world-economy," chapter 10 in this volume; also "The withering away of the states," chapter 5 in this volume.

13 ❧ Revolutionary movements in the era of US hegemony and after

The moving finger writes ...

Social change is an ambiguous phrase. Change can imply either historic novelty or historic alternation. Social change in the first sense is a recording of the ceaseless flow of the stream of history. "Nor all thy piety nor wit shall lure it back to cancel half a line." Social change in the second sense is a recording of the many cyclical rhythms of which social life is composed. A concentration on either of these components tends to give us sterile interpretations which are often tautologous and in any case offer little guidance as to how we can intervene in the construction of our collective destiny.

Both the ceaseless flow and the cyclical rhythms are there, of course, and what we see is simply a matter of how we cut into the "blooming, buzzing confusion." A good part of the problem of social analysis is that explanation requires concepts, and that concepts are reifications of our perceptions of past phenomena which, however heuristic, are always distortions. Hence we are condemned to explain the historically unique by the sociologically general. Not only is this difficult but our standard methodologies seldom take this into account.

An inappropriate methodology merely invalidates social-science analysis; it incapacitates social movements. Revolutionary movements can only succeed to the extent that they know how to maneuver in the dark forest of the present with concepts inevitably derived from the past. It is this subject to which I wish to address myself – the evolving strategies of these movements since the Second World War.

I will not argue here, but merely restate in capsule form, my conception of the structure and history of the capitalist world-economy up to that point, and the internal contradictions in the system. I believe capitalism to be the mode of production of an historically singular phenomenon, a world-economy that originated in Europe in the sixteenth century and which, by its internal logic and dynamic, expanded over time to absorb all other areas on the globe, and hence to destroy all other social systems.

To describe this world-economy as capitalist is to assert that it is a single social division of labor based on the integration of complementary production processes, and that the institutions of this world-economy are structured in such a way that they reward more often than not those whose activities are predicated upon the endless accumulation of capital. Over time, the operations of such a system tend to result in the formal rationalization of the extraction of surplus-value, and to the extent that rationalization is achieved, it eliminates structures which counteract a polarization of the class structure.

A moment's reflection reveals that the formal rationalization of the system undermines its substantive rationality and thus in the long run its political viability. It is therefore the success of capitalism as a world-system (and not its difficulties) that will bring about its demise. Both Marx and Schumpeter saw this with lucidity, and we will do well never to lose this apothegm from sight. The path to the success that is failure is, however, slow and sinuous. Its byways are determined by the three basic dilemmas of the system, which we may label provisionally the economic, the political, and the ideological dilemmas.

The "economic" dilemma is that those activities that maximize the profits of individual economic enterprises in some short run do not optimize the continuing capacity of the class of entrepreneurs to obtain profit in some longer run. Specifically, reducing the wages of the workers of a given enterprise may increase the profits of that enterprise. Because however every enterprise tends to do the same, the cumulative effect is to reduce global effective demand and thereby make it more difficult for the collectivity of entrepreneurs to realize profit. This leads to the contradictory actions which account for the repeated long-term cycles of expansion and stagnation.

The "political" dilemma is that those who are globally rewarded by the institutions are a minority. The majority are constantly resisting this state of affairs. They are expressing their resistance within, through, and to the institutions in various ways and with varying and shifting efficacity. The dilemma is that resistance changes the *rapport de forces* and results in new political compromises. Whenever these new

compromises favor the movements of resistance (and of course sometimes they do not), it involves weakening the holders of power in the
system by reducing both their short-run political power and their
long-run capacity to accumulate capital. However, every compromise
has its ransom. The very fact of the compromise reincorporates the
movements of resistance into the framework of political stabilization of
the system.

The "ideological" dilemma results from the ambivalent roles of two
key institutions of the capitalist world-economy, the states and the
nations. The states and the nations are both creations resulting from
the ongoing processes of the world-economy. They are not only created
institutions; they are institutions that are being constantly re-created.
The states are defined by and constrained by their membership in an
interstate system. The nations are defined by and constrained by their
necessary relationship to a state-structure. The problem for the
accumulators of capital is that they need to utilize state-structures as a
crucial intervening mechanism in the construction and constant reconstruction of the world market. In order, however, to do that, they have
to foster nationalism as the social glue of these structures, which in turn
makes the state-structures a force for internal social compromise that
puts limits on the accumulation of capital. The problem for the
movements of resistance is that they need to acquire power within the
state-structures to achieve their ends, and they foster nationalism in
large part in order to acquire state power. However, the acquisition of
state power and the growth of nationalism have acutely negative as
well as positive aspects for movements of resistance.

I call these two problems an ideological dilemma because both the
capitalists and their opponents are forced to fight their battles using
concepts seen through the distorted ideological prisms which the
institutions of state and nation construct and constantly reconstruct.
Whereas therefore the economic dilemma of the capitalist world-
system is primarily a problem for the party of order and the political
dilemma primarily one for the party of movement, the ideological
dilemma is one both sides share. This explains some of the curious
convolutions we have seen up to now on questions relating to the
evolution of the interstate system, the rationalization of state
machineries, and the fostering of nationalist sentiments.

As I said, however, I wish to consider these dilemmas from the point
of view of revolutionary movements. Where in fact did the world stand
in 1945 at the end of the Second World War? The interstate system had

just emerged from a long reshuffle of alliances. This reshuffle had begun in 1873 with the decline of British hegemony. It had culminated in the third Thirty Years' War, that of 1914–45, between the two contenders for the succession, Germany and the United States. The US was the unequivocal victor of this long war and emerged as the new hegemonic power of the capitalist world-economy.

The Second World War marked the turning point as well of a Kondratieff cycle. The B-phase of stagnation which commenced more or less in 1920 had ended, and a new and dramatically expansive A-phase was beginning and would last until circa 1967. The efficiency of US productive enterprises was at that point unmatched anywhere, and this provided a secure base for US control of world trade and finance as well as for US military supremacy.

The only significant constraint on US power was the USSR. The Soviet regime was the product of the Bolshevik Revolution of 1917, a major expression of a steadily expanding network or family of world antisystemic movements that had first emerged on the scene in the nineteenth century and had become a major geopolitical force in the twentieth. Although the USSR was not as strong, either economically or militarily, as anyone pretended, it was just strong enough to create world-systemic space for various anti-hegemonic and antisystemic forces.

The strategy of the antisystemic movements had been decided upon long before. It had in fact been conceived in the nineteenth century and confirmed by crucial decisions during the 1914–45 period. In the period from 1945 on, this strategy has paid off in enormous successes. Despite this fact, there seems to be a widespread feeling that these movements are in some sort of cul-de-sac. To understand this paradox, we must first review the historic development of their strategy.

I talk of antisystemic movements, but of course this is not nineteenth-century language. The nineteenth-century analysts and activists talked of two phenomena, the social movement and the national movement. What was meant by the social movement were all those forces being organized by and on behalf of the working classes – one should really say, the urban working classes – to defend their rights against a triumphant bourgeoisie and to assert their claims in the distribution of reward and power. What was meant by the national movement were all those forces that defended the rights and asserted the claims of "peoples" who did not control their own state-structure. These two movements were seen as quite different and, to a great extent, antithetical. Furthermore, they tended at first to be located in different places. The social movement emerged first in western Europe, the national movement in various parts of the Austro-Hungarian and Ottoman Empires. There were of course places where, from the very beginning, both existed – for example, Italy, Russia, Ireland – and in these countries the relations of the two kinds of movements were ambivalent at best, often hostile.

Still the two movements, if their social composition and their themes seemed to be quite different, followed strikingly similar trajectories in terms of their strategic options. Both kinds of movements went through a fundamental debate about their relationship to the state, about whether or not the basic strategy of social change was to be the acquisition of state power. Once that was decided by both movements in favor of the state-power strategy, both of them suffered a basic split in terms of modalities by which state power would or could be acquired.

It was by no means obvious in the early nineteenth century that the optimal way to assert the claims of the working classes or of the oppressed peoples was through acquiring state power. One major alternative was withdrawal into utopian communities. Another major alternative was the mobility of individuals, each climbing the ladder of social stratification by isolated, persistent effort. A third major alternative was terrorism which was intended to bring about the collapse of the existing order. All three alternatives have had their advocates and indeed still do.

Somewhere in the middle third of the nineteenth century, however, those who advocated the creation of permanent organizations designed to mobilize large numbers of people in the struggle to achieve power in specified states won the day worldwide both within the social movement and within the national movement.

The two key elements of this strategic option are in the phrases "permanent organizations" and "specified states." Both elements have had enormous consequences. Permanent organizations had the strength of cumulative power and of constant readiness for tactical battle. They had the less desirable side effect that the perceived needs of organizational survival led to tactical compromises in contradiction to strategic objectives. The fact that power was sought in specified states focused political energy in an efficacious manner on a realizable goal, and the movement could reasonably expect that power in specified states would have meaningful outcomes for the masses organized by the movement. It had the less desirable side effect that seeking power in specified states in practice excluded seeking other kinds of power. Furthermore, power in specified states, once achieved, turned out to be less great than anticipated and the perceived needs to survive in state power led to further tactical compromises in contradiction to strategic objectives.

To repeat, once the state-power strategy was adopted, the question arose about the modalities of achieving this power. The basic fault line has lain between those who argued for a creeping, gradual acquisition of state power versus those who argued for a cataclysmic, sudden acquisition. Much went with one or the other option, which came to be known as reformism vs. revolution. The reformists argued the possibilities and the merits of compromises with the existing holders of power, the utility of education as a tactic, the desirability of creating organizations whose very massiveness would be a mode of persuasion. They tended to argue that objective reality was on their side and that they were really fulfilling the best of previous ideals (bourgeois ideals for the social movement, Western ideals for the national movement) rather than destroying them. The revolutionaries asserted the opposite on all of these propositions. Compromise was said to be neither desirable nor possible, education a mirage, and mass organizations inefficacious unless guided by a cadre (or vanguard) party. Objective reality was seen as operating in their favor only via subjective organization and transformation, and the previous ideals were castigated as hypocritical and deceptive. A new culture was to be constructed which would draw inspiration from the cultures of the oppressed masses who would now be able to realize new possibilities in an arena of freedom.

What is striking about this reformist–revolutionary debate, viewed from a global vantage point over 150 years, is how it has passed through three phases, not merely in individual locales, but globally: (a) the prevalence of reformist views; (b) the conquest of primacy in very many locales of the revolutionary views; (c) the very frequent *de facto* reformulation of views by revolutionary organizations in the direction of reformism.

It is very easy to see how this has all operated since 1945. The distinction between the social movement and the national movement had definitely begun to blur, but let us maintain it provisionally. The social movement, largely in the guise of communist parties, came to power in a number of countries. If we omit those where Soviet military power mattered much more than local revolutionary forces, we have at a minimum the cases of China, North Korea, Vietnam, Laos, Cambodia, Yugoslavia, and Albania. As for the national movement, decolonization promoted by such movements swept Asia, Africa, and the Caribbean. How one characterizes the movements in the independent states of Latin America is debatable, but they too are surely part of this historic sweep to power of antisystemic movements.

How do we explain that at the very moment of American hegemony there was simultaneously, in state after state, an unprecedented string of victories of antisystemic movements, a process which seems to be continuing unabated today? Leaving aside the fantasies of the devil theorists, there are two plausible but quite contradictory explanations.

One explanation, offered quite frequently by the spokesmen of antisystemic movements, is that victory was the outcome of the inherent popular base of antisystemic movements which made of the US and world capitalist forces more of a "paper tiger" than was realized. Some would add as an additional element in the equation the role of an existing bloc of socialist states. This is what I would call the "triumphalist" theory and points to a continuing onward progression to a new world order.

In the 1960s an alternative explanation began to be offered. The coming to power of antisystemic movements, far from being their triumph, was a gigantic lure of global corporate liberalism, a mechanism to defang the movements, co-opt their elites, giving them the form but not the substance of victory. The truly dangerous face of America was not that of J. F. Dulles but that of J. F. Kennedy. "Revisionism" was said to be rampant throughout the revolutionary forces, with only a few and diminishing exceptions (Today, the Albanian Party of Labour asserts it is the last significant exception left, but so in effect does the Brigati Rossi.) This theory, which I shall call the "co-optation" theory, points to a difficult road ahead, in which only steadfastness of purpose and purity of vision can offer any hope.

I find neither of these explanations very satisfactory as intellectual constructions of reality. I find both of them disastrous as prescriptions for policy. Both the "triumphalist" and the "co-optation" theory, it should be noted, leave the strategy of state power untouched. The former merely says that whatever its limitations the global balance-sheet of this strategy is positive. The latter says that while the global balance-sheet is negative, this is because of subjective failures of the revolutionary parties which can be corrected by acts of will.

Obviously we all know there are problems about "post-revolutionary" states. The very first problem is what falls in this category. The term itself to be sure was invented as a more neutral substitute for "socialist states." (But even what falls in this latter category is uncertain: is, for example, Mozambique included?) I would however like not to specify the term further but rather to extend it to any state which has had any kind of "revolution" – thus, all the decolonized states which went through any serious anti-colonial mobilization (say, Algeria or Guinea, or even India); states with post-independence revolutions like Iran or Syria or Libya, or Mexico; and even European states which have had a merely "social democratic" kind of mobilization and acquisition of state power, say Sweden and maybe the France of Mitterand. Perhaps you will feel that I am putting together a mess of pottage, and perhaps I am. But let us see if the complaints about all the various kinds of "post-revolutionary" societies are not in fact similar, if to different degrees in different states.

Complaint number one is that these post-revolutionary states are insufficiently egalitarian. Whereas in most cases certain glaring strata of local parasitic *rentiers* (in one guise or another) have been eliminated, the new system of distribution provides for significant economic and life-chance inequalities between occupational strata, and (it is being increasingly observed) between men and women.

Complaint number two is that despite the change in ownership of the means of production, the work process has remained largely unchanged. Whatever was alienating to labor previously is still there. Whatever was repressive of individual freedom is still there.

Complaint number three is that despite the development of productive forces and even the expropriation of foreign companies, the state in question still manifests economic dependency in the world-system, either because transnational corporations still extract surplus-value in one way or another or because the post-revolutionary state still serves as a conveyor-belt for the accumulation of world capital.

Complaint number four is that however internationalist a particular movement claimed to be before the revolution, once power was achieved it reduced its willingness to aid antisystemic movements elsewhere. Indeed, it counseled prudence and moderation to these other movements. In the worst of instances, a post-revolutionary state became a subimperial power.

All of these complaints (and of course they could be developed in greater detail, and the specificities of the changes to be sure vary enormously) amount to arguing that whatever the post-revolutionary state claimed to be, it was insufficiently different from the pre-revolutionary state to argue that a successful revolution had occurred. This is the heart of the "co-optation" thesis, and one can see that this view is shared by a far larger group than supporters of the Albanian Party of Labor or the Brigati Rossi.

I do not propose to analyze the validity of each of these charges, and even less to determine what are the variations in truth according to the kind of post-revolutionary state with which we are dealing. Rather, let us look at the defense by the advocates of the "triumphalist" theses. Most triumphalists will admit, at least in private, that there is something in each of these complaints. But they will say the complaints are grossly exaggerated and that the difficulties are transitional. This response, however, is not the bottom line. The bottom line is the argument that, for each of these revolutionary movements, there was no effective choice, that the difficulties of transition were the inevitable price of a state-power strategy within a capitalist world-economy, and that a state-power strategy was the only strategy that offered any prospects *at all* for the success or even the very survival of antisystemic forces.

This is a very powerful argument. But so is the argument that "real existing socialism" (not to speak of the other varieties of post-revolutionary states) has reproduced so much of what was to have been transformed that the masses are now forced to make revolutions in so-called post-revolutionary societies (witness Poland).

To be sure, the illusions and disillusions of revolution are an old story. I would however like to contend that what lies ahead is not simply the same old story, that neither the "triumphalist" nor the "co-optation" explanation helps us to understand our current reality, and that a collective global reappraisal of strategy is what is called for.

It is not that the strategy of the seizure of state power was wrong. It may indeed be reasonable to argue that there was no effective choice, and even that this remains true today in many parts of the world-economy. I surely would not have advised PASOK that there was no point in seeking to win the Greek elections. And I surely would not say today to the FDR in El Salvador that state power is not a relevant, indeed crucial, organizational objective.

The question does not lie in whether Castro's Cuba is not preferable to Pinochet's Chile. It is unquestionably preferable in my view. The question is whether we shall arrive at a socialist world order by cumulating a series of revolutionary victories state by state until somehow a majority of post-revolutionary states (or is it two-thirds?) tips us over some global balance. I simply do not believe this to be the case and I see little in the history of the years since 1945 that would encourage us to believe such a thing.

The opposite is more probably true. Precisely because of the many state-by-state victories of antisystemic movements in the twentieth century, we are today faced with a new global political situation which is forcing us to rethink received modes of social analysis[1] (including that of the antisystemic movements) and therefore to rethink the strategies of the movements themselves insofar as these strategies derive from those older modes of social analysis. In short, I want us to take seriously the concept of *Aufhebung*, so central to Marx's own analysis.

At this point, you may legitimately expect me to have a program to offer you. I do not. Instead, I have an image of what will probably happen in the next ten years, and I have a series of questions about strategic choices.

(1) I believe that the decline of US hegemony, combined with acute economic competition between the US and both western Europe and Japan, and between the latter two, in a period of world economic stagnation, is leading to a serious reversal of interstate alliances. I expect the emergence of two new *de facto* blocs, that of Washington–Tokyo–Beijing on the one hand (already in an advanced stage of construction) and that of Bonn–Paris–Moscow on the other (the bases of which are being laid now). I have developed elsewhere the economic and political components of such a deal.[2]

Such a development would of course mean the end of NATO. It might eventually, if not immediately, mean political changes such as the reunifications of Germany, Korea, and China. My guess would be that different OPEC states would end up on different sides, most or all of the Arab states probably in the Bonn–Paris–Moscow camp and the outer oil states (Indonesia, Nigeria, Venezuela) more likely to be in the other camp.

(2) Suppose that is right. What would it mean in terms of ideology? The answer is easy: incredible confusion. Since the states in each camp would profess quite varying ideologies and states holding ostensibly similar ideological views would be in opposite camps, it would become

[1] This theme is argued in "The development of the concept of development," chapter 17 in this volume.
[2] "Friends as foes," chapter 6 in this volume.

increasingly difficult to convince people that the ostensible ideological categories reflected either different social locations or different social objectives.

Such a development would be in part the consequence, in part the instrument, of the intellectual metamorphosis through which I have just stated we are presently going.

(3) What will this mean in terms of social conflict? While I think the geopolitical realignments will decrease, not increase, the possibility of world war, I think it will increase, not decrease, the prospects of acute social conflict within states or at least within many states. In fact, dividing the world into four zones, I can see increased social conflict in three of them.

The first is the now classic zone of tempests, the largely peripheralized states of Asia, Africa, and Latin America, especially those which are not psychologically "post-revolutionary." Here there will not only be social conflict; it will be in formal terms the continuation of the previous antisystemic thrusts of this century. That is to say, from South Africa to Colombia, from India to Morocco, it is highly probable that we shall see movements, at once social and national, which shall seek by a combination of prolonged warfare, urban unrest, and the disaffection of military forces to achieve revolutions (via state power) in the mold of the other revolutions this zone has known.

The second zone is the United States. Unseated from its role of economic and military hegemony but nonetheless still immensely strong, faced with a relatively declining standard of living, containing an internal class structure in which the correlation of class and ethnicity is extraordinarily high and with strata roughly equal in size, and having developed a pattern of geographic dispersion which concentrates the underclass in the large cities, the US is on a path where it will be difficult in my opinion to avert *de facto* civil war. That is to say, I foresee social unrest that will be far more widespread and violent than what the US knew in the late 1960s.

Such a state of affairs in the US could conceivably drag in its wake (for analogous reasons) Canada and Great Britain, and even perhaps Australia and New Zealand (though the latter two instances seem less likely).

The third zone is that of the socialist countries, or rather of that segment of them which assert their fidelity to Marxism–Leninism. Poland indicates the problems and the limited options of those in power. If Solidarity has become the incredible political force that it has become, it is because of the depth of working-class support. Solidarity is a social movement of the same kind once led by Marxist–Leninists. Only the "paper tiger" this time has been not the US but the USSR, which has not responded to a very real challenge to its political system because it has not been able to do anything that would not weaken its position even further.

The "victory" of Solidarity is a qualified victory, to be sure, and eventually this victory may raise questions about whether Poland's "post-post-revolutionary" society is merely another partial break with and partial reintegration into the system. But in the meantime, the worst fears of the party hardliners will be fulfilled. For the message of Solidarity will indeed spread throughout eastern Europe, to the USSR itself, and perhaps beyond to the Asian communist countries. The greatest disturbances will be in the USSR because of its combination of bureaucratic clumsiness and multinationality. When all is said and done, however, the difficulties of the communist countries will probably produce a gentler form of social turmoil than that of the peripheral zone or of the United States, but it will be social turmoil nonetheless.

The fourth zone is Europe, and it is the only zone in which I anticipate relative social peace, abetted by a relatively favorable world economic position which will permit the extension rather than the contraction of the welfare state.

Somewhere around 1990, I expect a worldwide economic upturn that will permit a renewed world accumulation of capital and will relieve some of the economic pressures that will have fueled the social turmoil of this decade.

Where does such a picture leave us in terms of the construction of a socialist world order, the real objective from the outset of the anti-systemic movements? I believe that if we are collectively going to traverse the next 50–150 years so that the end product is a relatively egalitarian world order in which production for exchange and the endless accumulation of capital is not the predominant dynamic of the world-system, we are going to have to do more than continue on the same path we have advocated for the past 50–150 years. We shall have to stop maneuvering in the present with antiquated concepts derived from the past.

I have no doubt myself that the capitalist world-economy is an untenable mode of social organization in the long run. I have no doubt that it will be destroyed by its successes, by its ability and its unquenchable thirst to commodify everything. But I also do not doubt the endless ingenuity of those who wish to maintain privilege and inequality. When the rats jump off a sinking ship, it is not their intention either to drown or to cease being rats. The mode of production that will emerge as the dynamic of the successor historical system will be egalitarian, will enhance human freedom, only if we so construct it. And I think we will construct it through our movements primarily.

I have argued that the state is not the framework within which social action occurs but merely one of the institutions created to sustain and promote the interests of various actors in the real social arena, the capitalist world-economy. It follows that any transformation of capitalism can only be a transformation of this whole. The acquisition of state power by an antisystemic movement can therefore only be what the acquisition of state power by anyone else is, an instrument with which to maneuver in the political arena of the world-economy. It is not the only such instrument. It may not always be the most important instrument. And, like all instruments, it is only useful when placed within a continuing, global strategy.

Since the personnel of institutions inevitably seek to turn means into ends, if the means are to remain means the movements must devise mechanisms to set up counterpressures to this bureaucratic tendency. This was the rationale behind the Chinese Cultural Revolution, and we must not allow its political failure to dissuade us from the importance of the task. Solidarity represents a second try with a different technique. It may fail too. The search will continue.

We must take active account of the growing multiplicity of the forms of antisystemic movements. Scylla is to assume that only one form, a party form, is legitimate. Charybdis is that everything goes. In between we must recognize that the combined and uneven development of the world capitalist system has led and will continue to lead to a combined and uneven development of antisystemic movements, and that a world struggle involves necessarily serious transnational movements. The tricky question is how movements in "pre-revolutionary" states relate to movements in "post-revolutionary" states. What is changing today is that the increased number of post-revolutionary states and the increased ideological confusion bred by the histories of real existing socialism lead bit by bit to an erosion of the relevance of the distinction "pre" and "post" for the purpose of trans-state alliances of movements. There will be multiple movements in post-revolutionary states (there are already) and those which will be in power will not always represent the antisystemic thrust.

If I am vague in my prescriptions, it is because we are all feeling our way, emerging out of a strategy which was created in the nineteenth century, and which seemed to work then but has worked less and less well as the twentieth century proceeded, toward a new strategy that is relevant now. Let me specify the problem once again. When the ruling classes were self-confident and brutal, it was logical to seek power to destroy them. When the ruling classes have ceased to be self-confident, and are therefore trying to survive in new ways (even in the guise of a transformed world), the acquisition of state power is far from enough to destroy them. It may even perpetuate them. If our objective is not a stratified, commodified world (which ultimately could dispense entirely with quiritary ownership) but rather an egalitarian, substantively rational world, then our work is only beginning now, and it must begin inside and through the antisystemic movements themselves.

Part III

The civilizational project

14 ✤ The quality of life in different social systems: the model and the reality

Introduction

There have been thus far in the history of the world three different kinds of social systems: reciprocal mini-systems, redistributive world-empires, and the capitalist world-economy. The latter, which is the only extant system at the present time, is in crisis, and the world is in the beginning of the transition to a fourth prospective type, a socialist world-government. I have discussed previously what causes such world historical change, and how it comes about.[1] I should like here simply to outline what each such system looks like in two versions: the model its ideologues present of its functioning, and the way it really works, given the contradictions inherent in the structure.

Each such system is based on a different mode of production, composed of the ways by which, within a given arena, labor is divided among individuals and groups, decisions are made as to how much will be produced of goods and services, and goods and services are allocated among these individuals and groups. The most influential discussion of the historical evolution of modes of production is the *Communist manifesto* of 1848.[2]

Since these various modes of production have been (in all known

---

[1] Immanuel Wallerstein, "The rise and future demise of the world capitalist system: concepts for comparative analysis," *Comparative Studies in Society and History*, 16 (Dec. 1974), pp. 387–415.
[2] Karl Marx and Frederick Engels, *The communist manifesto* (New York: International Publishers, 1932).

instances) based on unequal contributions of labor-power and unequal distribution of the surplus, there have been groups who have profited from others and were able to maintain their economic advantage by relative control of the political and cultural structures of the system. One major element in such control has been the image these groups have fostered of how the social system operated. This is the model.

The reality has always been different from the model. In part this is because the model is obfuscation, both deliberate and subconscious, designed to secure specific kinds of behavior, not only from the exploited workers but from the privileged cadres of the system, behavior which might not be forthcoming as readily were the reality clearly perceived by all. But the fact of distorted understanding is only part of the story. If everyone saw clearly what was happening, the system might nonetheless still continue to function (at least for a while) because of the concentration of force in the hands of the privileged. It would eventually break down, however, because the system itself is based on certain contradictory pushes whose disruptive clashes wear down the tissue that holds the system together. The reality becomes both too clear and too grim. The alternative seems too desirable and too possible for too many, and they force fundamental change.

Reciprocal mini-systems

A reciprocal mini-system is a somewhat awkward name for what people in the nineteenth century used to refer to as a "primitive society." In the twentieth century, we have come to be more prudent in our language, if not in our private thoughts. Basically, these are small-scale systems, covering a limited geographical area, within which all that is essential for the survival of the collectivity is done. We might think of such systems as bearing the motto: one economy, one policy, one culture. That is to say, the boundaries of the division of labor, the structures of governance, and the values, norm, and language which are current are more or less the same.

Such a system exists where the technological base that conditions man's relation to nature is weak, and thus it becomes difficult to obtain much of a surplus, that is, much production that exceeds the quantity necessary simply to reproduce the collectivity over time. The division of economic tasks is limited, but such as there exists is governed by rules of reciprocity, that is by the giving of "gifts" that one expects will be reciprocated, according to some fairly clear set of rules. The term "reciprocal" to describe this, like the term "redistribution," is taken from the work of Karl Polanyi.[3]

The model of the reciprocal system is rather simple. The society is a relatively small collection of families, each family producing for its own needs and sharing communally. The families are linked together loosely in some larger system on one or another principle of kinship (partially fictive), a system large enough to permit a limited specialization of labor if necessary, and to join forces to produce needed common infrastructure and defense capabilities. Each family tends to be governed "autocratically" by an elder or elders and the larger system by some council of these heads of families, with perhaps a great elder or chief. Thus the model is "family sharing and the authority of age."

Such a system presumably has some clear advantages. Given simple technology and low surplus produced, the relatively (but quite imperfectly) egalitarian distribution combined with the tight control by the elders presumably maximizes the collective effort. The major problem of the system is to get its members to work hard enough so that all will survive. Occasionally this may be not too difficult, and work will cease when the target is reached, as judged by the head of the family and tightly controlled by the collectivity beyond the family. More frequently, however, the problem is the reverse – maintaining a high level of work-input in the absence of physical or market coercion. When this does not succeed, the group dies out.

Given this problem and given the fact that the limited surplus does not permit the creation of a specialized stratum of "intellectuals," a system that links authority to age at least maximizes the likelihood that such wisdom as is bred by experience will govern collective decisions.

The other side of this rosy picture is not hard to draw. There is no place within this system for the bright young man (and usually even less for the bright young woman). If ecological conditions are such that times are good, the elders merely suppress these potential troublemakers. But if times are bad, conditions become ripe for rebellions. Since such reciprocal mini-systems existed for the most part in times and places where land was relatively plentiful, such a rebellion usually took the form of migratory secession by a sub-group within the society.

The second contradiction derives from the problem of the disposition of windfall. Windfalls, by definition, are occasional, but they do

[3] Karl Polanyi, "The economy as instituted process" in Karl Polanyi *et al.* (eds), *Trade and market in the early empires* (Chicago: Henry Regnery Gateway edition, 1971).

occur in such societies because of climatic variation or other happenstance of nature, technological advance, or conquest of suddenly weaker neighbors. In such a case, the surplus exceeds expectations. If it is evenly distributed, it makes more possible the "secessions." If (more likely) it is not evenly distributed, it violates the "sense of justice" of the society and creates discontent which can lead to secessions or internal strife – or to the evolution of a "state" structure to contain the strife, which will result in a change in the "mode of production."

The third contradiction is that the functioning of such a system presumes secure boundaries, a condition that is in fact largely dependent on isolation. Whenever strong states arise in the general vicinity, these states tend to conquer such mini-systems, exacting tribute which transforms such a reciprocal mini-system into something quite different, a segment of a redistributive world-empire.

And the "quality of life"? Such a life seems at first glance to have the virtues of simplicity and relative equality. One can see how people not living in it can romanticize such a life. But the reality was far from idyllic. The systems operated by the oppressiveness of custom (which is how age maintained its authority). Minor warfare was frequent and death from warfare, both of men and women, had something of the quality of roulette. The systems themselves were not too long-lived, probably having minor secessions and accretions in each generation, and major upheavals every five or six. Negative natural windfalls were probably more frequent than positive ones, and the consequence of these was often starvation or violent death. In short, it would not be untrue to perceive of such social systems as ones in which life was "solitary, poor, nasty, brutish, and short."

Redistributive world-empires

Both the evolution of technology and the contradictions led to the creation of "states," which in fact took the generic form of redistributive world-empires: one economy (as single division of labor), one polity, but many cultures. The mode of production here was quite different. The political rulers required the production by each direct producer of a surplus, the total of which would be sufficient to sustain the needs of the non-productive classes, most of whom were in fact administrative officials of the state, arranged in a hierarchical pattern. The way in which this worked is that the state exacted from each direct producer a tax (largely of primary products) which, if collected from a group as usually was the case, is called tribute. The producers were *forced* to create sufficient surplus to pay the tribute, whose level was defined at the center in terms of the size of the bureaucratic machinery and the costs of maintaining the infrastructure. The centralized tribute was then redistributed in the form of incomes for the bureaucracies and the costs of public works. This is why the mode of production is called redistributive (or sometimes tributary).

The states were of varying sizes and internal forms. They were sometimes very extensive over time and space with elaborate bureau-cracies (Ancient Rome, China), sometimes smaller but still very centralized, or extensive but with a very atrophied center (as in feudal Europe in the early Middle Ages). Of course the variation in forms of these structures had important consequences. In a sense a large part of the corpus of Weber's works[4] is devoted to analyzing these variations.

But, as a *mode of production*, all the variations retained the same essential core: the ruling groups pressed the direct producers to produce a specified surplus over their direct consumption needs (which amount could vary), but they also produced no incentive (and some positive disincentives) for producing *more than* the specified surplus.

Because technology was more complex, and the set of positions in the social system were varied, the division of labor was more complex, and the issue arose of how persons and groups were allocated to specific roles. The model of the redistributive world-empire was quite straight-forward: the various occupations were publicly defined in certain clear categories (estates, castes, etc.) and individuals were perpetually assigned to position by descent. The lower orders produced the food and other essentials of physiological sustenance for everyone, and the higher orders engaged in the military, administrative, and intellectual tasks, from which then the lower orders were both kept out and exempt. The model of an extended family was borrowed from the mini-systems but became a very stretched metaphor.

There were presumably two great justifications for a redistributive over a reciprocal mode of production. One was that it was more efficient in guaranteeing the physical safety of its members against the depredations of nature and human enemies. The second is that it permitted the development of a "high culture" by the reservation of part of the surplus to the sustenance of producers and bearers of such a high culture. The second was true, but the first was doubtful.

[4] Max Weber, *Economy and society* (3 vols.), ed. by Guenther Ross and Claus Wittich (Totowa, N.J.: Bedminster Press, 1968).

The contradictions of such a system were several. Since the allocation to occupational roles was essentially the arbitrary result of prior warfare, no allocation was in fact perpetual. Access to the privileged stratum, and to higher places within the hierarchy, could always be reopened by new uses of force. Thus, since control of the political machinery was the only key to privilege, the system invited recurrent internecine warfare, especially between different groups of the elite within a system. This being the case, those at the center of the system had no choice but to seek constantly to expand their internal bureaucracy to control potential rivals from within and to expand their frontiers to control predators from without.

This pressure led to the second contradiction. An expanded bureaucracy required expanded income which required increasing the tribute obtained from the direct producers. Over time, as the demands on the rural workers mounted, so did their resistance. Furthermore, as the control mechanism (the bureaucracy) expanded, so did the need for a meta-control mechanism – either a para-bureaucracy, or further bribes of the existing one. In either case, there came a point where the whole process was self-defeating. The expanded bureaucracy more than ate up the expanded tribute the collection of which was its raison d'être.

Collapse then of the imperial network came both from lassitude at the center and from opportunistic linkages with regional peasantries by regional agents of the center, leading to secessions. It is no wonder then that such redistributive world-empires were constantly expanding and contracting over historical time, and elites were "circulating" as described by Pareto[5] and so many others. The speed of such cyclical shifts and the size of imperial domains at their high point were a function of the state of technology, the state of the terrain, and the particular political mechanisms that different variants of the redistributive mode developed. It should be noted, a not unimportant detail, that the level of technology never permitted these "world"-empires in fact to expand to include the entire surface of the globe, and that therefore several, even many, of these systems coexisted as did a number of reciprocal mini-systems. The cyclical pattern seemed unending until the sixteenth century, when a particlar conjuncture of pressures combined with certain technological advances to permit the creation of the capitalist world-economy.

[5] V. Pareto, *The rise and fall of the elites: an application of theoretical sociology* (Totowa, N.J.: Bedminster Press, 1968).

As for the quality of life in redistributive systems, it is not clear that it was that much better for the individual than the reciprocal mini-systems. Presumably, the individual was promised greater security. But the reality was that the aristocrat was faced with the insecure life of the perennial warrior, the direct producer with the pressure to expand his efforts with no benefit to himself, and the merchant classes with the constant prospect of expropriation to meet the voracious needs of the center to expand its bureaucracy or even merely to prevent the formation of quasi-autonomous centers of power. No wonder so many individuals in such systems sought the refuge (the life-preserving refuge, first of all) of religious institutions.

As for the collective quality of life, no doubt such systems did create a collective cultural patrimony that we have inherited and which has both enriched us and made possible technological progress. But the costs of producing these cultural products were extremely high in human sacrifice.

The capitalist world-economy

In the sixteenth century, in Europe, a capitalist world-economy came into existence which eventually expanded to cover the entire globe, eliminating in the process all remaining redistributive world-empires and reciprocal mini-systems. It was not the first world-economy to exist, but it was the first to survive over time and allow the coming to fruition of a capitalist mode of production. The particular circumstances of the transition have been treated elsewhere.[6]

The structure of a capitalist world-economy is *one* economy, *multiple* states, and multiple cultures. What needs to be clarified here is exactly how this mode of production differs from a redistributive one. The absence of a political center is the crucial difference from a redistributive system. In the redistributive mode, decisions on the quantity of production were made by the center in virtue of the amount of surplus required to maintain the overall system. In a capitalist mode, decisions on the amount of production are made by owners of productive enterprises (which can include states) in virtue of their *profitability*, that is the degree to which the product, once exchanged on a *market*, expands the initial investment of capital, in effect by absorbing through the market operation first of all the surplus produced by the workers who

[6] See Immanuel Wallerstein, *The modern world-system*, Vol. I: *Capitalist agriculture and the origins of the European world-economy in the sixteenth century* (New York and London: Academic Press, 1974).

created the original product and second of all, via the operations of unequal exchange,[7] a part of the surplus created by the workers who created other products.

The state machineries become one mechanism among several whereby the owners of productive enterprises can try to affect the operations of the market to maximize their profit. Since the owners compete with each other for optimal profit, the vector of their individual decisions is not collectively planned and can be shown to produce effects of permanent disequilibrium in the functioning of the world-market.

The model of the system is that of permitting each individual, freed from all constraints of custom and inheritance, to pursue his interests in the market, which presumably rewards effort and efficiency. The slogan is *la carrière ouverte aux talents*.

The advantages argued for this system are that it maximizes the use of the human skills in productive activities, instead of rewarding skills in military prowess, as did the redistributive mode.[8] This being the case, the use of technology is maximized and system-wide production is steadily expanded, making it possible to overcome the perennial shortfalls of production of previous systems. The prospect of an eventual cornucopia for everyone is said to be at the end of the rainbow.

The reality once again contradicts the model. Although the freedom of each individual to pursue his own good is supposed to be the basic premise of capitalism, the pursuit by each individual of his interest precisely requires efforts by him to constrain the freedoms of others through control of the state (creation of monopolies and destruction of rival ones, restraints on freedom of sale of labor, the socialization of loss but the individualization of profit, etc.).

While thus freedom of all the factors of production is a basic tenet of the system, and in particular the freedom of labor as a commodity, in fact the effective operation of the system requires the permanent maintenance of a state of "partial freedom" wherein some labor is sold as a commodity on the market and some labor is precisely not "sold" but coerced or semi-coerced, thus creating a large stratum of "semi-proletarian" workers who in fact are denied legal rights and live at a "subsistence" level.

The major social mechanism created presumably to allocate

[7] See A. Emmanuel, *Unequal exchange: a study of the imperialism of trade* (New York: Monthly Review Press, 1972).
[8] See J. A. Schumpeter, *Capitalism, socialism and democracy* (New York: Harper, 1942).

individuals to occupations by virtue of talent rather than descent – the educational system – in fact functions only among the "free" laborers, and even for them primarily as a way of maintaining descent lines by making exceptions for the very few (co-optation of bright individuals from the working classes) and thereby justifying the caste-allocation for the remaining vast majority. The justification is now more subtle and effective than that of redistributive systems: instead of the inevitability of fate or the will of God, caste-allocation is claimed to be the consequence of the application of human reason. Each individual is said to have a status he has achieved, rather than one ascribed to him.[9]

The expansion of total production, and therefore of the global surplus, is quite real. But the mechanisms of allocation exaggerate the inequalities of real income still further than in redistributive systems. While it is true that a larger percentage of the system's members are privileged than in the redistributive mode (since it requires a larger group of cadres to operate the more complex system), the privileged remain a minority within the world-economy, the majority still remaining at a "subsistence level," and the gap between this level and the average real life-income of the privileged cadres is considerably greater.

In addition, the expansion of global surplus has been achieved not merely by technological advance but by exacting greater workloads from the direct producer. The direct producer in medieval Europe ceased work at noontime. The direct producer of the peripheral areas of the world-economy today works the day long.

And the quality of life? The direct producers suffer a form of cultural alienation unknown in previous systems.[10] While destruction as a result of natural happenings has diminished, destruction by man-made means has expanded. It is not clear that the overall balance-sheet is positive. While childhood mortality has decreased, it is possible that adult mortality has increased (the probability, say, that a forty-year-old will live to eighty). Racism among the "semi-proletarian" sectors within the capitalist world-economy is far more destructive than anti-barbarism directed against those on the edges of redistributive world-empires. Anti-barbarism expressed itself for the most part theoretically and in the form of open warfare. Once the warfare was terminated and the barbarians were incorporated in the empire, the

[9] See Talcott Parsons, "An analytic approach to the theory of social stratification," in *American Journal of Sociology* 45 (May 1940), pp. 841–62.
[10] See Samir Amin, "In defense of socialism," in *Monthly Review* 26 (Sept. 1974), pp. 1–16, and Bertell Ollman, *Alienation: Marx's conception of man in capitalist society* (Cambridge: Cambridge University Press, 1971).

survivors no longer suffered special opprobrium. Racism, however, expresses itself continuously throughout the operation of the capitalist system as a basic ideological component of its operation, justifying inequality.

Finally, while capitalism has indeed expanded global production, it has done so in the least efficient rather than the most efficient manner, since decisions made in virtue of individual entrepreneurial profit do not take into account collective costs, thereby creating the various dilemmas we speak of today as "ecological."

A socialist world-government

A socialist world-government, that is, a world-system based on a socialist mode of production, does not exist today. Rather we are living in a period of crisis in the capitalist world-economy in which it seems that the most likely and desirable outcome over time is the establishment of a worldwide socialist mode of production.

In this transitional era, several state machineries have come under the control of socialist parties which are both seeking to bring about this worldwide transition and seeking to prefigure within their state boundaries some aspects of a socialist mode of production (such as collective ownership of the means of production, the institution of non-material incentives for productivity, etc.). It would be no more plausible to analyze how a socialist world-system would in fact function by a close look at these prefigurings than it would have been to draw a picture of the twentieth-century capitalist world-economy from a close look at its prefigurings in north Italian or Flemish city-states in the High Middle Ages, dominated though they were by bourgeois proto-capitalist strata.

In fact Engels argued this point in his letter to Conrad Schmidt on 5 August 1890:

There has also been a discussion in the *Volkstribüne* about the distribution of products in future society, whether this will take place according to the amount of work done or otherwise. The question has been approached very "materialistically" in opposition to certain idealistic phraseology about justice. But strangely enough, it has not struck anyone that, after all, the method of distribution essentially depends on *how much* there is to distribute, and that this must surely change with the progress of production and social organization, so that the method of distribution may also change. But to everyone who took part in the discussion, "socialist society" appeared not as something undergoing continuous change and progress, but as a stable affair fixed once for all, which must, therefore, have a method of distribution fixed once for all. All one can reasonably do, however, is (1) try and discover the method of distribution to be used *at the beginning* and (2) try and find the *general tendency* of the further development. But about this I do not find a single word in the whole debate.[11]

What we can do is outline the prospective model. A socialist world-system involves the reunification of the boundaries of economic and political activity. The idea is that on the basis of an advanced technology, capable of providing a rate of global production adequate to meet the total needs of all the world's population, the rate and forms of production will be the result of collective decisions made in virtue of these needs. Furthermore, it is believed that the amount of new labor-time to maintain such a level of productivity will be sufficiently low as to permit each individual the time and resources to engage in activities aimed at fulfilling his potential.

The global production required will be attained, not merely because of the technological base, but because the egalitarian collectivity will be interested in realizing the full "potential surplus."[12] This being the case, the social motivations for collective aggressive behavior will have disappeared, even if, in the beginning phases, not all the psychological motivations will have done so. Since collective decisions will be pursued in the common interest, then worldwide ecological balance will follow as an inherent objective.

In short, the socialist mode of production seeks to fulfill the objective of the rational and free society which was the ideological mask of the capitalist world-economy. In such a situation, repressive state machinery will have no function and will over time transform itself into routine administration.

What will the contradictions be? It is not possible to say. We can, as Engels suggested, try and discover the problems at the outset, not merely in the present transitional era, but in the future first phases of a socialist world-government. It is quite clear that the major contradiction at the outset will be that between the proclaimed norms of the system and the fact that many, indeed most, individuals will have been socialized in values appropriate to a capitalist mode of production, and families will tend to perpetuate such socialization. Until these patterns are changed – a long and arduous task – the social bases of the socialist mode of production will not be

[11] Karl Marx and Frederick Engels, *Basic writings on politics and philosophy*, edited by Lewis S. Feuer (Garden City: Doubleday Anchor Press, 1959), p. 396.
[12] See P. Baran, *The political economy of growth* (New York: Monthly Review Press, 1957).

secure, a cessation of the process of transformation would still be possible, and a class struggle reminiscent of the capitalist world-economy would continue in new but real terms.[13]

Presuming this long first phase of the socialist world-government were navigated successfully, contradictions might still persist, but there is no plausible way of predicting what they will be or whether they will be. Science is not necromancy, and history will not come to an end, even if a particular stage of historical development does.

---

[13] Mao Zedong, "Speech at the Tenth Plenum of the Eighth Central Committee, 24 September 1962" in Stuart Schram (ed.), *Mao Tse-Tung unrehearsed: talks and letters, 1956–71* (Harmondsworth: Penguin Books, 1974) pp. 188–96.

15 ✒ Civilizations and modes of production: conflicts and convergences

The main problem ... is that of the dialectic of the specific (the factor of nationality, of national culture, of civilization) and the universal (the syncretic civilization that will emerge out of the human species through the mediation of science and technology). In the first stage, the principal danger is not that of accentuating the dimension of nationality but rather that of imposing hegemonic molds that are asserted to be universal, and which will ensure, even more than previous ways, the denaturing of non-Western world civilizations, destined to be sub-products of technicality and productivism: economic, demographic, ethnographic reserves; an alienated underworld.

Anouar Abdel-Malek[1]

This long quote catches the fact that behind the central intellectual antinomy of the modern world, which Abdel-Malek calls the "dialectic of the specific and the universal," lie the parallel symbiotic dyads of barbarian and civilized, non-Western and Western, periphery and core, proletarian and bourgeois, the dominated and the dominant, the oppressed and the oppressors.

None of these pairs of terms involve two separate phenomena brought into (external) relationship with one another. Rather the terms represent positions on a continuum which are the outcome of a *single* process. The creation of the one was the creation of the other – both materially and ideologically. "Civilization gave rise to barbarism," said Owen Lattimore.[2] And hegemonic forces gave birth to social science. *Pax Britannica* ensured the intellectual triumph of the belief in universals – universals that could be circumscribed and tested, theorems that were defined as laws, realities that became imperatives.

[1] Anouar Abdel-Malek, "Marxisme et sociologie des civilisations" in *La dialectique sociale* (Paris, 1972), pp. 354–5.
[2] Owen Lattimore, "La civilization, mère de Barbarie?" *Annales ESC*, 17:1 (Jan.-Feb. 1962), p. 99.

Just as British power and capitalist enterprise came to pervade the furthest corners of the world, so did the presumptions about universal truths come to pervade and define our consciousnesses, our cosmologies, our moralities, our scientific efforts.

It was not new that a civilization saw itself as Civilization (singular), the center surrounded by barbarisms. What was new was that this attitude was no longer defended on the basis that it was *deduced* from a God-given construction of reality; rather it was said to be *induced* from existential experience. What before was known metaphysically was now known rationally. Progress resided in the fact that present and future inequalities were now said to be merited inequalities, the consequence of the presumedly autonomous inner efforts of individuals.

The whole argument is so inherently preposterous and implausible that it requires a wrench of our critical faculties to appreciate that such ideas did not merely receive *droit de cité* but very nearly expunged all opposing views from the academy, on the grounds that they were legacies of pre-rational thought. Such were the glitter and the power of a capitalist world-economy in its days of un-self-questioning splendor that it was not easy to gain a hearing for the other side.

Yet other side there was. Indeed, there were two movements to refute this apotheosis of one particular into the universal. The two movements represented two different strategies of rebuttal. One riposte was to argue that this particular was only one particular among several or many. The other riposte was to argue that this particular was not universal.

The distinction was subtle but full of implications. The first movement asserted that civilization was a term with a plural and no singular. There were *only* civilization*s*. The second movement asserted that this particular, which thought itself to be universal, was only a transitory phase of human existence. The first movement emphasized the cultural context of human production, human activity; the second, the social relations that underpinned them. The first movement led to scholarly elaborations of alternative civilizations – to Orientalism, in both its best and worst senses. The second movement led to scholarly and extra-scholarly effort to analyze and further the transitory quality of the dominant world structures.

I do not suggest for a moment that these two schools of thought were identical or even similar. But they both started as reactions to (as well as expressions of) dominant socio-ideological forces. And their paths have crossed constantly in *praxis*, even when the actors involved have refused to admit it. And thus I should like to review the conflicts and convergences between these two antisystemic *Weltanschauungen* and movements.

What is a civilization? An old question, and definitional games are not always fruitful. In this instance, however, we must be clear. The word "civilization" ought to be used to mean something different from and more than the term "culture" of long anthropological tradition; else, why have two terms? If so, it then must be something more than a set of collective norms and values of a particular group of any size in any place. Most of us tend in fact to use the world "civilizations" to describe only larger, more encompassing, more enduring "cultural" phenomena. We speak of Western civilization, of Chinese civilization, of Indian civilization. In these three cases at least, we refer to phenomena asserted to continue for millennia, and this despite the fact that the Europe of the eleventh century and the twentieth, the China of the Sung dynasty and of today, the India of the Delhi Sultanate and of today have only the most marginal similarities as social structures. And this statement would be *a fortiori* true if we pushed the comparisons back three thousand more years.

What is it then that permits us to speak of a "civilization"? There are, to start with, certain surface continuities. The languages or languages spoken, while far from identical, are historically linked, such that contemporary languages can be said to be derived from earlier ones. But even there we stretch our imaginations. Outside linguistic influences have intruded in the interim. Many languages have been extinguished. If we are tracing linguistic heritages (say, English out of Romance, and Germanic languages out of their Indo-European origins) we must also remember that there is a vast geographic shift. New York is indeed far from Athens.

Well, then, you may argue, it is less a relative epiphenomenon such as language than a broader cosmological unity as reflected in religion and philosophy which constitutes the continuity. I scarcely need to review both the similarities and the differences of ancient and contemporary cosmological views identified with these "civilizations." But let us note in passing that the cosmological lines are different from the linguistic ones – for example, it is frequently stated that contemporary Western thought has, at least in part, Hebraic roots, but clearly there is no linguistic link.

I could go on like this, but it is essentially a false path. There is no "essence" which defines a civilization. For each trait uncovered, one could list countless exceptions. There probably do not even exist any *dimensions* of definition common to all "civilizations." Rather, I think we should conceive of "civilizations" as historical mental constructs, created, dissolved, and re-created, as groups feel the need of asserting their particularity in a dyadic relationship with some other groups. "Civilization gave rise to barbarism," said Owen Lattimore. We could rephrase the same point: "One civilization gives rise to another civilization." One only exists in function of the other(s).

When groups seek to establish their particularities, they reinvent their histories. They look for "continuities" which at that moment in time will be congenial: linguistic, religious, philosophical, esthetic, racial, geographic. They endow artifacts with the status of prior moments in a progression. Needless to say, the civilizational past chosen by groups in the tenth century AD will have been quite different, perhaps radically different, from the civilizational past chosen by the twentieth-century groups who include particular tenth-century groups in their past.

Tradition is always a contemporary social creation. Civilizations are the way we describe our particularities in terms of millennial heritages. We are not free to be totally arbitrary. There must be some surface plausibility to the continuities asserted. They cannot, at least today, fly in the face of all the canons of empirical verification. But once that is said, there remains a vast gamut of pasts one can plausibly choose, a vast gamut of pasts that are in fact chosen. And of course conflicting interests argue for alternative pasts for the collectivity.

To say that civilizations are ever-changing, very impermanent creations of contemporary groups is not to denigrate in any way their importance or their reality. No one who has ever traveled around the world, or read in the world's literature, has any doubt that there are significant differences between the world's diverse "civilizations." But when it comes to drawing the boundaries and defining the differences, we seldom agree with each other.

Let me now turn to "modes of production," a quite different concept from "civilization," having a separate intellectual heritage and enjoying a quite segregated but equally lively contemporary renaissance and debate. Here too I must make clear my position. A mode of production is a characteristic of an economy, and an economy is defined by an effective, ongoing division of productive labor. Ergo, to discover the mode of production that prevails, we must know what are the real bounds of the division of labor of which we are speaking. Neither individual units of production nor political or cultural entities may be described as having a mode of production; only economies.

Given this premise, I have previously argued that there are only four possible modes of production, only three of which have been known thus far in empirical reality. They are reciprocal mini-systems, redistributive world-empires, a capitalist world-economy, a socialist world-government.[3]

From my perspective, the key difference in these modes of production is found in the *productive* process. In reciprocal mini-systems, all able persons are direct producers, but the process of reciprocal exchange results in an unequal distribution of real surplus – which, given the technology, is always limited – in favor of a sub-group of direct producers, usually older males. The primary concern of the privileged groups is to ensure that there is a surplus at all.

In redistributive world-empires, there is a stratum of non-producers. The surplus generated by the direct producers is pre-empted in the form of tribute paid to the (imperial) ruling stratum. This tribute is collected by an armed bureaucracy. The interests of the ruling stratum vis-à-vis the armed bureaucracy lead them to try to limit the creation of surplus by the direct producers for fear that the armed bureaucracy will be able to appropriate enough to make them (or part of them) independent of the ruling stratum. The slogan might well be: "Enough but not too much."

In a capitalist world-economy, the surplus generated by the direct producers is pre-empted in the form of profit distributed *among* the bourgeoisie via the market, as modulated by the multiple state-structures which seek to affect market distribution. The interest of the bourgeoisie taken collectively is *always* the expanded (and unlimited) accumulation of capital, since the dynamics of the system mean that stagnation always leads to regression.

We can only guess how a socialist world-government would operate. Presumably its defining features would be production for use, equitable distribution, and a collectively agreed-upon balance of use-values. How these objectives would or could be structurally ensured is a matter of continuing debate.

I have reviewed this taxonomy very cursorily because I wish to see

---

[3] See my two successive formulations of this position: "The rise and future demise of the world capitalist system: concepts for comparative analysis," *Comparative Studies in Society and History*, 16:4 (Sept. 1974), pp. 387–415, and "The quality of life in different social systems: the model and the reality", chapter 14 in this volume.

its relation to the concept of civilization. Historically, there have been countless mini-systems, a large but countable number of world-empires, a similarly large but countable number of world-economies (but only *one* that has survived and flourished for more than a brief period, that one being the modern world-system). A socialist world-government is an invention of the future.

Mini-systems have emerged and disappeared over the millennia. My guess is that few have survived for more than 150–200 years. We have virtually no direct knowledge of how they historically functioned. One of the ways (but only one) in which they disappeared was their incorporation into world-empires, at which point they ceased to be mini-systems with their own mode of production and became simply one more region producing surplus seized by the bureaucracy of a world-empire in the form of tribute.

Since world-empires operated structurally in a cycle of expansion and contraction, they were continuously abolishing mini-systems by absorbing them and later "releasing" zones within which new mini-systems could be created. World-economies were inherently much more unstable than world-empires, and were constantly either being converted into world-empires by conquest or disintegrating, allowing mini-systems to re-emerge.

Hence, up to about 1500, the history of the world was the history of the temporal coexistence of three modes of production – one without records, the mini-systems; one unstable and therefore transitory, the world-economies; one spectacular and encompassing, the world-empires. It is fundamentally the latter to which we now in retrospect give the name "civilizations." One of the reasons we do this is that each time a *new* world-empire was on the ascendant, it sought ideological legitimation by claiming a direct link with a prior world-empire, and in so doing it created certain continuities which we, the analysts of today, perceive as the distinguishing features of that "civilization."

In the sixteenth century, a new phenomenon occurred which was to change the rules of the game. For the first time, a world-economy did not disintegrate but survived, and became the world capitalist system we know today.

The modern world-system changed the rules of the game in two ways. In the first place, the operation of the rules of world-empires led to long-term geographical expansion followed by geographical contraction. The rules of the capitalist world-economy (the expanded reproduction of capital) involved expansion but no contraction –

periods of relative stagnation, yes; attempts of areas at tactical withdrawal, yes; but real contraction, no. Hence, by the late nineteenth century, the capitalist world-economy included virtually the whole inhabited earth, and it is presently striving to overcome the technological limits to cultivating the remaining corners: the deserts, the jungles, the seas, and indeed the other planets of the solar system.

This ceaseless expansion has meant that both mini-systems and world-empires have disappeared from the surface of the earth. Today there is only one social system and therefore only one mode of production extant, the capitalist world-economy. Does this mean that there is then only one civilization? Here we come to the second inportant change in the rules of the game. For the answer to my question is "yes" in one sense, and "quite decidedly no" in another.

On the one hand, something we might call "capitalist civilization" clearly dominates the thinking and action of rulers and ruled, oppressors and oppressed. It is the cosmology of "more," more of everything, more for everybody, but more particularly (or if necessary) for "me" or "us." There are seeming rebellions against this cosmology: "limits of growth" rebellions which often turn out to be hidden ways of defending the "more" of what is of interest to one group against the "more" of another group; "egalitarian" rebellions which often turn out to operate on the assumption that the route to equality is through more of the same, but this time for someone else, "us."

I do not need to develop this theme. The analysis of the pluses and minuses of capitalist civilization has dominated the literature, the philosophy, and the social sciences of the last century, if not of the last two. Nor am I even taking sides on what seems to me an historically pointless question: the "progressiveness" of capitalism. What is more to the point is to observe that capitalist civilization (singular) has bred modern nationalisms (plural).

When Western civilization sought to transform itself into civilization pure and simple by the Enlightenment trick of reifying capitalist values into secular universals, it was sure that not only God and history were on its side but that all rational men (by which was meant the elites throughout the system, including its periphery) would be on its side as well, at least eventually.[4]

Instead what has happened is that everywhere, and more and more,

---

[4] In this respect, Marxism was a quintessential child of the Enlightenment. See this viewpoint cogently presented by Tom Nairn, "Marxism and the modern Janus," *New Left Review*, no. 94 (Nov.–Dec. 1975), pp. 3–29.

nationalist particularism has been asserting itself. Indeed, if there is
any linear equation at all, it is the correlation of the expansion of
capital, the uneven development of the world-system, and the claims to
differentiation by groups ever more integrated into the system – in a
dialectical vortex of centripetal and centrifugal forces.

How are these nationalisms we know so well and the civilizations of
which we have been talking related? It is a question seldom posed, as
far as I know. The confusion is simple when we deal with China, or
India, or even the Arab world. (I say "even" because though there are
multiple Arab nations or at least states today, nonetheless we talk of an
"Arab nationalism.") But what of the large number of members of the
United Nations whose claim to "civilizational" status is less widely
accorded?

I have tried to think of an uncontroversial example, and I cannot.
This in itself tells us something. I cannot think of an uncontroversial
example of a present-day state that is clearly not the "heir" of a specific
"civilization," because any example that might seem plausible to me –
or to you – would probably give offense to the leaders and the
intellectuals of the state in question. For, be it well noted: every state
today, without exception, proclaims itself the continuation of a civilization, and in many (perhaps most) cases heir of a civilization unique to
it.

One of the rare persons with the courage to tackle this issue was in
fact Anouar Abdel-Malek who, at the Seventh World Congress of
Sociology in 1966, distinguished varieties of nationalism on the Three
Continents of Asia, Africa, and Latin America, singling out a category
which he called "renascent nations," which were those "supported by
a continuing millenary national tradition ... " He listed China, Egypt,
Iran "principally," but also Turkey, Morocco, Vietnam, Mexico,
Armenia. He said of these "nations" as compared to others in the
Three Continents: "the coefficient of propulsion to development ...
cannot but be different."[5]

No doubt, but is the difference fundamental? I am not sure. The
nationalisms of the modern world are not the triumphant civilizations
of yore. They are the ambiguous expression of the demand both for
participation in the system, assimilation into the universal, the elimination of all that is unequal and indeed different, and *simultaneously* for
opting out of the system, adhering to the particular, the reinvention of

[5] Anouar Abdel-Malek, "Esquisse d'une typologie de formations nationales dans les Trois
Continents' in *La dialectique sociale*, pp. 120–2.

differences. Indeed, it is universalism through particularism, and particularism through universalism. This is the genius and the contradiction of capitalist civilization which, precisely as it hurtles towards its undoing, becomes in the interim stronger and stronger.

Are renascent nations in a different position from "truly" new nations? Stronger perhaps, but different? Is not the real issue that we are all in the same boat, facing the same dilemma: that, within a capitalist world-economy, nationalism (and civilizational analysis as one expression of nationalism) is both the "ideology of weaker, less developed countries struggling to free themselves from alien oppression"[6] (which are *all* countries and quasi-countries except the momentarily hegemonic one) and also the ultimate expression of the form of rapacity that is peculiar to capitalism (power and privilege through unlimited growth)?[7]

If civilizations as a mode of legitimating new redistributive world-empires are no more, but civilizations as the epitome of contemporary cultural resistance within a capitalist world-economy are flourishing, what future do they have? Here we come not only to untrod ground, but to arenas about which thus far we have largely refused to think. If, as I believe is the case, we are living in the early moments of a long systemic change – the transformation of the capitalist world-economy into a socialist world-government – and if we think such a transition will probably be completed but not certainly, we ought to pose the following question: If the millennial particularism we label "civilizations" have redefined themselves as *intra*-systemic oppositional ideologies within a capitalist world-economy, will the transition to socialism complete the undermining of their material bases, or conversely provide them with the building-stones of true reconstruction?

It is not cowardice but wisdom to say we do not know the answer. In the first place, we really do not have more than the remotest idea of what a socialist world would look like in practice, and most certainly it would require a heroic leap of the imagination to envisage its cultural parameters. It is a bit like asking the burghers of thirteenth-century European city-states to sketch our twentieth-century world. Some might have risen to the challenge, but what they would have imagined might in turn seem hopelessly parochial to us.

[6] Nairn, "Marxism and the modern Janus," p. 5

[7] "'National liberation' in the essentially antagonistic universe of capitalism, with its blind, competitive, and wildly uneven development, bears a contradiction within itself. It simply cannot help lapsing into nationalism in the most deleterious sense because it is a form of

What I think we may plausibly assert is that a socialist civilization will not be a cosmological mélange of a bit of this and that from everywhere. The ideas, the values, the world-views that will emerge from a socialist mode of production will lead in new directions, reflecting very different material premises from either classical world-empires or the capitalist world-economy.

Those who are hopeful share the vision of Marx: "from the realm of necessity to the realm of freedom." For Samir Amin, this means that

The direct apprehension of use values is thus the bearer of diversity, not uniformity. In contrast to the uniformity brought about by capitalism's destruction of culture, here there is the richness of a rebirth of diversity. National diversity, doubtless, but also diversity that is regional, local, individual.[8]

I need hardly say that against this optimism the world is full of harbingers of doom.

The harbingers of doom reject the Enlightenment. The optimists fulfill it. This in itself might make us suspicious. Is socialism merely the last gasp of Western capitalism triumphant? And if it is, can we truly still see this as progress, as Marx saw British rule in India, and Engels French rule in Algeria? For me, surely not. There is, however, this to remember, in Tom Nairn's very perceptive words:

History was to defeat the Western Philosophers. The defeat has been permanent. This is perhaps the true, larger meaning of Marxism's "failure" over the National Question.[9]

What is crucial in practice I think is to try to bring together what might be called "civilizational analysis" with a clearer grasp of the functioning of modes of production, and in particular with the historically singular evolution of the world capitalist system, in order to construct our options for diverse potentials in the "realm of freedom." We cannot do this abstractly – academically, if you will. But we do need to think about the fact that civilization (singular noun, with adjective "capitalist") has not yet obliterated civilizations (plural noun, meaning ideologies of resistance drawing on but not based on millennial traditions) even while civilization (singular) has transformed and circumscribed civilizations (plural).

The game is far from over. And we are its players – free not to shape but to struggle.

adaptation to this universe." Tom Nairn, "Old nationalism and new nationalism" in *The red paper on Scotland* (Edinburgh, 1975), p. 50.
[8] Samir Amin, "In praise of socialism," *Monthly Review*, 26:4 (Sept. 1974), p. 16.
[9] Nairn, "Marxism and the modern Janus," p. 9.

16 ❧ The dialectics of civilizations in the modern world-system

The dialectics of civilizations cannot be discussed abstractly or ahistorically. It has to be considered differently at three separate moments of world-time: the period before the sixteenth century, when no area of the world had a capitalist mode of production; the period from the sixteenth century to today, when the European world-economy with a capitalist mode of production spread to incorporate all areas of the globe within its economic boundaries; the period which began in the twentieth century, and which will continue for an uncertain length of time, which constitutes the world transition from capitalism to socialism.

About the first period of world-time, that prior to the sixteenth century, we need only note two things. First, in the constant rise and fall of world-empires in various parts of the earth, intellectuals and rulers at later points in time sometimes laid claim to continuity with earlier world-empires that had disappeared. Secondly, the cultural parameters of these various "civilizations" – loosely linked series of world-empires – differed in significant ways, undoubtedly more than their economic parameters.

For reasons we will not explore here, in Europe in the sixteenth century there grew up a structure which today we call a capitalist world-economy, whose *economic* parameters were fundamentally different from those of any other structure coexistent on the planet. One central economic parameter was the unremitting drive to ceaseless accumulation, which meant that, by fits and starts, this world-economy would expand, successfully expand, to incorporate over four centuries all the rest of the earth within its boundaries.

A second central feature of capitalism as a world-system was that it was constructed around an axial division of labor between core zones and peripheral zones between which there was unequal exchange. As the system expanded, incorporating new geographical areas, these areas were forced to play certain economic roles, a process we call peripheralization. It involved transforming the productive processes, including both what was produced and how the labor was controlled. We call this the creation of export cash-crops and of forms of coerced and semi-coerced labor. It involved transforming the indigenous political structures, either eliminating them altogether (colonialism) or weakening them vis-à-vis state-structures in core zones (semi-colonialism).

It involved finally a number of pressures at the level of culture: Christian proselytization, the imposition of European languages, instruction in specific technologies and mores, changes in the legal codes. Many of these changes were made *manu militari*. Others were achieved by the persuasion of "educators," whose authority was ultimately backed by military force. I am of course speaking of the complex of processes we sometimes label "Westernization" or, even more arrogantly, "modernization."

There were two main motives behind these enforced cultural changes. One was economic efficiency. If given persons were expected to perform in given ways in the economic arenas, it was efficient both to teach them the requisite cultural norms and to eradicate competing cultural norms. The second was political security. It was believed that were the so-called elites of peripheral areas "Westernized," they would be separated from their "masses," and hence less likely to revolt, and surely less able to organize a following for revolts. This turned out to be a monumental miscalculation, but it was plausible and did work for a while. (A third motive was *hybris* on the part of the conquerors. I do not discount it, but it is not necessary to invoke it in order to account for the cultural pressure, which would have been just as great in its absence.)

This cultural pressure wrought significant changes in the behavior of the populations located in the peripheral areas of the capitalist world-economy. But the changes, however great, were far less than the propagators of the faith had wanted or expected. In the first place, "Westernization" never went very deep, in the sense of affecting the large majority of these populations. In the second place, the "Westernized elites," or significant segments of them, became in a second or third generation the very leaders of a cultural resistance centered around the "renaissance" of their own civilizational heritage, which as we know became quickly transformed into political resistance, or modern nationalism.

At that point, the dialectics of the economy took over. As organized centers of politico-cultural resistance in the peripheral zones of the capitalist world-economy grew stronger, they found that the realization of power pushed them simultaneously in two opposite directions: more intensive integration with the capitalist world-economy; and withdrawal from it. I am not talking here of a split between conservative, so-called "pro-Western" or "moderate" movements and radical, so-called "socialist" movements. I am speaking of the contradictions felt *within* the socialist national liberation movements.

Each of these movements, without exception, has been caught in the dilemma of deciding whether the construction of socialism means the progressive, dialectical fulfillment of its predecessor – of capitalism, science, the Enlightenment – or is a radical break with it – economically and cosmologically. Some movements have tried to bridge the dilemma by a theory of two stages: the first fulfillment, the second an eschatological rupture. The problem with this solution is that the first stage is a living reality, the second a messianic aspiration.

This is very pertinent to the question "civilizations, one or many?" For in the world of socialism – not of pre-capitalism, nor of capitalism – will there be one or many civilizations? (I put this in the future tense, because we are not yet in the world of socialism.) We could debate this issue on the level of moral desirability. Almost everyone today would opt for the virtues of diversity. This is reinforced by modern biological theory which sees in diversity a necessity for survival of the genus.

The question, however, is not in our pious intentions but in the realities of our behavior. We may not be living in the world of socialism but we are living in the midst of the worldwide transition from capitalism to socialism. How do the movements who support this transition, who indeed propel it, act? They act, as already suggested, in contradictory manners.

We are not really capable of imagining the future following a change as fundamental as the one through which we are living. Socialized as we *all* are into the values of the present world, we are not even aware of all the blinkers which hinder our view. We are in Plato's cave and see only the shadows.

Nonetheless, let us explore the implications of a socialist mode of production, a mode based on production for use-values. It involves some kind of collective decision-making about social production to which we may give the shorthand label of "planning." As long as planning is at the level of states, it is ultimately planning for a "firm" and not for an "economy" and cannot eradicate the law of value. The clear implication is that planning must be at a world level, the only kind of production for use that can eliminate unequal exchange. Thus one implication is the eventual creation of a socialist world-government, however distant that may seem.

But if world socialism also implies, as the nineteenth-century theorists felt, a "withering away of the state," this "world-government" presumably will *not* be one of our contemporary forms of state government writ large.

Where then do civilizations come in? Will the logic of efficiency, the relative absence of struggle, eliminate the pressures for separate identity, or quite the contrary, will it release a cultural unfolding of variegation never before known? And will such a world still have a category of intellectuals to manipulate these symbols of variation, or will every man be his own priest?

Lest we be swept up in utopian vagaries, we should remember that the point is not how we will one day act, but how we are now acting. As long as we still live within a capitalist world-economy, the renaissance of civilizations is a mode of resistance, but only up to the point that the detour becomes the journey. It is a delicate game we all play in this transition to socialism, and how we play it may in large part determine whether we may succeed in completing the transition. On the one side is the Scylla of self-defeating particularisms which will sustain the present world-order by their inability effectively to mobilize world opposition to it. On the other side is the Charybdis of neo-Enlightenment universalism in socialist garb which will substitute a technocratic bourgeoisie for a more enterpreneurial one but retain the basic system. In between is a path that leads to the world transformation that could be the "negation of the negation," as Sartre said in his analysis of Negritude, and will lead to a world in which it may be that the question "civilizations, one or many?" will cease to have any meaning.

17 ✝ The development of the concept of development

A case can be made for the assertion that the concept of development is not merely one of the central components of the ideology both of Western civilization and of world social science, but is in fact the central organizing concept upon which all else is hinged.[1] I am not interested here however in the history of Western civilization. I am interested rather in the history of social science, indeed in the very concept that there is something called social science, or (to be more accurate) that there are various disciplines that collectively make up the social sciences. This is not, as any rapid glance at the historical evolution of the organization of universities will show us, a self-evident idea. What today are called the humanities have long been studied. What today are called the natural sciences have a very long history. The social sciences however were invented and inserted into the curriculum only in the nineteenth century.

This is itself a remarkable fact which is insufficiently observed and/or celebrated. For example, the *International encyclopedia of the social sciences*, published in 1968, does not even have an entry for "social science(s)" as such.[2] This is no accident but in fact reflects the dominant ideology of world social science.

---

[1] "Of all metaphors in Western thought on mankind and culture, the oldest, most powerful and encompassing is the metaphor of growth." Robert A. Nisbet, *Social change and history: aspects of the Western theory of development* (New York: Oxford University Press, 1969), p. 7 (Nisbet uses "growth" and "development" as interchangeable for this discussion). To be sure, the point of Nisbet's book is summed up in the title of the last section, "The irrelevance of metaphor," but Nisbet's insistence on the "priority of fixity" does not undo this observation on intellectual history. Indeed, his book is the *cri de coeur* of someone who feels very much in a minority.

[2] It is true that the *Encyclopedia of the social sciences*, published in 1937, is opened by an essay entitled "What are the Social Sciences?" But it is a very weak essay, of a chronologically descriptive, discursive nature.

The invention of the social sciences required a particular extension of modern secularism. The natural sciences are based on the assumption that natural phenomena behave in predictable (or at least analyzable) ways, and are therefore subject to intervention and manipulation. The struggle to establish the legitimacy of this perspective encountered, as we all know, the resistance of many religious authorities and of all those who believed that such a view would stimulate man's *hybris* and undermine social stability. We have little patience today for any who still preach such a backward form of resistance to scientific enquiry.

The social sciences basically make a parallel assertion: social phenomena behave in predictable (or at least analyzable) ways, and are therefore subject to intervention and manipulation. I do not for a moment suggest that this belief was unknown before the nineteenth century. That would be an absurd suggestion. But I do suggest that such a perspective did not really have *droit de cité* before then.

The French Revolution in many ways crystallized the issues involved in this concept and served as an ideological turning point. By legitimating the concept of the rights of man, the revolutionary process bequeathed us the legitimacy of deliberate social change which no amount of conservative ideologizing since has been able to undo. (Note that conservatives are reduced these days to arguing that social interventions ought to be "cost-effective," a dramatic comedown if ever there was one.)

If social intervention is legitimate, it can only be because what is is not perfect but is perfectible. It is in the end only some variant of the idea of progress that justifies the enormous social energy required by social science, the most complex of all forms of knowledge. Otherwise, the whole exercise would be an esthetic game, in which case poetry or mathematics might be more appealing modes of activity. And if what is is not perfect but is perfectible, we may be drawn to portray the alternatives as an antinomy of reified forces. This is of course what did happen historically. In the wake of the French Revolution and all the ideological turmoil it generated, social commentators of human "development" began to make a distinction that was crucial for all subsequent analysis – the distinction of society and state.

In general, the state represented what was, and was not perfect, and society represented the force that was pushing towards the perfectibility of the state. But at times, as we know, the imagery has been reversed. No matter! Without the distinction of society and state, social science, as we know it, would not have existed. But it is also true that without the distinction of society and state, the social movement, as we know it, also would not have existed. For both social science and the social movement have claimed to incarnate views about the underlying society against the pieties of officially stated analyses and policies.

Thus, the epistemological links between social science and the social movement are profound, which to be sure justifies the great suspiciousness which political conservatives have always shown towards the enterprise of social science.

Let us look more closely at the antinomy of society/state. An antinomy involves a permanent tension, a permanent misfit or contradiction, a permanent disequilibrium. In some sense, the intent of both social science and the social movement is to reduce this antinomy, whether by harmonization or by violence or by some *Aufhebung* (transcendence) of the pair.

The question of course immediately arises, which society, which state? The difficulties involved in answering this query have been so enormous that the query itself has, for almost two hundred years, been largely skirted. To skirt a query is not however to neglect to answer it. It is to answer it secretly, shamefully, by burying the answer in a largely unspoken premise.

The premise was that the state was those states that were "sovereign," that is, those states which reciprocally recognized each other's legitimate existence within the framework and the norms of the interstate system. There were in addition aspirants to this status, entities not yet existing whose existence was advocated by various national movements. And there were candidates for elimination, usually small-sized units which larger states wished to absorb, and whose legitimacy was thereby put into question by some ideologues.

But generally speaking, everyone "knew" which the states were, and a large part of the enterprise of nineteenth-century (and indeed twentieth-century) history has constituted essentially a reading back into the past of a continuing history for such "states."

If then "society" was to remain in permanent tension with the "state," and the states were particular geographically bounded, juridically defined entities (which however had histories), then it seemed to follow that each state was a society or had a society, and each society had a state. Or at least, it seemed to follow that this is how it ought to be. Nationalism is the name which we give to such an analytical credo in the realm of politics and culture.

This thrust to parallelism of boundaries of society and state had immense hidden implications for the epistemology of social science as it in fact historically evolved. For it determined the basic unit of analysis within which almost all of social science has been written. This basic unit was the state – either a sovereign state or a politico-cultural claimant to state status – within which social action was said to have occurred. The "society" of such a "state" was adjudged to be more or less cohesive, more or less "progressive" or "advanced." Each "society" had an "economy" which could be characterized, and which had "home markets" and "foreign markets." Each "society" had a culture, but it also had "minorities" with "subcultures," and these minorities could be thought of as having accepted or resisted "assimilation."

You may be thinking that anthropology at least presented an exception. Anthropologists scorned the modern state and usually concentrated on some other entity – a "tribe" or a "people." But in fact all the anthropologists were saying was that in what today we call the peripheral areas of the world-economy, which were in the late nineteenth century largely dominated by colonial powers, the formal state was a thin social layer lying over the real political entities which were the so-called "traditional" political structures. The starting point for an anthropologist dealing with an acephalous society was the same as for an historian dealing with central Europe – a primordial and largely fictive politico-cultural entity which "governed" social life, within which the *real* society existed.

In this sense, both the anthropologists and the Germanic historians of the nineteenth century could be spurned by hard-nosed British empiricists as incorrigibly romantic. For myself, much as I think the "romantics" were wrong, they seem to be less wildly off the mark than our hard-nosed arrogant empiricists. In any case, the subsequent transformation of vocabulary indicates the stateness-orientation that was always there. Central European *Völker* and Afro-Asian "peoples" who came to dominate a sovereign state thereupon became "nations." Witness the Germans and the Burmese. Those that didn't get to dominate a sovereign state became instead "ethnic groups," entities whose very existence has come to be defined in relation to one or more sovereign states. Poles are an "ethnic group" in the US but a "nation" in Poland. Senegalese are an "ethnic group" almost everywhere in West Africa except Senegal.

Thus, the state came to provide the defining boundaries of the "society," and the "societies" were the entities which were comparable one to the other – in the famous billiard-ball analogy, comparable to individuals within all of human society.[3] "Societies" were seen as collective entities going along parallel paths in the same direction. That is to say, it was societies that were "developing." "Development" (or, in older terminology, "progress") was a measurable (or at least describable) characteristic of societies.

This use of "societies" as the basic unit of social science had two clear consequences. It rendered plausible two fundamental options of the philosophy of social science there were widely adopted in the nineteenth century. I call these two options "universalization" and "sectorialization."

Universalization is the presumption that there exist universal laws applicable to all of human society or rather all of human societies. The objective of social science is said to be the clear statement of these universal laws (in the form of propositions that are "falsifiable"). The limits to our ability to state these laws are the limits of our present ignorance. The enterprise of social science is the search to reduce this ignorance. This is a realizable task. Once such laws, or a significant number of them, are stated, we shall collectively be able to deduce applications that can be used at the level of policy. That is to say, we shall be able to "intervene" effectively in the operation of these laws. The model obviously is that of classical physics and its applications in technology and engineering.

Of course, one can state or discover "universal" laws about any phenomenon *at a certain level of abstraction*. The intellectual question is whether the level at which these laws can be stated has any point of contact with the level at which applications are desired. The proponents of universalization never seriously debated whether such a conjuncture of levels was theoretically probable. Recognizing gaps in current ability to make these applications, the proponents merely insisted that these gaps could be bridged in some near future by the earnest application of scientific intelligence.

There were to be sure some who emphatically denied the existence of such laws. But these "particularizers" tended to go to the opposite extreme. They expounded a so-called idiographic as opposed to a nomothetic view of social science. They argued that no generalizations

---

[3] A famous American textbook of the 1950s was Kingsley Davis's *Human society* (New York: Macmillan, 1948). The message was that each separate society follows a set of rules which is that of "human society" as a generic category.

at all were feasible, since everything was unique, and only empathetic understanding was possible. Or in a slightly less restrictive version, it was argued that only very low-level generalizations were feasible. A great deal of huffing and puffing between the two schools of thought occurred. But in fact the idiographic school shared not merely the central unit of analysis with the nomothetic school. They also shared the presumed parallelism of all "societies" – in one case because they were all alike, in the other because they were all different.

What both schools excluded, and what was largely absent from mainstream work, was the possibility that a *via media* exists, that a significant level of generalizations (the analysis of structures) was not only possible but essential, but that this level was below the arena of "all societies" and rather at the level of what I would term "historical systems."[4]

The effective exclusion of this methodological *via media* was quite consonant with the other philosophical option of modern social science, which may be called "sectorialization." Sectorialization is the presumption that the social sciences are divided into a number of separate "disciplines," each of which comprises an intellectually defensible distinct focus of discourse. Over the past 125 years, we have collectively more or less settled on the following categories of "disciplines" – history, anthropology, economics, political science, and sociology (with some reservations one might add geography). You will recognize here the names of academic departments in most universities and the names of national and international scholarly associations. Of course, there were/are other candidates to the status of "discipline" – e.g., demography, criminology, urban planning – but by and large these other candidates have not found widespread support.

The reason is simple. If one takes the five agreed-upon disciplines, we find they reflect the assumptions of nineteenth-century liberal thought. Civilized life was organized in three analytically (and politically) separate domains – the economy, the political arena, and what was neither the one nor the other (which received the label of "social").

---

[4] For a brief exposition of what is involved in the *via media* see my "The *Annales* School: the war on two fronts," *Annals of Scholarship*, 1:3 (Summer 1980), pp. 85–91. This *via media* is not at all the same as Merton's "theories of the middle range." Merton advocated "special theories applicable to limited ranges of data – theories, for example, of class dynamics, of conflicting group pressures, of the flow of power and the exercise of interpersonal influence..." (Robert K. Merton, *Social theory and social structure*, rev. and enlarged ed. (Glencoe, Ill: Free Press, 1957), p. 9). This refers to the *scope* of the data, but Merton's objectives are to develop "universal" theories of the middle range, not theories which are valid only for given historical systems.

Thus we have three nomothetic disciplines: economics, political science, and sociology. History was reserved to the largely idiographic account of each separate society.

Anthropology was given the domain of the non-civilized. (If a society was exotic but was in some sense thought to be "civilized" – that is, to have a literature and a major religion – then it was consigned to "Orientalism," a kind of bastard combination of history and philology). Anthropologists had a hard job deciding whether they wanted to be nomothetic analysts of grand historical sequences or idiographic recorders of "pre-historical" structures. Since they tended to do a bit of everything, their domain was safe only as long as their "peoples" were colonized and ignored. With the political rise of the Third World after the Second World War, everyone else began to impinge on the anthropologists' domain, and hence for survival the anthropologists returned the favor, with the emergence of such new concerns as "urban anthropology."

Before we can do an "archaeology of knowledge" we should see clearly the "architecture of knowledge." The rooms were "societies." The designs were "universalizing" and "sectorializing." The ideology was that of British hegemony in the world-system. As of 1850, the British dominated the world-economy and the interstate system virtually without challenge. They were the most efficient producers of the most high-profit products. They were the leading commercial power and largely imposed an ideology of free trade upon the world. They secured this doctrine by their naval power. The gold standard was in effect a sterling standard, and the banks of the City of London centralized a great proportion of world finance. Of this period, the so-called "golden age of capitalism," it has been said that "between 1846 and 1873 the self-regulating market idealized by Adam Smith and David Ricardo came nearer to being realized than ever before or since."[5]

It was natural then that Great Britain should set the tone not only in world science but in the newly emerging social sciences. French social thought was no counterbalance. It was basically on the same wavelength as the British, as for example is attested by the correspondence between John Stuart Mill and Auguste Comte. One might even make the case that Saint-Simon expressed the spirit of

[5] Dudley Dillard, "Capitalism after 1850" in Contemporary Civilization Staff of Columbia College (eds.), *Chapters in Western civilization*, 3rd ed. (New York: Columbia University Press, 1962), Vol. II, p. 282.

nineteenth-century capitalist entrepreneurs even better than Smith or Ricardo.

The profoundest legacy left us by this group of thinkers is their reading of modern history. The questions they felt called upon to explain were (1) Britain's "lead" over France, (2) Britain and France's "lead" over Germany and Italy, and (3) the West's "lead" over the East. The basic answer to question one was "the industrial revolution," to question two "the bourgeois revolution," and to question three the institutionalization of individual freedom.

The three questions and the three answers are really one catechism which justified, indeed glorified, monumental and growing inequalities in the world-system as a whole. The moral implicitly preached was that the leader merited the lead because he had somehow shown his devotion earlier and more intensely to human freedom. The laggard had but to catch up. And the social scientist had but to pose the question incessantly: what explains that a particular laggard has been and still remains behind?

There were some who refused to play this game, the schools of resistance as I think of them: the proponents of historical economics in Germany, later the *Annales* school of French historiography,[6] and from the beginning (but outside the universities) Marxism. What these resistants shared was rejection of both the universalizing and the sectorializing postulates of modern social science. But these movements were weak in numbers, largely separated from each other, and ultimately ineffective on a world scale in limiting the spread of the dominant ideology.

Their ineffectiveness came in part from their dispersion. But it came in part from a fundamental error in judgment. While all the movements of resistance rejected the epistemology of the dominant social science, they failed to challenge the historiography. They accepted without too much thought the "Industrial Revolution" in England at the turn of the nineteenth century and the French Revolution as the two watershed events of the modern world. They thereby accepted the premise that the construction of a capitalist world-economy itself represented "progress" and in this way implicitly accepted the whole underlying theory of "stages of development" for each separate society. By surrendering the historiographic domain, they undermined fatally their resistance in the epistemological realm.

The consequences of this contradictory stance of the schools of

[6] See my brief *"Annales* as resistance," *Review*, 1:3/4 (Spring-Summer 1978), pp. 5–7.

resistance became clear in the period after 1945. At that time, the United States had become the new hegemonic power, replacing a long-since displaced Great Britain. Despite the enormous geographical expansion of world social science, American social science played an even more dominant role in the period 1945–67 than had British in the period 1850–73.

The counterpoint to American hegemony was at one level the USSR and its "bloc" of states, which were in acute politico-military controversy with the US. But it was also, at a perhaps deeper and more long-range level, the rise of the national liberation movements throughout the peripheral areas of the world-economy. Bandung was made possible by the conjunction of three forces: the strength of social and national movements in the periphery, the political and ideological forces incarnated in the Soviet bloc, and the needs of American capitalists to eliminate the monopolistic access that west Europeans held to certain economic zones. Thus American hegemony and the rise of the "Third World" were linked in both symbiotic and antagonistic fashion.

This contradictory link was reflected in the ideology of social science. On the one hand, there was a renewed triumph of scientism, of a pervasive and often specious quantification of research, in terms of which the newly discovered research arenas of the peripheral countries were simply one more source of data. On the other hand, the complexities of the study of these areas pushed toward the building of area studies on an "interdisciplinary" basis – a timid questioning of sectorialization, so timid that the very name reinforced the legitimacy of the historic "disciplinary" distinctions. The reconciliation of these two thrusts was in the invention of a new vocabulary to restate nineteenth-century verities: the vocabulary of "development" – economic, social, political – subsequently subsumed under the heading of modernization theory.

At the level of ideology, the world of official Marxism turned out to pose no real opposition to modernization theory, despite the fact that it was derived from an ideology of resistance. The official Marxists simply insisted upon some minor alterations of wording. For society, substitute social formation. For Rostow's stages, substitute Stalin's. For Britain/US as the model, substitute the USSR. But the analysis was the same: the states were entities that "developed," and "development" meant the further mechanization, commodification, and contractualization of social activities. Stalinist bureaucrats and Western experts competed as to which one could be the most effective Saint-Simonian.[7]

As we know, the frenetic certainties of the 1950s began to come apart in the 1960s. The US and its allies began to find their power undermined by the growing militance and successes of the movements of the Third World, without and within. The problems of the real world became the problems, both social and intellectual, of its ideological centers, the universities. The explosions of 1968 (and thereabouts) were the result.

It is fashionable these days to play down the importance of these rebellions of the late 1960s on the ground that the student rebels of that period have since largely become either reintegrated into or expelled from the social fabric and that the successor student generations are quiescent. What good, it is asked, did the New Left really serve? The answer is really very simple. It was the meteoric flames of this rebellion that were primarily responsible for burning away the tissue that maintained Establishment liberalism as the unquestioned ideology of US universities in particular and of Western universities in general. It is not that the Establishment was destroyed. But since then it has been unable to exclude competing views as illegitimate, and this has permitted the 1970s to be a time of much intellectual fertility.

The explosions in Western universities were matched by the destruction of the sclerotic world of official Marxism. The death of Stalin, Khrushchev's report, the Sino-Soviet split, the triumphs and then the failures of the Cultural Revolution have all resulted in what Henri Lefebvre has called "Marxism exploded."[8] Here too we should not be misled. The fact that there are today a thousand Marxisms amidst a situation in which more and more people claim to be Marxist does not mean that orthodox Marxism (whatever that be) has disappeared as a major ideological force. It simply no longer has a monopoly in its corner.

The disappearance of both *consensuses* – the liberal and the Marxist – is not independent of the changing geopolitics of the world. With the demise not of American power but of American hegemony, which I would date as from 1967, there has been a steady movement towards a restructuring of the alliances in the interstate system. I have argued elsewhere that the *de facto* Washington–Beijing–Tokyo axis which

---

[7] On the role of the Saint-Simonian element in the Marxist tradition, see Luca Meldolesi, *L'utopia realmente esistente: Marx e Saint-Simon* (Rome and Bari: Laterza, 1982).

[8] Henri Lefebvre, "Marxism exploded," *Review*, 4:1 (Summer 1980), pp. 19–32.

developed in the 1970s will be matched in the 1980s by a *de facto* Paris–Bonn–Moscow axis.[9] Whatever the reasons for this regrouping (in my opinion they are largely economic), it is clear that it makes no ideological sense at all, certainly not in terms of the ideological lines of the 1950s.

This geopolitical shift, itself linked to the ideological-cum-political explosions in both the Western and the socialist countries, has begun to open up, for the first time since the 1850s, both the epistemological and the historiographical premises of social science.

In terms of epistemology, we are seeing a serious challenge to both universalization and sectorialization and an attempt to explore the methodology of holistic research,[10] the implementation of that *via media* that had been excluded by the nomothetic–idiographic pseudo-debate of the nineteenth century. For the first time, the imagery of the route of scientific advance is being inverted. Instead of the assumption that knowledge proceeds from the particular towards ever more abstract truths, there are some who wish to argue that it proceeds from the simple abstractions towards ever more complex interpretations of empirical – that is, historical – reality.

This epistemological challenge has been made before as we have already noted, but it is being made more systematically and solidly today. What is really new, however, is the historiographical challenge. Once our unit of analysis shifts from the society-state to that of economic worlds, the entire reification of states, of nations, of classes, of ethnic groups, even of households falls away.[11] They cease being primordial entities, Platonic ideas, whose real nature we must somehow intuit or deduce. They become constantly evolving structures resulting from the continuing development of long-term large-scale historical systems.

In such a context, the British "Industrial Revolution" of 1760–1830 or the French Revolution do not disappear. But they may be seen in better perspective. There will be an end to the incredible formulation of

[9] See my "Friends as foes," chapter 6 in this volume; also my chapter "Crisis as transition" in S. Amin, G. Arrighi, A. G. Frank and I. Wallerstein, *Dynamics of global crisis* (New York: Monthly Review Press, 1982).

[10] See Robert Bach, "On the holism of a world-systems perspective," with commentaries by Christopher Chase-Dunn, Ramkrishna Mukherjee, and Terence K. Hopkins, in Terence K. Hopkins, I. Wallerstein *et al.*, *World-systems analysis: theory and methodology* (Beverly Hills: Sage, 1982), pp. 159–91. See also in the same volume Terence K. Hopkins, "World-system analysis: methodological issues," pp. 145–58.

[11] See my "The states in the institutional vortex of the capitalist world-economy," chapter 3 in this volume.

intellectual problems in the form: "Why did not Germany have a bourgeois revolution?"; "Can the Kenya bourgeoisie develop an autonomous capitalist state?"; "Is there a peasantry in Brazil (or Peru or ...)?"

We are living in the maelstrom of a gigantic intellectual sea-change, one that mirrors the world transition from capitalism to something else (most probably socialism). This social transition may take another 100–150 years to complete. The accompanying ideological shift will take less time, however – probably only another twenty years or so. This ideological shift is itself both one of the outcomes and one of the tools of this process of global transition.

It follows that the intellectual tasks before us are important ones, that our intellectual responsibilities are moral responsibilities. First of all, we must (all of us) rewrite modern history – not merely the history that scholars read but the history that is infused into us in our elementary education and which structures the very categories of our thinking.

We must learn how to think both holistically and dialectically. I underline the words "learn how." For much of what has claimed in the past to be holistic and dialectical was merely all-encompassing, sloppy, and unduly motivated by the needs of propaganda. In fact, a holistic, dialectical methodology is infinitely more complex than the probabilistic quasi-experimental one that is so widespread today. We have scarcely begun to explore how it can be done seriously. Most of us are more frightened by its difficulties than by those of linear algebra.

We must then use this methodology to invent (I deliberately use the strong word "invent") new data bases. The ones we use now (or 98% of them) are the results of collecting for 150–200 years data about states. The very word "statistics" is derived, and not fortuitously, from the word "state." We do not have serious data about the capitalist world-economy (not to speak of other and prior world-systems). No doubt there are manifold intrinsic and extrinsic problems in the manufacture of such data. But the methodological ingenuities of the last thirty years, which have opened up for quantitative research fields, such as medieval history, once thought entirely recalcitrant to the application of hard data, give reason to hope that enough energy applied with enough intelligence might bring us thirty years from now to the point where we have at least as much hard data on the functioning of the modern world-system as a system as we have today on the functioning of the various states.

We must use this new data to theorize anew, but hesitantly. Too much damage has been done in the past by prematurely jumping into the saddle and creating reified constructs which block further work. It is better for the time being to have fudgy concepts which are too malleable than to have clearly defined ones that turn out to be poorly chosen and that thereby serve as new Procrustean beds.

Finally, I am convinced that neither using a new methodology nor theorizing will be possible except in conjunction with praxis. On the one hand, it is the function of intellectuals to reflect in ways that those who are at the heart of politics cannot, for want of time and distance. But on the other hand, it is through action that unexpected social truths (not only about the present and future, but about the past as well) are revealed, and these truths are not visible (or at least not at first) except to those whose very activities are the source of the discoveries. The intellectual who cuts himself or herself off from political life cuts himself or herself off from the possibility of truly perceptive social analysis – indeed, cuts himself or herself off from the truth.

The epistemological links between social science and the social movement were there from the inception of both. There is no way this link can be cut without destroying both. No doubt there are dangers to both in this close tie, but those dangers pale by comparison with the dangers of surgical separation. This is what was tried in the late nineteenth century, and it would not be too strong to assert that the many horrors of the twentieth were, if not caused by, then abetted by this putative separation.

The likelihood is that this long-standing alliance between social science and the social movement will take on a new direction and a new vigor in the next twenty years. Neither social science nor the social movement will be able to emerge from the cul-de-sac in which both are presently without a transformation of the other. This of course makes the change doubly difficult. Not only is each being called upon to question (and reject) long-standing premises, but each is being called upon to recognize its dependence on the other's progress for its own progress. There is no guarantee that these fundamental hand-in-hand changes will occur, but it is likely.

Index

Abdel-Malek, Anouar, 159
accumulation of capital, *see* capital
Adler, Victor, 114, 116
Afghanistan, 63, 90
Africa, 60, 63, 67, 77–8, 81, 87, 109–10, 120,
  129, 138, 142, 166
Agnew, Spiro T., 72
Akins, James, 61
Albania, 90, 118, 120, 138, 140
Algeria, 139, 168
anarchism, 48, 86, 113, 115, 124
anthropology, 176, 179
antisystemic movements, 20–2, 24–5, 49, 52–7,
  59, 63, 67, 77–9, 82–96, 98, 104–8, 111–12,
  114–15, 117, 123–4, 127, 130–45; *see also*
  national(ist) movements; social movements
appropriation of surplus-value, *see under*
  surplus-value
Arab states, 14, 166
Argentina, 46
Armenia, 166
Arusha Declaration (1967), 80
Asia, 60, 66, 87, 90, 120, 135, 142–3, 166;
  southeast, 63, 81, 109–10, 125
Atatürk, Kemal, 126
Australia, 81, 142
Austria, 114–15, 136

Bakunin, Mikhail, 48, 113
balance of power, 17, 38–9, 45, 50, 71, 100,
  108
Bernstein, Eduard, 114
bifurcating turbulence, 38
Bismarck, Otto von, 71
Blanquism, 113, 116
Bohemia, 115
Bolshevism, 48, 86–8, 114–17, 124, 135; *see also*
  communist parties, Soviet Union
bourgeoisie, 4, 10–11, 17, 19–20, 22–5, 34–6,

48, 84, 93, 99–104, 112, 114–16, 118–20, 123,
  127–9, 135, 137, 156, 159, 163, 180
Boxer Rebellion, 82
Brazil, 61, 110
Brest-Litovsk, Treaty of (1918), 70
Bretton Woods, 42
Brigati Rossi, *see* Red Brigades
Brzezinski, Zbigniew, 75
bureaucracy, 30, 33, 41, 45, 48–9, 88, 124, 130,
  143–4, 150–3, 163–4, 181
Bush, George, 76

Cambodia, 74, 90, 92, 107, 130, 138
Camp David, 66
Canada, 120, 142
capital: accumulation of, 3, 6–7, 11, 15–16,
  18–19, 22, 29, 34, 38, 43–4, 46, 53–4, 59, 80,
  93, 98, 133–4, 139, 143, 163, 169; as factor of
  production, 19, 29, 31, 41, 44, 81
capitalism: origins of, 97, 129, 133, 153;
  principles of, 3, 33, 43, 98, 101–3, 123,
  126–7, 130, 133–4, 154, 156, 165, 167, 169;
  strength of, 9, 18, 49, 51, 55, 97, 106, 127,
  133, 160, 179; transition from, 11–12, 52, 55,
  57, 86, 89, 95, 107, 111, 113–14, 123–31, 133,
  144, 167, 169, 171–2, 184
capitalist world-economy: characteristics of, 2,
  10, 13–14, 21, 29, 36–7, 55, 80, 105, 127, 132,
  158; crisis of, 23–4, 26, 29, 46, 52, 55, 57–8,
  63, 103, 119, 126, 129, 131, 134, 147; cyclical
  pattern of, 6, 14, 16, 23, 37, 40, 43, 46, 58, 68,
  85, 99, 101–3, 128, 131, 133; development of,
  4, 6, 13, 18–19, 23–4, 29–30, 37, 39–40, 48,
  52, 59, 80, 97–8, 100, 104, 123, 126, 130–3,
  143, 147, 153–6, 160, 164–7, 169, 171–2, 180,
  184; expansion of, 6–7, 23, 58, 63, 73, 80,
  99–100, 102–3; incorporation into, 80–1,
  102–4; institutions of, 7, 14, 18, 20, 22, 100,
  102–3, 107, 127, 133–4, 144, 163; interstate

system and, 8, 14, 25, 33, 38, 50, 70, 80, 82–4, 94, 106–8, 134; secular trends of, 14, 17–18, 26, 37, 40, 58, 104, 108, 127, 131; states and, 4, 20, 25, 33, 36, 50–1, 69, 80–2, 94, 127
Caribbean area, 63, 81, 138
Carter, Jimmy, 63, 73, 75–6
caste, 151, 155
Castro, Fidel, 126, 140
catching up, 21, 54–5, 65, 89, 92–3
Central America, 63
Chile, 140
China, 60, 62, 65–6, 75, 77, 81–2, 89–92, 109–10, 116, 119, 122, 125, 130, 138, 141, 144, 151, 161, 166, 182; Sino-Soviet relations, 62, 65, 182
Christendom, 49
Civil Rights Act (1965), 73
civilizations, 23, 25, 159–72
class, 8–10, 12, 14, 18–20, 22, 29, 32–4, 36, 76, 83–4, 89, 91, 100–2, 127–9, 133, 183
class struggle, 4, 6, 10, 16, 32, 36, 56, 62, 91–2, 99, 107, 109–10, 112, 124, 127, 131, 142, 158
Colombia, 142
colonialism, 80–2, 87, 170, 176
Comintern, *see* Third International
commerce, 3, 5, 39–40
commodification of factors of production, 18, 19, 54, 59, 93, 101, 127–8, 143, 154, 181
commodities, *see* production, factors of
commodity chains, 2–4
Commune, 113, 115–16
communism, 48, 71, 86, 89, 93, 119, 124–5
communist parties, 33, 71, 89–90, 93–4, 106, 121, 125, 137, 143; Albania, 138, 140; Cambodia, 138; China, 60, 91–2, 106, 119, 122, 125, 138; Cuba, 122; Czechoslovakia, 109; Europe, 112–22; France, 119–20; Germany, 119–20; Italy, 119–21, 126; Korea, 138; Laos, 138; Poland, 95; Soviet Union, 48, 62, 88–92, 106, 115, 121, 124–5; Spain, 120; Vietnam, 119, 122, 125, 138; Yugoslavia, 138
Comte, Auguste, 179
Concert of Europe, 42
contractualization, 18, 127, 181
convergence, 55
co-optation, 53–4, 128, 138, 140
core areas, 4–5, 8, 15–16, 29, 53, 99–100, 103, 105, 159, 170
core processes, 7, 20, 45, 50, 103
core states, 9, 17, 22, 24, 51, 56–7, 61–2, 65, 71, 74, 104, 109
crisis: fiscal, 109–10; of capitalism, *see* capitalist world-economy; of feudalism, 23, 52, 97; of socialism, *see* socialism
Cuba, 116, 122, 125, 140
Cultural Revolution (China), 90–2, 109–10, 125, 144, 182

cyclical patterns, *see* capitalist world-economy; Kondratieff cycles
Czechoslovakia, 66, 90, 109–10, 121

Debray, Régis, 9
deflation, 42
demand, 6, 16–17, 23, 98–9, 110, 133
détente, 62, 65, 75, 89
Deutscher, Isaac, 95
development, concept of, 21, 173–85
division of labor, *see* labor
Dominican Republic, 46
Dubček, Alexander, 109, 121
Dulles, John Foster, 76, 138

economy, concept of, 2, 8, 13
Egypt, 166
Eisenhower, Dwight D., 75
El Salvador, 46, 77, 140
Engels, Frederick, 47, 147, 156–7, 168
England, *see* United Kingdom
Enlightenment, 165
entrepreneurs, 15–17, 33–4, 43–5, 49, 51, 57, 99–101, 103, 133
ethnic groups, 2, 8, 12, 20, 29, 36, 41, 72, 74, 100–1, 110, 142, 176, 183
Eurocommunism, 109, 112–22
Europe, 29, 37, 43, 46–7, 49, 50, 52, 58–60, 62, 64–7, 71, 74–5, 80, 82, 87, 90, 97, 105–6, 109–10, 112–22, 126, 129, 133, 136, 139, 141, 143, 151, 155, 161
European Economic Community, 65
exchange: processes of, 4, 15; unequal, 5, 11, 15, 21, 38, 45, 80, 82, 103, 154, 170
expansion, *see* capitalist world-economy; production

factors of production, *see* production
fascism, 70–1, 76–7, 118–19
feudalism, 23, 52, 93, 97, 151
finance, 5, 39–40
First International, 86, 113, 124
First World War, 35, 42, 69, 114
forces of production, *see* production
Ford, Gerald, 75
France, 31–2, 34, 42–3, 49, 60, 75, 77, 86, 113–15, 117–18, 120, 139, 141, 168, 180, 183
free trade, 5, 6, 61
French Revolution, 1, 174, 180, 183

Germany, 42–3, 66–7, 69–71, 75, 77, 86, 88, 113–15, 118–21, 135, 141, 180, 183–4
Gramsci, Antonio, 119, 122
Greece, 89, 118, 140
Grotius, Hugo, 5, 49
guerrilla movements, 116
Guinea, 139

Hague Congress of the International
    Workingmen's Association (1872), 113
Haig, Alexander, 76
hegemony, 5, 17, 22, 30, 37–46, 51, 58–60, 62,
    67–71, 74, 77, 85, 105, 132–45, 159, 167, 179,
    181
historical systems, 27–8, 37, 46, 178
Hitler, Adolf, 70
Ho Chi Minh, 126
Hobsbawm, Eric J., 9, 11, 96
Holy Roman Empire, 49
Holy See, 49
households, 14, 16, 18–19, 22, 29, 33, 36, 53,
    100–4, 111, 127–8, 183
Hungary, 90, 121, 136

imperialism, 5, 7, 75, 82, 119
incorporation, *see under* capitalist
    world-economy
India, 81, 110, 139, 142, 161, 166, 168
Indonesia, 131, 141
industrial revolution, 180, 183
inflation, 42, 61–3, 78
International Socialist Bureau, 114
Internationals, *see* First Int.; Second Int.;
    Third Int.
internationalism, 10, 21, 114, 124, 139
interstate system: balance of power in, 38–9,
    45, 50, 71, 100, 108; capitalist
    world-economy and, *see* capitalist
    world-economy; development of, 17, 30,
    49–50, 57–9, 81, 134; politics of, 7–8, 20–2,
    46, 49, 56, 62, 65, 84, 89–90, 92, 94, 129, 131,
    141, 179; restructuring of, 77, 81, 104, 110;
    workers' movements and, 11, 25, 49, 57, 83,
    106, 108
Iran, 56, 61, 63, 82, 110, 139, 166
Ireland, 136
Israel, 66
Italy, 49, 70, 113, 118, 120–1, 126, 136, 180

Japan, 43, 46, 59–60, 62, 64–5, 70, 74–5, 77,
    103, 110, 126, 141, 182

Kampuchea, *see* Cambodia
Kennedy, John F., 60, 72, 138
Kissinger, Henry, 62, 75
Kondratieff cycles, 16, 45, 59, 72, 99, 109, 135;
    see also capitalist world-economy
Korea, 90, 138, 141
Kronstadt rebellion (1921), 125
Khrushchev, Nikita, 89, 121, 125, 182

labor: as factor of production, 3–4, 11, 18, 31,
    33, 41, 44, 59, 81, 127–8, 148, 154, 170;
    division of, 2, 8, 13, 15, 18, 20, 22, 25, 28, 38,
    50, 58–9, 61, 80, 90, 92, 94, 103, 133, 147–8,
    150–1, 163, 170

land, *see* production, factors of
Laos, 138
Latin America, 87, 120, 138, 142, 166
League of Nations, 70, 89
Lefebvre, Henri, 113, 182
Lenin, Vladimir, 4, 7, 48, 52, 70, 81, 87, 114,
    125–6, 142–3
liberalism, 41, 45, 59–60, 76, 138, 182
Libya, 139
Locarno Pact (1925), 89
logic of domination, 25
logic of socialism, 24
logic of the civilization project, 25
logistics, 42, 45–6
Lomé Convention, 65

McCarthyism, 60, 72
Mao Zedong, 90–1, 95, 107, 126, 131, 158
Marchais, Georges, 121
mare liberum, 5
markets, 13, 15, 18, 31, 43–5, 64–5, 153–4, 163
Marx, Karl, 11, 55, 86–7, 101, 113, 123, 126,
    133, 141, 147, 168
Marxism, 2, 10, 48, 86–7, 89, 91, 113–16, 124,
    142–3, 165, 180–2
mechanization, 16, 18, 59, 127, 181
Menshevism, 86–7, 114–15, 124
mercantilism, 41, 86–96
Merton, Robert K., 178
Mexico, 77, 139, 166
Middle East, 63, 66–7
Miliband, Ralph, 87
military power, 17, 41, 58, 60–1, 63, 66, 70–1,
    73, 75, 77, 81, 83, 88, 90, 137
Mill, John Stuart, 179
mini-systems, *see* reciprocal mini-systems
minority groups, 20–1, 72, 76–8, 176
Mitterand, François, 139
mobility: of individuals, 9, 72, 136; of states, 9,
    72, 136
monarchies, 10
monopoly, 3, 33, 100–1, 154
Morocco, 142, 166
Morosini, Giuseppe, 120
Mozambique, 116, 139
multinational corporations, 3, 53–4, 62, 64,
    77–8, 93, 139

Napoleonic Wars, 42, 104
Nasser, Gamal Abdel, 126
national(ist) movements, 8–12, 20–1, 31, 35,
    56, 59, 62, 77, 82, 104–5, 109, 114, 120,
    122–31, 134–7, 142, 165–7, 171, 175, 181
nationalization, 55–6
nations, 20, 29, 31, 35–6, 100–1, 134, 183
nation-states, 20, 129–30
Nazism, 70–1
Nemec, A., 115

Netherlands, 5, 17, 34, 39, 42–3, 49, 58, 113; *see also* United Provinces
New Deal, 69–70, 73–7
New Zealand, 142
Nigeria, 31, 141
Nisbet, Robert A., 173
Nixon, Richard, 65, 73–5
North Atlantic Treaty Organization, 65, 75, 141
nuclear war, 25, 57, 75

oil prices, 61–2, 109
Organization of Petroleum Exporting Countries, 61, 109–10, 141
Ottoman Empire, 81, 136

Padovani, Marcel, 121
Palestine Liberation Organization, 66
"pan-" movements, 21
Paris Commune, 113, 115–16
parties, 8–10, 12; *see also* Bolshevism; communist parties; Menshevism; socialist parties
pasok, 140
peoples, 14, 20, 22, 129, 135
peripheral areas, 5, 8–11, 15–17, 19, 29, 54, 79, 99–100, 105, 110, 155, 159, 170–1, 176, 181
peripheral processes, 7, 103
peripheral states, 45, 57, 62, 80–5
Persia, 81
petty proprietorship, 3
Pinochet, Augusto, 140
Pol Pot, 90, 92, 107
Poland, 95, 121, 140, 142–4
Portugal, 5, 109
post-revolutionary states, 139–42, 144
price structures, 4, 31, 44
primitive society, 148
production: expansion of, 5–6, 10, 16–18, 40, 98, 101, 111; factors of, 2, 18–19, 25, 29, 31, 33, 41, 43–4, 55, 59, 81, 89, 98, 103, 154; *and see* capital, labor; forces of, 11, 25, 54, 84, 90, 92; mode of, 3, 4, 6, 8–9, 14–15, 25, 32, 38, 43, 94, 126, 133, 144, 147, 150–1, 153, 156–7, 159–69; processes of, 2, 8, 13, 16, 18, 22, 25, 28, 31–3, 39–40, 50, 59, 64, 80, 98–9, 104, 133, 139, 170; relocation of, 16, 35, 61, 64, 78, 99, 103
profit, maximization of, 5, 16, 34, 128, 133, 154
proletarianization, 11, 16–19, 23–4, 53, 100, 102–4, 111, 127–9
proletariat, 4, 10, 34–6, 48, 91, 101–2, 104, 113, 115, 119–20, 124, 127–9, 159

quasi monopolies, 3–7, 30, 50

race consciousness, 8, 35, 101
race war, 78

racism, 22, 70–1, 76–7, 155–6
Rapallo, Treaty of (1922), 70
Reagan, Ronald, 69, 75–6
reciprocal mini-systems, 147–51, 163–5
Red Brigades, 113, 138, 140
redistribution, 6, 15, 23–4, 100, 129, 147, 149–53
redistributive world-empires, 147, 150–3, 163–5, 167–9
reformism, 21, 137
revisionism, 47, 124, 138
revolution, 9, 77, 82–96, 106, 112, 114–15, 117, 123–6, 130, 132–45
revolutionary movements, *see* antisystemic movements
Ricardo, David, 179–80
Roman Empire, 126, 151
Roosevelt, Franklin D., 69–71, 73
Russia, *see* Soviet Union
Russian Revolution, 24, 47, 70, 77, 87–8, 115–17, 135

Saint-Simon, Claude Henri Comte de, 179, 182
Saudi Arabia, 61
Schmidt, Helmut, 62
Schumpeter, Joseph A., 11, 51, 133
Second International, 35, 87, 113, 116, 124
Second World War, 10, 42, 62, 69–71, 77, 90, 109, 112, 118, 120, 125, 132, 134–5, 179
semiperipheral areas, 10, 11, 15, 17, 99–100, 103–5, 110–11
semiperipheral states, 7, 20, 22, 50–1, 57, 61, 64
semiproletarianization, 11, 16–17, 19, 154–5
Serbia, 114–15
Smith, Adam, 179–80
social formation, 2
social movements, 20–1, 25, 53, 59, 77, 79, 82, 90, 93, 104, 116, 120, 122–7, 130–1, 135–7, 142, 171, 175, 181, 185; *see also* antisystemic movements
social sciences, 1–2, 11–12, 17, 22, 132, 159, 165, 173–81, 183, 185
social systems, 147–58
socialism: crisis of, 126, 131; evolutionary, 114, 124; logic of, 24; transition to, 11–12, 52, 55, 57, 86, 89, 107, 111, 113–14, 123–31, 140, 144, 167–9, 171–2, 184; world, 25–6, 57, 84–7, 90, 92, 123–31, 140, 143, 147, 156–8, 171
socialist parties, 47, 104, 112–13, 117, 156; Austria, 115; Bohemia, 115; France, 115, 117; Germany, 115; Greece, 140; USA, 71
socialist states, 25, 64, 79, 86–96, 107, 138–9, 142
socialist world-government, 156–9, 164, 167, 171
society, concept of, 1–2, 27–8, 174–7, 183
Solidarity, 142–4